Theophilus of Antioch

Theophilus of Antioch

The Life and Thought of a Second-Century Bishop

Rick Rogers

LEXINGTON BOOKS
Lanham • Boulder • New York • Oxford

LEXINGTON BOOKS

Published in the United States of America
by Lexington Books
4720 Boston Way, Lanham, Maryland 20706

12 Hid's Copse Road
Cumnor Hill, Oxford OX2 9JJ, England

Excerpts from *Theophilus of Antioch: Ad Autolycum*, text and translation by Robert H. Grant (1970), © Oxford University Press 1970. Reprinted by permission.

British Library Cataloguing in Publication Information Available

Library of Congress Cataloging-in-Publication Data

Rogers, Rick, 1950–
    Theophilus of Antioch : the life and thought of a second-century bishop / Rick Rogers.
        p.   cm.
    Includes bibliographical references and index.
    ISBN 0-7391-0132-3 (cloth : alk. paper)
    1. Theophilus, Saint, 2nd cent.   I. Title.

BR1720.T47 R64   2000
270.1'092—dc21
[B]   00-023374

Printed in the United States of America

Contents

Acknowledgments

The work on this book was begun in the Department of Near Eastern Studies at The University of Michigan in 1992 and was continued in the History and Philosophy Department at Eastern Michigan University. My gratitude to all those who supported me at both institutions can only be incompletely expressed. I wish to thank Serena J. Leigh, Ginger M. Strader and their staffs at Lexington Books and the Rowman and Littlefield Publishing Group for their professionalism and kind assistance in all matters of production. To my loving and beloved wife, Susan Kesling Rogers, I dedicate this book.

PART ONE:
BACKGROUND

Chapter 1

Theophilus' Life

Theophilus is truly a remarkable personality. This second-century bishop from Syrian Antioch was an apologist, a biblical exegete, a chronologist, an evangelist, an heresiologist, a teacher and a theologian. Yet, in spite of his fine literary contributions and highly regarded work, Theophilus is one of the most underappreciated authors and activists of his time. He is overshadowed by the mystique surrounding the martyrs Ignatius and Justin and the litigious polemics of Athenagoras and Tatian, not to mention the extensive theological contributions of Irenaeus and Tertullian.[1] However, I believe the primary reason modern scholars pay less attention to Theophilus than to these other personalities is due to his undefined theology. Theophilus' thought appears to reflect a Jewish-Christian background. Jewish Christianity is, in many circles, considered heretical. Before taking an in-depth look at that theology in part two of this book, let us consider what we actually know about Theophilus and his work.

In the ancient church only Eusebius (ca. 260-339) and Jerome (ca. 347-419/20) tell us anything regarding his career.[2] I will begin with the later and briefer testimony. According to Jerome, scripture scholar, translator, polemicist and ascetic,[3] in his *Lives of Illustrious Men:*

> Theophilus, sixth bishop of the church of Antioch, in the reign of the emperor Marcus Antoninus Verus composed a book *Against Marcion,* which is still extant, also three volumes *To Autolycus* and one *Against the Heresy of Hermogenes* and other short and elegant treatises, well fitted for the edification of the church. (*Lives* 25)

Jerome knew Theophilus was the sixth bishop of the church at Antioch and an author of a number of treatises—three of which he mentions by name: *Against Marcion, To Autolycus,* and *Against the Heresy of Hermogenes.* While he specifically characterizes some unnamed Theophilian documents as "short and elegant treatises," he seems to have appreciated the quality of Theophilus' entire corpus. The only distinguishing mark about *Ad Autolycum* is that it was a three-volume work. Far more noteworthy is his claim that all of these documents by Theophilus were "well fitted for the edification of the church." Out of the 135 early-church personalities Jerome comments on in his *Lives,* this is the only set of documents for which he makes this claim. While one should not make too much of this observation, especially given the higher praise he lavishes on several more-famous authors, neither should one underestimate the value he seems to be placing on *Ad Autolycum.*[4] Here is a collection of texts obviously addressed to a "pagan,"[5] and yet, according to this famous biblical scholar, deemed useful for the instruction and improvement of the church.

Immediately following the above text, Jerome speaks of other works said to belong to Theophilus:

> I have read, under his name, commentaries *On the Gospel* and *On the Proverbs of Solomon* which do not appear to me to correspond in style and language with the elegance and expressiveness of the above works. (*Lives* 25)

This passage not only reasserts his appreciation for the literary quality of all the earlier works, especially in comparison with a couple of Theophilian commentaries, but it also may resonate some concern regarding the authenticity of these poorer works which have come to Jerome "under his name." That such a recognized master of style and language, should have called this sort of attention to Theophilus' "authentic" treatises is significant. It is equally remarkable, however, given his proclivity for at least a brief theological comment, that Jerome chose to say nothing about the bishop's thought. This would seem to suggest that he found no objectionable content in Theophilus' theology, or in any of the bishop's particular works when considered in terms of his larger literary contribution.

Eusebius, bishop of Caesarea and the first major church historian, is only slightly more informative.[6] His testimony, which as we have seen was later confirmed by Jerome, is that Theophilus was the sixth bishop of Antioch "from the Apostles" (*EH* 4.20.1) This phrase no doubt refers particularly to Peter (and perhaps Paul) as representative of the apostolic tradition, whose oversight role in Antioch is well documented in the New Testament.[7] Eusebius then goes on to offer the following list of Antiochene bishops who preceded Theophilus: Evodius, Ignatius, Heron, Cornelius and Eros (*EH* 3.22.1 and 4.20.1).[8] It is important to notice that there is nothing in Eusebius' discussion of Theophilus to suggest that the sixth bishop of Antioch was not theologically consistent with his predecessors, particularly Ignatius.

According to Eusebius, however, Theophilus is more than just an overseer of a local community of Christians. He says:

> Of Theophilus, whom we have mentioned as bishop of the church of the Antiochenes, three elementary treatises are extant, addressed to Autolycus, and another with the title, *Against the Heresy of Hermogenes,* in which he has quoted the Apocalypse of John, and there are also extant some other books of his on instruction. (*EH* 4.24.1)

I would like the reader to focus for a moment on Eusebius' use of the ambiguous adjective, "elementary."[9] Is Eusebius making a pejorative comment on the style of Theophilus' books?[10] I do not believe he is. It is interesting to note that Jerome seems to think of these books as a collective unit, referring to them as "three volumes *To Autolycus*," while Eusebius appears to view them as more independent, speaking of them as three treatises "addressed to Autolycus."[11] Given that the third "treatise" is introduced in an obvious epistolary manner, it is possible that Eusebius took them all to be lengthy independent letters.[12] Thus, the term, "elementary," could have been his assessment of their relative size when compared to other documents of Theophilus. However, he may also be commenting on their relative value to the Christian community. Eusebius' additional observations, that Theophilus made use of the Apocalypse of John and composed "other books . . . on instruction," suggests to me that he is discussing only the content of Theophilus' works and not their size or literary quality. After all, as was pointed out above, the bishop's books to Autolycus are written to a pagan audience and not to those Christians who are better informed in the doctrinal matters of the church. Therefore, their pedagogical value for one such as Eusebius would of course be "elementary."[13] If this is true, Jerome seems slightly more impressed with the ecclesiastical value of *Ad Autolycum* than does Eusebius.[14] Nevertheless, neither seems to have questioned the bishop's literary style.

Whatever else Theophilus may have written about, the fact that he is a formidable presence who chose to deal with one of the most serious of contemporary issues, namely, heresy, ultimately determined his value for Eusebius. In the historian's words regarding an additional book:

> It is clear that Theophilus joined with the others in this campaign against [heretics] from a noble treatise which he made against Marcion, which has been preserved until now with the others that we have mentioned. (*EH* 4.24.1)

A reference to "the heretics" is mentioned a few sentences earlier in this paragraph. It is on this crucial issue that Eusebius appears to find Theophilus a soul mate. The historian continues:

> [The] heretics were even then no less defiling the pure seed of apostolic teaching like tares, and the shepherds of the churches in every place, as though driving off wild beasts from Christ's sheep, excluded them at one time by rebukes and exhortations to the brethren, at another by their more complete exposure, by unwritten and personal inquiry and conversation, and ultimately correcting their opinions by accurate arguments in written treatises. (*EH* 4.24.1)

It is entirely possible that this tradition of Theophilus as heresiologist, along with the approval of Eusebius, preserved the bishop's name from the fate of those whom some scholars have claimed he anticipated, namely, Paul of Samosata (fl.

ca. 260-268) and Marcellus of Ancyra (ca. 280-374)—both of whom were declared heretics by the later church.[15] Eusebius appears to be claiming Theophilus as a "shepherd" of the primitive church who, along with others, made a "campaign" against Marcion,[16] Hermogenes and other such heretics of his day. With this important testimonial, it would seem that Theophilus' reputation as an "orthodox" bishop was firmly established in the eyes of the Catholic Church.[17]

In addition to Jerome's and Eusebius' contributions, information about Theophilus and his career can be inferred from his own words in his only extant works, the three books of the collection called *Ad Autolycum*. The title of Theophilus' collection was probably derived from an opening comment in the second book, where he acknowledges the name of his dialogical partner. It seems that Theophilus was having an ongoing conversation with someone he usually referred to as "O man" (first in *Ad Autolycum* 1.2)[18] and twice as "O friend" (1.1, 14).[19] Theophilus treats his interlocutor as an inquiring pagan gentleman, eventually addressing him as "O excellent Autolycus."[20] Given the nondescript character of these references to Autolycus and the fact that these documents do not really seem like personal letters, one could make a reasonable case for "Autolycus" being nothing more than a rhetorical construct, that is, a fictional character posing the theological questions Theophilus is prepared to discuss.[21] However, one should also consider the fuller nature of the implied relationship between Theophilus and Autolycus in these documents. In their initial conversation, Theophilus accuses Autolycus of having personally "attacked" and "ridiculed" him (1.1, 12). Before they began their second conversation, however, Theophilus' mood seems to have changed and he reminds Autolycus, "we parted from each other with great friendliness when each went to his own house" (2.1). Occasionally the reader of *Ad Autolycum* will sense Theophilus' affection for Autolycus, although it is usually tied to a respect for his learning and eagerness to know more, as is apparent in the following passage:

> As far as the other writers whose works you have read . . . you have [an] accurate knowledge . . . . He who loves learning must really love it . . . . Meet with us more often, so that by hearing a living voice you may accurately learn what is true. (2.38)[22]

Later in their third discussion, Theophilus implies that Autolycus is a hardworking historian who is deservedly called "a lover of learning" (3.15).[23] This language throughout *Ad Autolycum* of specific encounters, of familiarity with intellectual development, and of commitment to personal growth, not to mention the conversational tone of all three books, seems an excessive contrivance if Autolycus were no more than a literary fiction. The bishop appears to invest considerable energy in this relationship, leading me to conclude that it is unlikely that Autolycus was a rhetorical invention.[24] Nevertheless, while I think based on the above observations that Autolycus was a real person, Theophilus clearly signals a wider readership. His carefully composed presentations are more like a series of treatises than epistles, and thus he would not have intended them to be merely private affairs. Whether Autolycus is real or fictional, I take him to be the perfect nemesis and foil for my educationally minded bishop—this curious and perhaps sympathetic pagan who does not speak back.[25]

What about dates? While it has been suggested that Eusebius may not have known the third book in this collection addressed to Autolycus, as we have seen, he clearly says that "three elementary treatises are extant" (*EH* 4.24.1)[26] The problem is that Eusebius' *Chronicle* dates Theophilus' episcopate from 169 to 177 even though the death of Marcus Aurelius (March 17, 180) is mentioned in the third book (3.27, 28).[27] While the first two books could have been composed as late as the monarchy of Commodus, the evidence of the third book demands its post-180 date. Actually, this is the only certain date we have concerning Theophilus' career, although there is no reason to doubt the 169 reference.[28] He may well have died around 188 CE, for Maximinus, his immediate successor, is said to have been made bishop of Antioch in that year.[29]

Theophilus' books do not inform us about his episcopacy or even that he was a resident of Antioch. In one passage where he is discussing the location of Eden in relation to the Tigris and Euphrates rivers, he makes an off-the-cuff remark that these rivers border on "our own *klimata* " (2.24). This term, *klimata,* usually refers to some sort of climatic zones, although it is best translated in this context as "regions."[30] While it is probably safe to say that Theophilus was a Greek-educated Syrian, how much more biographical information can be gleaned from his books is uncertain. A couple of scholars have ventured to suggest, on the vaguest of Theophilian comments, that he was born "near" the Euphrates River of "pagan parentage," was "a slow learner," lacked oratorical skills, was not a library night owl and was "probably married."[31]

Theophilus' most substantial personal revelation comes in a carefully crafted account of his adult conversion, which slides back and forth between pedagogy and proselytism.

> Do not disbelieve, then, but believe. I too did not believe that resurrection would take place, but now that I have considered these matters I believe. At that time I encountered the sacred writings of the holy prophets, who through the spirit of God foretold past events in the way that they happened, present events in the way they are happening, and future events in the order in which they will be accomplished. Because I obtained proof from the events which took place after being predicted, I do not disbelieve but believe, in obedience to God. If you will, you too must obey him and believe him, so that after disbelieving now you will not be persuaded later, punished with eternal tortures. (1.14)

Theophilus' opening imperative is noteworthy on at least two counts. First, his words are not unlike Jesus' words to Thomas in John 20:27—"Do not be faithless, but believing"[32]—which the bishop may be echoing. The "Doubting Thomas" story is unique to the Gospel of John, which is the only New Testament book Theophilus mentions by name (2.22).[33] Thomas is an important figure in the bishop's Syrian church.[34] Therefore, this story may have been familiar and the phrase idiomatic even to a Syrian pagan like Autolycus. Second, Theophilus' words to Autolycus are a gentle prod introducing the reason for his belief in what he earlier called "the general resurrection of all men" (1.13). Of course, in John, the phrase is much more of a reprimand of Thomas for not believing in the resurrection of Jesus.

After his opening salvo, Theophilus tells his readers that he became a believer because of his encounter with "the sacred writings of the holy prophets" and his conviction of their valid predictions. The bishop then turns from this personal revelation to his central point, telling Autolycus that he had better pay attention now, for persuasion from disbelief is inevitable and, if necessary, severe. Theophilus' God demands acknowledgement and obeisance, even if these gestures must be exacted "with eternal tortures." Theophilus does not seem to be preoccupied with God's vengeance in *Ad Autolycum*, but he does occasionally raise the specter.[35] He is, however, a man highly committed to "the sacred writings of the holy prophets." As we shall see, his theology features the role of these prophets who were the agents of his own transformation from a doubting Theophilus to one who could say, "I do not disbelieve but believe."

With this brief account of his conversion in the first book of *Ad Autolycum*, Theophilus has established the importance of prophecy in his religion. Earlier, however, in this same document, he informed his readers about whom he was. In the midst of what seems a seriously contentious argument he identifies himself, saying:

> You call me a Christian as if I were bearing an evil name, I acknowledge that I am a Christian. I bear this name beloved by God in the hope of being useful to God. It is not the case, as you suppose, that the name of God is offensive. Perhaps you yourself are of no use to God and therefore think about God in this way. (1.1)[36]

On the one hand, Theophilus' pronouncement that he is a Christian includes a rather transparent attempt to educate Autolycus about the etymological elements of his name. Theophilus' name actually means "beloved by God." Given this explanation his pagan friend might quickly conclude that "Theophilus" and "Christian" are nearly interchangeable notions. On the other hand, Theophilus' suggestion of a phonetic similarity between the Greek word "christ" (*christos*) and the term "useful" (*chrestos*) is never fully developed by the bishop, but left to his readers imagination.[37]

While his definition of a Christian will be explored in chapter six of this book, let me conclude this chapter by focussing attention once again on a particular point which I believe is highly significant. Theophilus was not only a bishop but also an author who composed several books known as *Ad Autolycum*, which were judged by no less an authority than Jerome as "fitting for the edification of the church." Given that Theophilus' immediate audience does not appear to be the Christian community, it seems reasonable to assume that the theological substance of these documents is ecclesiastically "elementary," following Eusebius' observation. Nevertheless, while Eusebius' comment is not necessarily contradicted by Jerome's, the later scholar seems more appreciative of the theological content of *Ad Autolycum*. Perhaps with a slight preference for Jerome's language, I would also add that *Ad Autolycum*, as an expression of the bishop's religious opinion, represents the essentials of his Christian faith. This is an extremely important point given the premium Theophilus puts on the role of the "holy prophets" (as I argue in chapter five). With this presentation of the bishop's life, let us now turn to his writings.

Notes

1. Theophilus is usually classified as one of the four most faithfully preserved and highly productive apologists of the early church. Therefore, it is fascinating to compare the scholarly literature on him with his three vastly better-known counterparts, Tatian the Syrian, Athenagoras of Athens and Justin the Martyr. Recently a fine study tool for patristic studies has been published by Everett Ferguson called *Encyclopedia of Early Christianity* (New York: Garland, 1990). (This first edition of Ferguson's work is used so often in the following endnotes that the full citation is, from this point on in my book, referred to as simply *EEC*.) Comparing the bibliographical entries in that edition for Theophilus with these other contemporary theologians, one finds that while Tatian has eight, Athenagoras has ten and Justin has eighteen, Theophilus has only four (two being patristic sources, one being a modern English edition of Theophilus' books and one lonely article). J. Quasten's *Patrology. Volume One: The Beginnings of Patristic Literature* (Utrecht and Brussels: Spectrum, 1950), which offered Tatian eight and a half pages of analysis, Athenagoras seven and a half pages and Justin twenty-four pages, offered Theophilus only five and a half pages. E. J. Goodspeed's *A History of Early Christian Literature* (Chicago: The University of Chicago Press, 1983) was somewhat more fair. Nevertheless, this treatment of Theophilus is standard in most of the dictionaries, encyclopedias and compendiums in the field of patristics and early church history today, going back at least to 1907 with Geffcken's brief two pages (250-52) in *Zwei griechische Apologeten* (Leipzig and Berlin: Teubner, 1907).

Several fine books and monographs have been published detailing the religious and theological contributions of Justin, Tatian and Athenagoras. To mention only the most prominent, W. L. Barnard, *Athenagoras* (Paris: Beauchesne, 1972) and *Justin Martyr: His Life and Thought* (Cambridge: Cambridge University Press, 1967), O. C. Edwards, *Barbarian Philosophy: Tatian and the Greek Paideia* (Ph.D. diss., University of Chicago, 1971), M. Elze, *Tatian und seine Theologie* (Göttingen: Vandenheock and Ruprecht, 1960), E. R. Goodenough, *The Theology of Justin Martyr* (Amsterdam: Philo Press, 1968), E. F. Osborn, *Justin Martyr* (Tübingen: Mohr, 1973) and A. E. Osborne, *Tatian: A Literary Analysis and Essay in Interpretation* (Ph.D. diss., University of Cincinnati, 1969) have written important intellectual biographies on these three apologists. But no comparable book-length study had been done on Theophilus until my, *Salvation By Law: The Protreptic Theology of Ad Autolycum* (Ph.D. diss., University of Michigan, Ann Arbor, 1996).

2. In R. M. Grant's impressive book *Greek Apologists of the Second Century* (Philadelphia: The Westminster Press, 1988), 140-47, and several other earlier patrologies listed in the bibliography, we have only modest presentations of the data regarding Theophilus' life.

3. See *EEC*, 484-86 for a brief discussion of Jerome's significance in early church history. For a biography on Jerome, see J. N. D. Kelly, *Jerome: His Life, Writings and Controversies* (New York: Harper and Row, 1975).

4. While he spoke positively of the personal contributions of Ignatius (*Lives* 16) and Justin (*Lives* 23), he did not address the ecclesiastical value of their writings as he did with Theophilus. Consider a sampling of Jerome's critical comments. Regarding Theodorus, bishop of Heraclea, he says his works "are written in a polished and clear style and show an excellent historical sense" (*Lives* 90). Of Victorinus the rhetorician, he says "yielding himself to faith in Christ [he] wrote books . . . in dialectic style and very obscure language, books which can only be understood by the learned" (*Lives* 101). Jerome read Ephraim of Edessa in translation (a Greek volume translated from the Syriac), and said that he still "recognized even in translation, the incisive power of lofty genius" (*Lives* 115).

5. The adjective "pagan (*paganus*)" is not used by any second-century Christian writer. The Christian usage of the term, *pagani*, first appears, says R. L. Fox, *Pagans and Christians: Religion and The Religious Life From the Second to the Fourth Century A.D.* (San Francisco: Harper and Row, 1986), 30-31, "in Christian inscriptions of the early fourth century and remained colloquial, never entering the Latin translation of the Bible." Nevertheless, the term has become a useful generalization for most church historians and so will be used through out my book in that manner; following R. L. Fox; W. H. C. Frend, *The Rise of Christianity* (Philadelphia: Fortress, 1984); R. M. Grant, *Greek Apologists;* E. R. Dodds, *Pagan and Christian in an Age of Anxiety* (New York: Norton, 1965); R. MacMullen, *Christianizing the Roman Empire: A.D. 100-400* (New Haven: Yale University Press, 1984); E. Pagels, *The Origin of Satan* (New York: Random House, 1995), 112-48; and S. Benko, *Pagan Rome and the Early Christians* (Bloomington: Indiana University Press, 1984), who defines paganism (25, fn. 9): "as a general term for all members of the Roman empire who were not Christians. They may have been devotees of Greek and Roman state cults, initiates of mystery religions, followers of philosophical schools that demanded a certain conduct of life, or even people having a particular interest in spiritual matters." None of these historians uses the term in a derogatory sense, but as a designation for Christian opponents who were not Jews or heretics.

6. See *EEC*, 325-27, for an assessment of Eusebius' contributions to the history of the early church. Also, see R. M. Grant, *Eusebius as Church Historian* (Oxford: Clarendon, 1980) and T. D. Barnes, *Constantine and Eusebius* (Cambridge: Harvard University Press, 1981). Eusebius' *Ecclesiastical History* will hereafter be referenced as *EH*.

7. See Galatians 2 and Acts 11-15.

8. Eusebius seems to offer another tradition (found in *EH* 3.36.2), certainly less valued if it is one, in which Peter, rather than Evodius, was considered the first bishop of Antioch with Ignatius succeeding him. However, Eusebius may be simply calling attention to Ignatius as a bishop who was "second after Peter" while Evodius was first after Peter. For a further discussion of the problem regarding these two traditions in Eusebius, see G. Downey, *A History of Antioch in Syria from Seleucus to Arab Conquest* (Princeton: Princeton University, 1961), 284ff.

9. Eusebius' Greek word στοιχειώδη may also be translated as "basic" or "fundamental." In this context, I would have preferred either of these to "elementary."

10. R. M. Grant, *Greek Apologists*, 144, thinks so. He says: "The style of Theophilus is resolutely 'plain'. . . . Eusebius described the books as 'elementary,' a term he also applied to the *Shepherd* of Hermas to indicate its lack of style and sophisticated theol-

ogy." I would disagree with Grant on both Theophilus' style and his understanding of Eusebius' comment on this bishop.

11. Notice that the translator of Jerome's comment takes the name of the stated recipient of these volumes to form the title of the work, while the translator of Eusebius does not.

12. The three books of Theophilus' *Ad Autolycum* are arguably independent of one another, as is demonstrated in chapter two, where their epistolary style is also briefly discussed. See S. K. Stowers, *Letter Writing in Greco-Roman Antiquity* (Philadelphia: The Westminster Press, 1986), for a current discussion of the variety of early Christian epistolary compositions. Perhaps at some time between Eusebius and Jerome this collection of independent works was treated as an inseparable unit and designated by the single title that Jerome seems to know.

13. Eusebius' likely criterion for this judgment is his probable observation regarding Theophilus' purpose in composing this collection of books for a particular audience, a point which will be clarified in chapter two.

14. One should keep in mind, however, that Jerome speaks of *Ad Autolycum* as appropriate for the "edification" of the church and not the "education" of the church. While it is unlikely that Jerome saw *Ad Autolycum* as sufficient theology, he seems to have appreciated the books as legitimate church theology to a greater degree than did Eusebius.

15. Paul of Samosata was condemned for his teachings by the Synods in Antioch in 264 and 268. See M. McHugh, "Paul of Samosata," *EEC*, 703. Marcellus of Ancyra, who attended the council of Nicaea in 325, was condemned for his views at councils held at Antioch in 341, at Sardica in 343, again at Antioch in 345, and finally at Constantinople in 381. See R. Lyman, "Marcellus of Ancyra," *EEC*, 566-67. While an analysis of the claim that Theophilus anticipated Paul and Marcellus is well beyond the scope of my book, it must be mentioned as an intriguing possibility. R. M. Grant's assessment of the possibility in *Jesus After the Gospels: The Christ of the Second Century* (Louisville, KY: Knox, 1990), 76, 80-82, 100 and 108, and in his *Gods and the One God* (Philadelphia: Westminster Press, 1986), 133-35 is very much to the point and adequate for our purposes here. His conclusions are based in part on those of R. L. Sample in his book, *The Messiah as Prophet: The Christology of Paul of Samosata* (Ph.D. diss., Northwestern University, 1977), 159ff. and 193ff.

16. Eusebius, of course, is not suggesting by his use of this Greek word "campaign" (στρατευσάμενος) an "expedition" (στράτευμα), but the waging of an intellectual war against those of a decidedly different Christian position. The importance of Theophilus as an anti-Marcionite, as both Jerome and Eusebius contend that he was, must not be underestimated as we attempt to describe the bishop's theological teachings.

17. See F. W. Norris, "Theophilus of Antioch," *EEC*, 985, and the treatment of the bishop by A. C. Coxe, who adds occasional notes, in *The Ante-Nicene Fathers* (Grand Rapids: Eerdmans, 1953), hereafter cited as *ANF*, volume 2, 87-88. Also, see T. Halton, "Catholic Church," *EEC*, 187-88. Ignatius of Antioch (*Smyrnaeans* 8) was the first to use the adjective καθολικός when he said: "Where the bishop is, there let the community be, just as where Jesus Christ is, there is the catholic church." Here the term means "universal," "general" or "whole," probably conveying organic unity. However, by the time of Clement of Alexandria καθολικός is used as a technical term for a community in contradistinction to others, when he says (*Stromateis* 7.17.107): "It is evident that these later heresies and those that are still more recent are spurious innovations on the oldest and truest church . . . . We say that the ancient and catholic church stands alone in essence and idea and principle and preeminence."

18. This Greek phrase, ὦ ἄνθροπε, occurs only in the first book and nine times in all (*Ad Autolycum* 1.2, 3, 6, 7, 10, 11, 13). With this first citation of a Theophilian passage, let me say that most texts and translations of Theophilus' *Ad Autolycum* referenced in my book are taken from the recent edition of that work by R. M. Grant, *Theophilus of Antioch: Ad Autolycum* (Oxford: Clarendon, 1970). Hereafter, Grant's edition will be cited *AA*, but the Theophilian texts themselves will be referenced by merely book and chapter numbers, e.g., in parenthesis as (1.2).

19. R. M. Grant translates both instances of ὦ ἑταῖρε "my friend."

20. This Greek phrase, ὦ ἀγαθώτατε Αὐτόλυκε, is used in 2.1. The third book, 3.1, is also clearly addressed to Autolycus. These are the only two occurrences of this rare Greek name in Theophilus' books, a name that was also used of a fourth century BCE Greek astronomer. See Liddell and Scott, *A Greek-English Lexicon* (Oxford: Clarendon, 1989), xx. The superlative ἀγαθώτατε is an unexpected choice. While Luke 1:3 (κράτιστε Θεόφιλε) and *The Epistle to Diognetus* 1:1 (κράτιστε Διόγνητε) chose the more common term for polite address, I doubt that much can be made of Theophilus' preference. See W. F. Arndt and F. W. Gingrich, *A Greek-English Lexicon* (Chicago: The University of Chicago Press, 1957), 450a regarding the more popular κράτιστε. With this first citation of a biblical text it should be noted that all New Testament Greek texts are taken from K. Aland, *The Greek New Testament,* second edition (New York: United Bible Society, 1968) and all New Testament translations come from H. G. May's and B. M. Metzger's edition of the Revised Standard Version known as *The New Oxford Annotated Bible* (New York: Oxford University Press, 1973). Furthermore, all Septuagint (LXX) texts and translations are taken from L. C. L. Brenton, *The Septuagint with Apocrypha: Greek and English* (Peabody, MA: Hendrickson, 1986), unless otherwise noted.

21. Cf. *The Epistle to Diognetus* and Justin's *Dialogue With Trypho*. See D. E. Aune, *The New Testament in Its Literary Environment* (Philadelphia: The Westminster Press, 1987), 200f., which discusses the convention of the imaginary opponent in Greco-Roman rhetoric. Among several features, he mentions the author's addressing his opponent using the vocative form, "O man," accusing his opponent of inconsistency, ignorance or error, and responding generally to his opponent's specific objections.

22. Although an argument from silence, this statement may suggest to some readers that Autolycus knew of a regular meeting location and time in which he could engage the bishop.

23. The Greek term he uses for "historian" (3.1) is συγγραφεύς. One might infer from this passage that Autolycus is a chronologist and mythologist as well. Nevertheless, clearly he is represented as a man eagerly engaged with intellectual matters.

24. Actually, in the first two books, Theophilus treats Autolycus as though he were his student, employing criticism and affirmation as a mentor would toward his protégé. In the third book, Theophilus is less effusive and somewhat more businesslike with Autolycus, much as a former teacher would be with a maturing peer. This might suggest that the third book was written a few years after the first two books, when the relationship between the two men had grown. Nevertheless, it has been rightly said of Theophilus' three books, by J. Bentivegna, "A Christianity Without Christ by Theophilus of Antioch," *Studia patristica* 13 (1975), 107, that there is a "warmth" in them shown toward the reader (who obviously possesses an opposing point of view) that is not found in any of the other so-called apologetic works of the second century.

25. Theophilus' dialogical partner, Autolycus, is paraphrased from time to time without, it would seem, the full voice of a quotation. A possible meaning for the name "Autolycus" could be "the silent one" or one who is practicing self (auto)-imposed silence. See Liddell and Scott, 1064b-1065a, where it is pointed out that the Greek word

λύκος, which usually means simply "wolf," is given some extended meanings. To see a wolf, λύκον ἰδεῖν, can mean, "to be struck dumb." However, the term λύκος is also used for a crow, a fish, a hook-shaped object (perhaps a nose) or even as a nickname for the pederast. Consider 1.2, where Theophilus rhetorically asks Autolycus if he is an ἀρσενο-κοίτης (one who lies with men), a term which R. M. Grant translates "pederast." This question of Autolycus seems a personal affront that could suggest less than a cordial relationship between the two. It could also suggest, along with the cryptic meaning of his name, that Autolycus is a literary fiction created by the bishop as a tool for presenting his ideas. Whatever the case may be, it is questionable whether the person or persons represented by Autolycus could have been a friend(s) with the bishop in the normal sense of the word.

26. R. M. Grant, *Greek Apologists,* 143, does not think that Eusebius knew the third book.

27. R. M. Grant, *Greek Apologists,* 143, offers a rather elaborate explanation of how Eusebius arrived at these dates on the basis of faulty conjecture; for Eusebius was aware of the third book, as I have shown above. Eusebius was probably a little careless, as I think he was with his listing of Peter as first Antiochene bishop rather than Evodius in *EH* 3.36.2. Another possibility, which is perhaps improbable, is that Theophilus retired from his office as bishop some three years before he wrote his third book. G. Downey, in his *A History of Antioch,* 300f., prefers to blame Jerome for the mistake, the translator and continuator of Eusebius' *Chronicle.* Downey, however, does not give reasons why Jerome's work should be disparaged.

28. G. Downey, *A History of Antioch,* 301; W. H. C. Frend, *The Rise of Christianity,* 252; R. M. Grant, *AA,* ix-x; F. W. Norris, "Theophilus," *EEC,* 895, and J. Quasten, *Patrology,* 237; all agree on the early date. R. M. Grant, from his analysis of Eusebius' contributions on Theophilus, in the article "The Problem of Theophilus," *Harvard Theological Review* 43 (1950), 180, concludes that at least the first two books addressed to Autolycus were "in the library at Caesarea or Jerusalem, and that [Eusebius] had not read them carefully."

29. G. Downey, *A History of Antioch,* 301, discusses the evidence for this date.

30. Regarding this translation of the Greek word κλίματα, see the comment by R. M. Grant, "The Problem of Theophilus," 179.

31. See J. Quasten, *Patrology,* 236 and R. M. Grant *AA,* ix, who refer to 1.14; 2.1, 25 and 28 and 3.4. However, I find their suggestions a conjectural stretch. For example, Theophilus' tongue-in-cheek claim to be "unskilled in speaking" (2.1) is probably no more than a literary affectation of Paul, who himself adds "but not in knowledge" (2 Cor. 11:6). One might even suggest, in this line of provocative observations, that Theophilus may have been the product of a very strict home, a supposition derived from 2.25 where he seems to speak beyond his own metaphor regarding paternal discipline. The bishop says: "For a father sometimes orders his own child to abstain from certain things, and when the child does not obey the paternal command he is beaten and receives chastisement because of his disobedience. The commands themselves are not the blows; the disobedience results in beatings for the disobedient one."

32. Καὶ μὴ γίνου ἄπιστος ἀλλὰ πιστός. Cf.Theophilus' Μὴ οὖν ἀπίστει, ἀλλὰ πίστευε.

33. With this first mention of Theophilus' use of a New Testament text, a couple of comments should be made regarding his knowledge of a New Testament canon. While Theophilus quotes from eight books and alludes to some sixty-four texts from the New Testament (see chapter two for a demonstration of the distribution of biblical texts in Theophilus' three books), he never mentions a New Testament canon or collection. It is

uncertain, however, whether or not he was familiar with the concept of a new covenant (see Hebrews 8:8 and Jeremiah 31:31 [LXX], which speak of a καινή διαθήκη, and Hebrews 12:22 and 24, where the author says, in a sermonic invitation, προσεληλύθατε . . . Ἰησοῦ μεσίτη διαθήκης νέας ["You have come . . . to Jesus, the mediator of a new covenant"]). With respect to the origin of the New Testament as a canon, B. S. Childs, *The New Testament As Canon: An Introduction* (Philadelphia: Fortress, 1985), 18, says: "It should be noticed that a remarkable consensus among modern scholars has emerged regarding certain features of the history of the canonization of the New Testament. There is broad agreement that the canon of the New Testament gradually developed as a part of the larger growth of the Christian church during the second century. By AD 200 the four gospels were widely reckoned as Scripture on a par with the [Hebrew Bible] along with a corpus of Pauline letters. However, the process of determining the out limits of the apostolic writings developed, often in heated debate, until the end of the fourth century at which time both the Eastern and Western branches of the church reached a decision regarding the canon's scope which then generally became normative for the ancient church."

34. See B. Layton, *The Gnostic Scriptures* (Garden City, NY: Doubleday, 1987), 359-65.

35. 1.3; 2.8, 14, 25, 26, 36, 37, 38; 3.7 and 11.

36. Once again, it seems to me that the emotional level and personal nature of his language in passages such as this one go some distance toward suggesting the reality of his encounter with an actual person whose debate encouraged him to compose these documents.

37. This important and fascinating passage from 1.1 will be discussed at length in chapter six. The term "Christian(s)" is used in 1.1, 12; 2.33; 3.4, 15.

Chapter 2

Theophilus' Writings

Having discussed the testimony about Theophilus of Antioch, the internal information regarding the title of his only extant books, his dates, and some of his
personal revelations, let us consider the genre and rhetorical development of *Ad
Autolycum*. In so doing I intend to make a case for defining the bishop's religious thought in this particular collection of books as "protreptic theology."

The Genre of *Ad Autolycum*

Theophilus' books,[1] or at least various parts of them, have been called apology,
biblical exegesis, chronology, mystagogy, christianology and theogony.[2] As a
collection, *Ad Autolyum* is a complicated mix of materials.[3] On the one hand, the
critical reader might see these books as three independent caches for Theophilus' disheveled thoughts. On the other hand, the casual and receptive observer,
perhaps charmed by their conversational tone and intensity, would probably
overlook what is occasionally a cacophony of ideas. Fortunately, Theophilus
himself is very helpful in describing his work and what it is that distinguishes his
three books from each other. The first set of three descriptive terms used above,
apology, biblical exegesis and chronology, can actually be applied to each of the
books, respectively, as marks of distinction rather than inclusive characteriza-
tions of the collection itself. But let us first consider the bishop's own language
in this regard.

Theophilus uses three terms to designate each of his books; however, they
are probably not of sufficient technical value to be considered generic descriptions. Nevertheless, they will be used throughout my discussions of *Ad Autolycum* for the simple reason that Theophilus chose them. The first book is,
according to Theophilus, a *homilia*.[4] It is from this word that we get the English
term "homily," a religious or moralizing sermon that may be either oral or written. Furthermore, "homiletics" is generally understood to be a branch of theology dealing with the preparations of such sermons. The Greek term *homilia* has
been used in a variety of ways.[5] Theophilus uses the term to refer to an instruc-
tional discourse regarding the nature of the religion he is promoting. His

Homilia, which I will use from this point on as a title for this document, may have been the text of an earlier lecture he then revised in the form of a public letter. It has the features of a document that was originally tightly structured, perhaps for an oral presentation, but is now redesigned for purposes of displaying greater social interaction, like an ongoing dialogue. Whatever the circumstances of the formation of our text may have been, the *Homilia* clearly reveals that it is engaged not only in the promotion of a religious perspective, but in a highly developed polemic against Greek religion. This polemic is occasionally punctuated by a defensive stance against what Theophilus takes to be ridicule of his Christian faith. Thus, in a qualified sense, the book may legitimately be called apologetic, even though it is not a sustained "apology."

The second book is called a *syngramma* by Theophilus.[6] This designation does not do justice to the weighty content of the document, however. While meaning little more than a "treatise" in this context, it will serve quite well as a title. Theophilus' *Syngramma* is a sustained effort on the bishop's part to give his friend (and perhaps his own church) a theological study. It is a theological text carefully constructed around the exegesis of a key biblical passage. The *Syngramma* possesses, as we shall see, a significant commentary on the early chapters of Genesis and developed reflections on a variety of doctrinal matters that I believe are highly important to his religious perspective.

The bishop calls his third book a *hypomnema.*[7] I take him to mean that he will provide Autolycus with an extended set of "memoranda" or informal summaries of subjects that have been under discussion for some time. These memoranda, which alone among his three books possess the most obvious element of the epistolary form, a salutation,[8] are arranged in two parts. The first part of the *Hypomnema,* which is my title for the document, deals with questions of morality—the inherent deficiency of Autolycus' values over agaiₙ.ₜt a Christian ethic. The second part is an attempt to organize a collection of sources so as to provide a chronology that would support the thesis that Christianity is older and truer than Autolycus' pagan religion. Having identified some of the distinguishing marks of Theophilus' extant writings, what can be said on behalf of their collective unity?

The second set of descriptive terms used above, namely, mystagogy, christianology and theogony, represents a creative attempt on the part of a couple of scholars to understand Theophilus' work as a unified whole. That is to say, these terms are more or less inclusive of all three books. J. Bentivegna uses the term "mystagogy" as a generic definition for Theophilus' work, but seems to prefer the designation he coined for the bishop's presentation of his faith, that is, "christianology." First, he defines mystagogy in a rather eccentric fashion as "the encounter between the Christian message and the cultural categories accepted by men."[9] The term is commonly used to refer to a document describing an initiation into a mystery cult, that is, into a community that possesses esoteric teachings.[10] Bentivegna does not believe, however, that Theophilus is introducing his readers to the esoteric features of his faith. Rather, he believes Theophilus is offering to make that which may be esoteric for some exoteric for all. It does seem that if one were to add the element of persuasion to Bentivegna's definition, an activity in which Theophilus clearly engages, then mystagogy would be a notion nearly identical to the missionary character of "apology." Thus, on first look, the new term, mystagogy, would appear to offer little to the discussion.

On second look, however, Bentivegna may be suggesting something that many readers of Theophilus have missed. It is true that the bishop is involved with proselytizing in *Ad Autolycum*. But, his proselytizing has a pronounced intellectual bent. He employs his intellect toward persuading, and sometimes intimidating, his audience to make room for his message. This message is essentially, what he calls his *theosebeia,* that is, the "mystery" of his religion.[11] In his *Hypomnema,* the bishop quotes from a Greek poet who asks: "What use is religion (*eusebeia*)?" (3.7). In reading Theophilus' books one senses that he is preoccupied throughout with this sort of question and thus perhaps with demonstrating how his *theosebeia* is to be distinguished from his pagan audience's *eusebeia.*[12] In fact he says just that at the beginning of his *Syngramma,* "I set forth the nature of my [*theosebeia*] for you" (2.1). Perhaps it is rather insightful after all on Bentivegna's part to suggest that Theophilus is a mystagogue, that is, one who interprets how his *theosebeia* is suitable for the uninitiated of his audience.

Bentivegna's other characterization of Theophilus' work, as christianology, offers an original term that is even more intriguing than his initial idea. He points out that Theophilus' extant teaching is "a Christianity without Christ," that is, Jesus in nowhere mentioned in his work, and so concludes that no one who had read *Ad Autolycum* "would have the slightest idea that Christian doctrine might have anything to do with the person of Christ."[13] Thus, Bentivegna claims, Theophilus does not offer his readers a christology, at least not a christology in the normal sense of the word. On the other hand, what the bishop does supply is an informed presentation of the essentials needed to be a Christian. While Bentivegna is correct in saying that Theophilus' *Ad Autolycum* does not promote any teachings *about* Jesus per se, a good case can be made that he promotes the teachings *of* Jesus. Nevertheless, it is Bentivegna's point that Theophilus presents in his extant collection of documents a Christianity that does not appear to be a religion centered on Christ, but a religion centered on what it means to be a Christian. This provocative observation by Bentivegna recommends accepting his designation of *Ad Autolycum* as christianology. Actually, both of Bentivegna's designations, mystagogy and christianology, are nearly coterminous in meaning. For him Theophilus' books exemplify persuasive instruction, leading to a knowledge of a particular type of Christianity that was intended to be attractive to a Greek pagan audience. Therefore, interpreted in Bentivegna's terms, as mystagogy and christianology, with the focus on the promotional elements of the bishop's theology, *Ad Autolycum* is Theophilus' invitation to the Christian life. Now let us consider one final suggestion, Cury's term "theogony."

It has been carefully noted by numerous scholars that Theophilus draws upon a host of literary sources like the Septuagint, Homer, Plato, Euripides, Orpheus, the Sibyl and others for information regarding the genesis of the pagan gods, the creation of the world and the origin of mortals, which in a broad sense is the material of a genre called theogony.[14] C. Cury, in this connection, is convinced that Theophilus uses the famous *Theogony* of Hesiod as a model and, further, he implies that the bishop is actually imitating Hesiod in the development of his own comparable theogony.[15] Cury says of Theophilus' method and motivation:

> [Theophilus] analyzed pagan accounts of theogonic materials and of-
> fered a Christian alternative. His purpose was to enlighten Autolycus
> concerning the one, true God, creation, and the history of man.
> Theophilus intended to demonstrate that the Christian account was
> the true one. He was aware that Autolycus had read "the histories and
> genealogies of the so-called gods" and was concerned because
> Autolycus did not realize that he was reading about the generations
> of men and not gods.[16]

Cury's use of the term theogony seems to offer a specific example of what Bentivegna was suggesting in his description of Theophilus' work as mystagogy. How does Theophilus interpret his *theosebeia* ? Cury would probably say that the bishop interprets the nature of his religion in terms of an alternative theogony. Actually, Cury is convinced that the structure and content of Theophilus' work proves his intent to develop a theogony. He points out:

> [Theophilus] demonstrates that he has pagan theogonies in mind as
> he relates the origin and nature of God, then the origin of mankind,
> and finally the establishment of the present order.[17]

Each of these three elements of Theophilus' theogony is, according to Cury, dealt with respectively by each of the bishop's three books.

Cury's designation of *Ad Autolycum* as theogony is useful in calling attention to an important aspect of Theophilus' work that is overlooked by Bentivegna, namely, the polemical elements of his theology. It is true that Theophilus intends to formulate an attractive invitation to his faith, as Bentivegna demonstrates, but the bishop did not do so in a way that compromised his understanding of the superior character of Christianity to Greek mythological thought. Cury makes clear that Christianity is for Theophilus a significant alternative position, even though the bishop does not actually set out to compare the two. Rather, Theophilus chooses to dissuade his audience using polemics. Homer, Hesiod and other Greek poets make theogonic claims that are for Theophilus usually insupportable and, more often than not, demonstrably false. Theophilus intends "to enlighten" his audience regarding the theogonic claims of the Christian account, which he maintains are supportable and demonstrably true. Given that there is no real demonstration of his point in the text, this becomes the language of polemics and not comparative analysis. Cury's contribution of this designation, theogony, for *Ad Autolycum,* with its focus on the polemical elements in Theophilus' theology, is a welcome addition to the discussion. However, it might serve us well to observe a few more comments by Theophilus himself before drawing up a general statement regarding the genre of *Ad Autolycum.*

Several of the designations given above are adequate for defining prevalent aspects of Theophilus' writings, namely, the promotional and polemical aspects, but they lack the descriptive breadth and generic precision that I am seeking. Theophilus views himself as a critic of philosophers, poets and historians in general. He says of them that they are inconsistent, foolish, useless, immoral and full of contradictions (2.3, 5, 15; 3.2-8). Of their writings, he says, they embellish and, in their attempt to be original, they fail by plagiarizing (1.14; 2.12, 37). Actually, "all the historians and poets and so-called philosophers are deceived in every respect, and so are those who pay attention to them" (2.28). These Greek authors are both deceived and deceivers, according to Theophilus. Therefore, to counter their deceptions one must become discriminating and employ critical reasoning. In his words:

> The intelligent listener and reader must pay close attention to what they say, as Simylos observes: "It is the custom to call poets equally those of exceptional nature and those who are bad; one must differentiate." In the same vein, Philemon says somewhere: "A bad thing is an unintelligent listener in his seat, for because of his stupidity he does not blame himself." One must therefore pay attention and understand what is said, critically examining the remarks of philosophers and of poets as well. (3.7)

Theophilus—standing before his class citing the appropriate quotations to his eager students, words that would motivate them and instill respect for his discipline—presents himself as a teacher of criticism.

As was stated above, each of Theophilus' books has its own generic qualities and its own distinguishable purposes. But what they all seem to share is a "didactic" character.[18] In the two passages cited above and in the one cited immediately below, each from a different book, Theophilus instructs his readers in the crucial art of "paying attention." This is didactic language or the discourse of a teacher intent upon instructing one in a discipline. The bishop consistently employs this style of discourse throughout *Ad Autolycum.* Consider this statement from his opening chapter in his first book:

> The man who loves truth, however, pays no attention to defiled language but examines the fact behind the word to see what it is and what it means. (1.1)

Theophilus would have his students know that learning how to pay attention through the application of critical examination is essential if one is to avoid deception.

As was suggested earlier, the first book is a discourse in which he sets forth the nature of his religion. The second book is a treatise which uses biblical commentary and theological discussion to demonstrate the inadequacy of the contemporary history texts for providing accurate religious truth. The third book is a set of memoranda in which he produces lengthy summaries of evidence for both the superior nature of his Christian ethic and the greater antiquity of his religion and scriptures. All three books are therefore highly didactic. Theophilus is an educator and his three books in the collection *Ad Autolycum* are presented to his readers much like modern classroom textbooks. As a man who loves truth, he teaches those who seek truth, how to learn truth. He claims that even the finest language can be defiled and therefore rhetoric should not be considered the source of truth. Obviously good students must go beyond the observation of language to obtain the truth. Theophilus is subtle, but he wants his readers to know and to feel confident that he is prepared to "lead them to a knowledge of the truth." Continuing the metaphor, at the end of each of these three textbooks, Theophilus offers advice to the student audience sitting in his classroom. First, says the teacher as promoter of his religion, "I advise you to fear [God] and believe him" (1.14). And second, says the teacher as promoter of his discipline, "he who loves learning must really love it . . . meet with us often, so that by hearing a living voice you may accurately learn what is true" (2.38). Last but not least, says the teacher as promoter of his sacred literature, "if you will, read these books carefully so that you may have a counsellor and pledge of the truth" (3.30).[19]

On the one hand, Theophilus' vocation is that of a professional church leader, a bishop, whose duties probably included some catechistic teaching. On the other hand, his avocation is that of a critical scholar and educator who wants to teach his intelligent listeners and readers the fine art of discovering the truth. Toward this end, he functions as both a professor of a particular perspective and a polemicist against any other viewpoint, while his three books, predominantly apologetic, theological and historical, respectively, are the pedagogical tools he uses. To imply, as do most patristic scholars, that all three texts are apology is to place his thought into such a narrow category that one might lose touch with his larger agenda as well as the focus of his theological work.

How should Theophilus be identified? The bishop does not fully share the inclination of Justin, Tatian and Athenagoras toward a defensively oriented rhetoric. He does not address himself to an antagonistic emperor or craft his material for an hostile Greek audience as do these three, but ostensibly makes a didactic presentation to a gifted "student" who although committed to Greek *paideia* is both skeptical and curious. There is tension between Theophilus and Autolycus, but the bishop's rhetoric throughout *Ad Autolycum* does not recommend identifying this entire collection of documents by the generalization, "apology." From the relative isolation of his profession and the shelter of his ecclesiastical walls, he could pursue his own agenda of interpreting and promoting Christianity with vigorous persuasion and intense polemic. He was probably not connected with a school and thus was not a professional scholar, as were most of the other Greek apologists. Rather he was an erudite pastor who enjoyed a scholarly avocation. While all three books can be read independent of each other, they share two features: a pseudo-dialogical style and a didactic nature.

They are the product of a bishop, an official of the church, who functions as a theologian and a *paideutes* (teacher of *paideia*). Again, it is imprecise to label him as a mere apologist and to treat his work in the expectation of finding only a variation on the literary approach and ideas of Justin, Tatian and Athenagoras. Thus, while *Ad Autolycum* might legitimately be called missionary literature or an invitation to embrace a particular *theosebeia,* to call Theophilus himself an apologist is far too limiting for my presentation of his theology and has led many readers to less than a full appreciation of that theology.

Trying to characterize Theophilus and his work by a single term is a difficult task. While the recent recommendations discussed above, mystagogy, christianology and theogony, pierce the cloud surrounding Theophilus' work as well as his persona, for purposes of my presentation it is much more useful to call him simply a theologian who produced material of a didactic nature. Moreover, the theological arguments made in these books are only what the bishop assumed were necessary to convince one like Autolycus of his need for conversion. The theology of *Ad Autolycum,* with its persuasive and dissuasive styles, and its promotional and polemical arguments, is seldom more than propaedeutic. The three books to Autolycus make up an invitation to take up a particular kind of theologically oriented life. In a sense then, *Ad Autolycum* can be called "protreptic literature."[20]

In summary, I think that in Theophilus' three books we are dealing with protreptic literature which contains the propaedeutic teachings of his religion in a form that could be called "protreptic theology," a theology designed to recruit converts to a moral life consistent with biblical law.[21] Let us now consider the rhetorical development of Theophilus' three books.

The Development of *Ad Autolycum*

Theophilus of Antioch was an important thinker within his church. His life is obscure, but judging from the evidence of his extant works, he was as engaged with the important theological issues of his day as any other second-century theologian. Before drawing our discussion of Theophilus' writings to a conclusion, where I will suggest a theory regarding the rhetorical development of his three books, let us first take a more detailed look at the structure and content of each book in *Ad Autolycum* and then address his use of biblical materials.

The *Homilia* (the first book in *Ad Autolycum*) is in many respects an apologetic discussion newly created from what appears to be a variety of catechistic materials which could very well have been developed by Theophilus at an earlier time and then pressed into service in a new format. Within the fourteen chapters of the *Homilia* there are seven primary subjects being dealt with, but not consecutively. Chapters one and twelve are linked together by Theophilus' treatment of the name "Christian." Chapters two and five offer a response to the philosophical problem inherent in Autolycus' request: "Show me your God!" Chapters three and four lay out the nature of God and his many attributes. Chapters six and seven address God's creative activity. Chapters nine through eleven deal with the absurdity of idolatry and emperor-worship. Chapters eight and thirteen challenge Autolycus' disbelief in the teaching of the resurrection of the dead. The last chapter of book one is Theophilus' own confession and testimony. These seven groupings of materials within book one, whether they were ever independent or not, are skillfully woven together to produce a suitable document for Theophilus' new purpose, namely, to introduce Autolycus to the bishop's religion (*theosebeia*).

Theophilus' *Syngramma* (the second of his books in *Ad Autolycum*), with its thirty-eight chapters, is far more like a "treatise" than the first book. How successful the *Homilia* may have been in gaining respect for Theophilus' *theosebeia* is not clear from what is said in this second book. Nevertheless, as his succinct introductory chapter makes plain, his *Syngramma* will "provide . . . a more accurate proof concerning the pointless labour and pointless religion (*threskeia*)" of Autolycus (2.1).[22] Where Theophilus insinuated, in his *Homilia,* that he had the resources to provide justifiable assurance regarding the truth of his religion he is now prepared, in his *Syngramma,* to give a more explicit demonstration proving the superiority of his religion. How will he provide such proof? By using a few of Autolycus' own history books, Theophilus will demonstrate that the Greek *threskeia* of his friend is no match for his own *theosebeia*. With this preface, we can see that the *Syngramma* does not possess the charming conversational tone that gave his first book its unique character, but rather it is a sustained effort on the bishop's part to provide his friend with an educational critique of his religion. His polemic, which at times is sarcastic, is directed at idolatry and mythology in chapters two and three, and at the philosophers, poets and historians in chapters four through seven. In chapters eight through ten Theophilus offers an introduction to a long discussion regarding the "origin of the world." What better topic to contrast *threskeia* and *theosebeia*? Chapters eleven through thirty-two consist of his commentary on the early chapters of Genesis and key reflections on Theophilus' logos speculation. With chapters thirty-three through thirty-eight the bishop returns to his polemic, but now carefully contrasting the Hellenistic and Christian understandings of prophecy and morality.

Theophilus' arrangement of materials in his second book is somewhat more controlled and deliberate. They fall into two main groups, the approximately fourteen chapters of his polemics (2-9 and 33-38) and the much larger twenty-three chapters of his exegetical treatment of Genesis (10-32). The concerns of chapters one, eight, nine, ten and maybe thirty-three as well, seem to have been conceived by Theophilus during the composition of his *Syngramma*. These chapters serve as fine introductions, conclusions and transitions for what were probably smaller independent tracts or lectures that now have a new purpose as a treatise and an address to Autolycus. Whether or not the polemical material itself ever existed as an independent document is less certain than that the commentary on Genesis surely did.[23]

Theophilus' *Hypomnema* (the third book in the collection) is promoted as a "brief" memorandum, although it is thirty chapters long. The introduction to this work, chapter one, makes clear that Theophilus intends to prove once and for all the antiquity of his scriptures over against the "nonsense" of Greek literature.[24] The body of the document is arranged in two parts. The first part, chapters two through fifteen, offers a critical discussion of the quality of the writings and the character of the authors that presumably Autolycus found authoritative. In so doing, Theophilus compares and contrasts pagan literature with biblical literature. Of course, the inherent deficiency of Autolycus' values over against a Christian ethic is emphasized. Chapters two through eight argue the uselessness, inconsistency and immorality of Greek authors. Chapters nine through fourteen juxtapose the merit, consistency and probity of the Law, Prophets and Gospels. Add to this the evidence of contemporary Christian conduct which is based on these writings, presented in chapter fifteen, and a powerful case has been made for the superiority of Theophilus' scriptures over Autolycus' Greek literature.

The second part of the *Hypomnema,* chapters sixteen through twenty-nine, is an attempt to organize a collection of sources to provide a chronology that would support the thesis that Christianity is older (and truer) than Autolycus' religion. Chapters sixteen through nineteen discuss the great flood and the Genesis account, with Theophilus attempting to set the record straight. Chapters twenty through twenty-three consider some details surrounding the exodus event and some chronological matters concerning the building of the temple, both on the basis of the witness of the historians Manetho, Menander and Josephus. Theophilus' analysis seeks to demonstrate that the report of these historians is so much later than the scriptures given through Moses. Chapters twenty-four through twenty-eight represent Theophilus' writing of chronological history from Adam to Cyrus of Persia to Marcus Aurelius. Chapter twenty-nine is a somewhat odd reassertion of his thesis with a few qualifications and the addition of a few more sources and arguments. The last chapter is Theophilus' final plea that his students read his sources and his books, and discover the truth for themselves.

To help us understand the development of these books, and given that their arguments depend so highly on the bishop's exegesis of scripture, it is worth our while to formulate a precise idea about Theophilus' use of particular biblical materials. While his explicit quotations (Q) from both the Septuagint (LXX) and the New Testament (NT) are numerous, his books are replete with biblical allusions (A). In Grant's edition of *Ad Autolycum,* he makes note of each quotation and allusion.[25] Being in agreement with most of his observations and speculations in this regard, I have constructed a distribution chart based on Grant's accounting. Consider the following statistics:

BIBLICAL QUOTATIONS AND ALLUSIONS IN *AD AUTOLYCUM*

Texts	*Homilia*		*Syngramma*		*Hypomnema*		Totals	
LXX	Q–1	A–36	Q–24	A–25	Q–19	A–17	Q–44	A–78
Law	Q–0	A–1	Q–7	A–13	Q–4	A–7	Q–11	A–21
Prophets	Q–0	A–3	Q–13	A–5	Q–13	A–7	Q–26	A–15
Writings	Q–1	A–31	Q–4	A–7	Q–2	A–0	Q–7	A–38
Apocrypha	Q–0	A–1	Q–0	A–0	Q–0	A–3	Q–0	A–4
NT	Q–0	A–24	Q–1	A–29	Q–7	A–11	Q–8	A–64
Gospels	Q–0	A–1	Q–1	A–7	Q–4	A–5	Q–5	A–13
Paul's Letters	Q–0	A–21	Q–0	A–19	Q–3	A–5	Q–3	A–45
The Rest	Q–0	A–2	Q–0	A–3	Q–0	A–1	Q–0	A–6

While there are many interesting observations that could be made about Theophilus' method and preferences, let me call to your attention several key points in terms of the present discussion. First, the *Homilia* (apologetic argument) appears to have less need for biblical quotations than the *Syngramma* (exegesis) and the *Hypomnema* (history and ethics). Second, while quotations from the Septuagint are evenly distributed between the *Syngramma* and the *Hypomnema* (particularly from the Prophets), quotations from the New Testament are more important for the bishop's work in the *Hypomnema* (despite the high number of allusions to Pauline material in the first two books). And third, while the Law and the Prophets are dominant in the *Syngramma,* as one might expect given the exegetical purpose of this book, the wisdom teachings of the Writings are essential to the arguments of the *Homilia.* Overall, the distribution of biblical materials (Septuagint and New Testament) goes to affirm the rhetorical purpose of each book.

Theophilus wrote his *Homilia* to Autolycus, a curious pagan friend, in order to convince him and his ilk of the legitimacy of the Christian faith. For this reason, this document may be properly called an apology. Theophilus' theological rhetoric in the *Syngramma* demonstrates that he wrote this document on a considerably higher level to a seemingly less hostile and better-educated reader. In the *Syngramma,* while still attempting to convince Autolycus of the value of Christianity, the bishop takes this opportunity to reveal far more of his theological perspective within a highly developed exegesis of a key biblical text. He seems to think Autolycus, or the audience he represents, was prepared to digest such material and could benefit from it. In fact, the *Syngramma* seems to possess material that would have been highly beneficial even to Theophilus' church. Such an observation may have led Jerome to exceed Eusebius' characterization of these documents as "elementary" treatises, saying of them that they were "well fitted for the edification of the church." The *Hypomnema,* while more concerned with historical data than the other two works, goes even further to lay out the essence of Christian theology as a matter of moral law. By the time of the publication of this document, Theophilus' attentive readers (students like Autolycus) were presumed to be better educated in Christian thought and therefore able to comprehend not only the superiority but also the utter necessity of Christian morality.

Now, in conclusion, let us consider a modest theory regarding the development of Theophilus' theological rhetoric in *Ad Autolycum*. It seems to me that we can observe an intended rhetorical development within the bishop's three books. Autolycus, as the bishop's nemesis in the *Homilia,* an interested skeptic in the *Syngramma,* and a protégé and potential convert in the *Hypomnema,* represents a lively Antiochene audience. The development that I believe exists within the books of *Ad Autolycum* reflects a growth in Theophilus' readership over a period of time, one which demanded his literary shift in purpose, and his willingness to add theological information appropriate for a maturing audience. But it should also be said that as a unit Theophilus' books maintained a certain consistency of purpose, that is, he intended by this collection to provide an attractive invitation to a Christian way of life. With these suggestions in mind, consider the following schematic of this development in *Ad Autolycum* in terms of audience, purpose and theology:

RHETORICAL DEVELOPMENT IN *AD AUTOLYCUM*

	Homilia	*Syngramma*	*Hypomnema*
Audience:	A slightly hostile reader whom the bishop considers a nemesis, who is well educated in Greek literature but who does not have much information regarding the Christian faith.	A more receptive reader whose hostility toward the bishop has subsided to skepticism regarding the bishop's religion and who is very curious and ready to engage in controversial biblical materials.	A reader who is highly informed about the Christian religion and deeply involved with the bishop, who may be prepared to consider conversion but needs to resolve some serious peripheral matters.
Purpose:	To introduce his audience to the philosophical foundations of his religion, and then to defend its veracity.	To educate his audience about the more refined nature of his religion and its literature, promoting its ethical demands.	To convert his audience by clarifying essential ethics and resolving any outstanding issues that may deter them from conversion.
Theology:	Among a variety of teachings about God, man, the logos and nomos, there is a theological focus on God's nature.	With the same variety of teachings, the focus has shifted to man's soteriological history and the role of the logos in that history.	With less attention on God and the logos, the focus is now on the content of nomos as a necessity to Christian conversion.

These documents could be described in terms of mystagogy or christianology, but with its mixture of didactic and polemical theology aimed at proselytizing, I prefer to speak of *Ad Autolycum* as protreptic literature which contains a protreptic theology. Theophilus' intellectual and religious environment was intense and challenging and he shows in his theological rhetoric in all three books a competitive spirit that was willing not only to defend his religion of biblical morality, a religion which he was committed to and called Christianity, but also to promote its sophisticated soteriology of law. While the bishop's only surviving writings contain a theological exposition of his faith, it is presented in the form of protreptic theology, that is, a theologically oriented invitation to "true religion." Therefore, it is *Ad Autolycum*'s "protreptic theology" that is promoted as a soteriology of law and not the bishop's "ecclesiastical theology" per se. It is important to be precise on this point so as not to suggest that the bishop promoted such a soteriology in his parish or among his mature converts. He could have, and I believe that he probably did in some fashion. But such an argument would be difficult to make without additional evidence. However, in choosing to expound his faith in the manner of these documents, it seems to me, he can be credited with theological ideas that were different from those of other second-century theologians, ideas which the later church actually found lacking in some essential ways.

As we shall see in the next three chapters of this book, Theophilus has a recoverable and rather complete theological perspective in *Ad Autolycum,* but it is not the perspective of an evolving orthodoxy—that is, the sort of perspective we would find in an Ignatius or a Justin or an Irenaeus.

Notes

1. R. M. Grant, *AA,* xix-xxi, provides information regarding the transmission of these books, and he says of the establishment of Theophilus' texts (on xix): "we are dependent upon a single manuscript now at Venice . . . written in the late tenth century or the early eleventh, and later corrected for orthography." The manuscript he is referring to is known as Codex Marcianus gr. 496 (folios 160 verso-185 recto).

2. While the first three terms are used widely in patristic scholarship and thus need no explanation, the last three are recent contributions. The terms "mystagogy" and "christianology" are used by J. Bentivegna, "A Christianity Without Christ by Theophilus of Antioch," *Studia patristica* 13 (1975), 107 and 128-30, respectively. The term "theogony" is used by C. Cury, "The Theogony of Theophilus," *Vigiliae Christianae* 42 (1988), 318-26.

3. One could make a similar claim regarding the extant apologies of Justin, Athenagoras and Tatian. The method employed in these works might be loosely called "stream of consciousness." This, of course, is occasionally the nature of the epistolary-type of composition, which the third of Theophilus' documents is clearly stylized to be. However, I think *Ad Autolycum* is less stream of consciousness and more organized than are the other documents of this general type. I believe the following discussion will show him to have had a plan for his "complicated mix of materials."

4. 2.1 uses the Greek word ὁμιλία, referring back to book one.

5. Arndt and Gingrish, 568b, points to its usage in Justin's *Dialogue with Trypho* 28 and 85, where ὁμιλίαν ποιεῖσθαι means "to deliver a sermon" or "to preach." Also, consider the range of usages in Liddell and Scott, 1222a-b, where ὁμιλία, in the right context, can even refer to the intimacy of "sexual intercourse."

6. 2.1. The common Greek word σύγγραμμα has a short range of meanings. The term is used in most instances to refer to a written "composition" or "speech." However, it occasionally designates a systematic prose work that one might refer to as simply a "treatise."

7. 3.1. The Greek word ὑπόμνημα is perhaps the most interesting of Theophilus' choices. This word has a wide range of meanings from "memorial" or "tomb" to "public records" of a transaction or "minutes" of a meeting, and from a "dissertation" by a rhetorician to a "commentary" on poetic works. It is also used to speak of a "draft" of a personal letter or a "petition" to a magistrate, as well as a "notification" of a birth.

8. 3.1—Θεόφιλος Αὐτολύκῳ χαίρειν ("Theophilus to Autolycus, greetings.")

9. J. Bentivegna, "A Christianity Without Christ," 107.

10. See the discussions by E. Ferguson, *Backgrounds of Early Christianity* (Grand Rapids: Eerdmans, 1987), 197-240, as well as L. H. Martin, *Hellenistic Religions: An Introduction* (New York: Oxford University Press, 1987), 11-12 and 58-89. For a specific study on mystery cults, consult H. R. Willoughby, *Pagan Regeneration: A Study of Mystery Invitations in the Greco-Roman World* (Chicago: University of Chicago Press, 1974).

11. The Greek word θεοσέβεια is used twice by Theophilus, in 2.1 and 3.7. Its meaning, in its broadest sense, is the "worship of God." Its only New Testament usage is in I Timothy 2:10, where it seems to be a "piety" or "reverence for God" defined by the "doing of good works." The most appropriate example is perhaps *The Epistle to Diognetus* 4.6, which says: "But as for the mystery of [the Christian's] own religion, do not expect to be able to learn this from man (τὸ δὲ τῆς ἰδίας αὐτῶν θεοσεβείας μυστήριον μὴ προσδοκήσῃς δύνασθαι παρὰ ἀνθρώπου μαθεῖν)." This instance of *mysterion* and *theosebeia* in the same sentence may be the conceptual source of Bentivegna's usage, although he does not share this information with his readers.

12. His *theosebeia* is, of course, true religion. However, when the bishop speaks of a "false religion," or one that is not his own, he uses the Greek term θρησκεία and not εὐσέβεια. See 2.1 and 6 for examples.

13. J. Bentivegna, "A Christianity Without Christ," 128. This article is also cited and supported by R. M. Grant in his two books, *Jesus After the Gospels: The Christ of the Second Century* (Louisville, KY: Knox, 1990), 69, and *Greek Apologists of the Second Century* (Philadelphia: The Westminster Press, 1988), 165.

14. Here, no distinction between theogony and cosmogony is made, even though the precise etymological usage of theogony concerns only mythology regarding the genesis of the gods. The precedent for this broader usage is of course Hesiod's *Theogony*. R. M. Grant, *AA*, xi, comments on Theophilus' non-biblical sources, claiming that the list of Greek authors in 3.3 was based on a school catalogue of "great books," that his poetic citations were from an anthology, that Homer and Hesiod were aspects of a school curriculum, that he probably read a few of Plato's dialogues, and that all in all he used popular handbooks. In R. M. Grant's book, *Greek Apologists*, 148-56, we have a thorough review of Theophilus' use of biblical and Greek sources.

15. C. Cury, "The Theogony of Theophilus," 318f. See 2.5-6, where Theophilus quotes from Hesiod, even though he does so in an unflattering way. Theophilus says Hesiod proclaimed the world created but "lacked the force [ἠτόνησεν] to say by whom it

was created" (2.5). Apparently, Hesiod was in some fashion "too weak" to tell the full story about creation. Furthermore, he said, "we find Hesiod talking absolute nonsense and contradicting himself" (2.6). However, Cury supports the comment by N. Zeegers-Vander Vorst, *Les citations des poètes grecs chez les apologistes chrétiens du IIe siècle* (Louvain: Publications Universitaires, 1972), 114, that Theophilus had "sous les yeux le texte complet ou tout au moins de très longs fragments de la *Théogonie.*"

16. C. Cury, "The Theogony of Theophilus," 318. Cury is quoting 2.2.

17. C. Cury, "The Theogony of Theophilus," 319.

18. The word διδακτικός is a good New Testament adjective. It is appropriate for describing the work of a bishop as is clear from its usage in I Timothy 3:2, where it says: δεῖ τὸν ἐπίσκοπον εἶναι διδακτικόν. In a similar connection, we read in II Timothy 2:24: δοῦλον κυρίου δεῖ εἶναι διδακτικόν. The next verse explains why this is necessary (see 2:25 in the NIV). It says: "Those who oppose him he must gently instruct (παιδεύοντα), in the hope that God will give them a change of heart leading them to a knowledge of the truth." As we shall see, παιδεύω is an important verb for Theophilus too (see 2.26).

19. M. Dods, in "Theophilus of Antioch To Autolycus," *ANF,* volume 2, 121, takes a particular manuscript reading of σύμβολον ("compendium") rather than Grant's σύμβουλον ("counsellor"). While Theophilus is probably saying that the biblical books are reliable sources of the truth (earlier in this chapter he spoke of αἱ ἱστορίαι τῆς ἀληθείας), there is another possible, though less probable, way of reading this last piece of advice. Given the perception of this final statement in the *Hypomnema* as a conclusion to his collection of Autolycian books, one could make a case for the bishop referencing his own three publications as educational tools.

20. In the words of A. J. Malherbe, *Moral Exhortation, A Greco-Roman Sourcebook* (Philadelphia: The Westminster Press, 1986), 122: "Protrepsis is designed to win someone over to a particular enterprise or way of life by demonstrating its superiority. First practiced by orators in the political arena and the law courts, it had become popular by the middle of the third century B.C. when the young Aristotle, in reaction to Isocrates, wrote his *Protrepticus,* which was an eloquent invitation to the philosophic life. Although preserved only in fragments, it appears to have contained a systematic argument in favor of philosophy. A follower of Isocrates replied to Aristotle in *To Demonicus* which redressed the balance by stressing the practical over the contemplative life. Protrepsis then continued to enlist recruits for the philosophic enterprise itself or for the moral life grounded in and guided by philosophy." Also, see S. K. Stowers, *Letter Writing in Greco-Roman Antiquity* (Philadelphia: The Westminster Press, 1986), 112-13, who says: "Protreptic . . . means those writings which fall broadly into the tradition of *protreptikoi logoi* (protreptic speeches), of which Aristotle's *Protrepticus* and Cicero's *Hortensius* are the most famous examples. These are exhortations to take up the philosophical life. Protreptic speeches can be traced back to the Sophists, who tried thereby to win students to their schools and to the wisdom which they taught. Protreptic works urge the reader to convert to a way of life, join a school, or accept a set of teachings as normative for the reader's life." Stowers believes that the "so-called apologies like the *Epistle to Diognetus* and Tatian's *Oration Against the Greeks* are actually protreptic works." Malherbe adds other second century works like the *Letter of Ptolemy to Flora* and of course Clement of Alexandria's, *Protrepticus.* It seems odd to me that neither Malherbe or Stowers considered *Ad Autolycum.* Regarding the protreptic nature of so-called apologetic literature, see especially H. Koester's *Introduction to the New Testament. Volume Two: History and Literature of Early Christianity* (Philadelphia: Fortress, 1982), 339-40. Koester dissents from many patristic scholars in their reading of "apologies" as merely

defensive literature. He claims: "The apologists were not primarily interested in the defense of Christianity against accusations that had been raised by the pagan world and by the Roman state—although this motive plays a considerable role. The primary model of apologetic works was instead the Greek *protrepticus,* that is, a literary genre designed as an invitation to a philosophical way of life, directed to all those who were willing to engage in the search for the true philosophy and make it the rule for their life and conduct."

21. My coinage of the term "protreptic theology" will be reconsidered in chapter six, after our consideration of the bishop's thought.

22. Theophilus uses the term "pointless labor" (ματαιοπονία) again when he opens book three (3.1), and some ten times he refers to positions other than his own by using a form of the adjective "pointless" (μάταιος) (2.1, 12, 35; 3.1, 4, 7, 26, 30). Such language suggests an ongoing polemic. However, that polemic is less intense and personal in this second book.

23. R. M. Grant, "Theophilus of Antioch to Autolycus," *Harvard Theological Review* 40 (1947), 234, suggests that this commentary could have been a first draft of Theophilus' *Adversus Hermogenem,* which Eusebius (*EH* 4.24) mentioned. Apparently, Hermogenes offered his own commentary on the Hexaëmeros, which was "one of the most rationalistic" of his day. See Tertullian's *Adversus Hermogenem* and J. Quasten's discussion of this commentary in his *Patrology,* 276. Who was Hermogenes? K. Rudolph, in his *Gnosis* (San Francisco: Harper and Row, 1985), 325-26, offers this pithy summary regarding the notorious gnostic about whom both Hippolytus and Tertullian wrote treatises: "[The painter Hermogenes] was probably born in Antioch (in Syria) and, in about 180, the bishop of Antioch [Theophilus] wrote a polemical tract against him which has not survived. Twenty years later Tertullian wrote against him in Carthage. This painter, of whom Tertullian maliciously opined that he married more than he painted, evidently influenced his disciples very much ideologically. He must have had a very original mind for, like the Alexandrian gnostics, he combined Greek Platonic ideas with gnostic and Christian ideas into a dualistic cosmology which Hippolytus included in his book of heresies."

24. Theophilus often calls pagan literature "nonsense" (2.6, 10, 12, 15, 30; 3.1, 7, 8, 16, 21, 26).

25. R. M. Grant, *AA,* 148-50.

PART TWO:
THEOPHILUS' THEOLOGY

Chapter 3

The Human Condition

The investigation underway now allows us to move forward with the task of entering into the theological home of Theophilus' *Ad Autolycum*. Finding our way in should be somewhat easier with the acknowledgement that we are dealing with protreptic literature. In other words, we are not necessarily privy to his ecclesiastical theology, but only to what I have called his protreptic theology, that is a theology accessible to potential converts and designed to meet their specific needs. Nevertheless, part of what motivates this project is the belief that by exploring his protreptic theology, one might recover at least nuances of the bishop's ecclesiastical theology, perhaps even enough to characterize his confessional community. Of the three primary teachings or doctrines in his protreptic theology, it is Theophilus' study of the human condition as delineated by the biblical books that is most convenient and will be treated first.[1]

There are two parts to Theophilus' analysis of the human condition. He has arranged his thoughts on the subject of man within an exegesis of the biblical paradise story that is truly striking in some of its features. This story first teaches of man's placement in and later banishment from paradise, and second reveals man's potential return to paradise. What is remarkable in the bishop's exegesis of this story is that he believes the biblical text answers the questions of why man was originally put in paradise and how man can return to paradise. In pursuing the first of these questions Theophilus focuses on man's "capacity" to function as a law-keeper. Thus, the first part of Theophilus' doctrine is formulated in terms of man's original role in paradise. More precisely, he speaks of man's original "opportunity for progress" toward immortality. In pursuing the second question—How can man return to paradise?—Theophilus focuses on man's "willingness" to function as a law-keeper. Thus, the second part of the bishops' doctrine is formulated in terms of man's new vocation after banishment from paradise. More precisely, he speaks of man's ensuing "occasion for repentance" until resurrection.

Therefore, these two Theophilian phrases, man's "opportunity for progress" and man's "occasion for repentance," serve as rubrics for the discussion that follows. This discussion will first analyze what Theophilus means by this "opportunity" for progress and this "occasion" for repentance, and then proceeds with the bishop's exposition on human destiny. The chapter concludes with a summary and a schematic presentation of my understanding of the Theophilian theory of man.

An Opportunity for Progress

After Theophilus quoted the biblical creation story and briefly discussed how God walked and talked in the garden, he then reiterates that:

> [1] God made man on the sixth day but revealed his formation after the seventh day, [2] when he also made paradise so that man might be in a better place and a finer location. (2.23)

This seems an odd or eccentric explanation of what happened after the sixth day's work. Consider the first half of this statement [1]. Is Theophilus saying the obvious, that the "formation" of man is identical to the "creation" of man, but God chose to reveal it in the biblical text only after a discussion of the seventh day? On the basis of this passage, this seems a safe assumption.[2] However, to take the first half of the bishop's statement as no more than a textual note is to lose sight of the second half, where he appears to be speculating that paradise was created post-Sabbath. Theophilus' reading of the Genesis creation account suggests to him that there are two continuous but different stories—a "creation" story and a "paradise" story. It is in the second of these stories that Adam's "formation" (πλάσις) is revealed and, even though he has already been created, he is placed in the garden of Eden or paradise.[3] The bishop appears to believe that creation was completed on the sixth day, that God rested on the seventh day and, presumably, that paradise was constructed on the eighth day.[4]

Earlier Theophilus addressed two potential misunderstandings. First, he was concerned that the references to "creating" man and "forming" man be taken as an inconsistency in the biblical text.[5] He said in an earlier passage in his *Syngramma:*

> And so that the formation of man might also be indicated—so that there might not seem to be an insoluble problem among men, since "Let us make man" had been spoken by God but man's formation had not yet been manifested—the scripture teaches us, saying: "A spring went up from the earth and watered all the face of the earth, and God formed man, dust from the earth, and breathed the breath of life into his face, and man became a living soul." (2.19)

By the terms "revealed," "indicated" and "manifested," in the two passages above, Theophilus is referring to the actual scriptural texts in the book of Genesis. Man's formation is revealed, or indicated, or manifested, by scripture only after it has narrated the story of creation. But again, this textual point is arguably not the major point he wants to make. For Theophilus, the shift in language regarding man's origin, from "creation" to "formation," is merely a clue to an important shift from the creation story to the drama of paradise.

There is a second potential misunderstanding some readers may encounter in the biblical account of man' creation. Theophilus takes Genesis 2:4-5 as a summary of the creation story up to that point. Given that the "summary" ends by saying, "there was no man to till the earth," after the text had already said that God created a man, the bishop is concerned that some readers may once again be confused or think there is an inconsistency in the story. So he tries to explain. He says of this biblical text:

> Hereby it reveals to us that at that time the whole earth was watered by a divine spring, and it had no need for a man to till it. The earth brought forth everything spontaneously in accordance with the commandment of God, so that man would not grow weary from labour. (2.19)

So, man lived in an earth that yielded fruit "spontaneously" for his nourishment. However, he did not need to work. While the biblical text said "there was no man to till the earth," according to Theophilus, one should interpret it as saying "there was no *need for* man to till the earth." Therefore, the biblical text is not inconsistent or even ambiguous if one knows how to interpret it correctly. It does not tell of two alternative stories about the one creation of man or speak of two separate creations of man, but rather two continuous stories, with the climax of the first story (the origin of man) serving as an introduction to the second story (the origin of paradise).

Now consider the second half of the passage with which this section began. Again, Theophilus said:

> [1] God made man on the sixth day but revealed his formation after the seventh day, [2] when he also made paradise so that man might be in a better place and a finer location. (2.23)

This second passage [2] states that paradise, as a post-Sabbath phenomenon, is a superior piece of land, designed it would appear for some special purpose. What is that purpose? Before answering this crucial question, the bishop attempts to describe paradise. What does paradise look like? How is it different from the rest of the earth? Theophilus begins with a general characterization:

> After forming man, God chose a place for him in the eastern regions, excellent for its light, brilliant with brighter air, most beautiful with its plants. In this he placed man. (2.19)

And more specifically:

> God then caused to come up from the earth every tree which was beautiful to see and good to eat, for originally there were only the plants, seeds, and herbs produced on the third day. The vegetation in

> paradise possessed greater goodness and beauty, since paradise is called a plantation planted by God. The other plants there were like those in the world, but the two trees of life and knowledge are found in no other land than in paradise alone. (2.24)

Paradise is a place with the best of everything, with the best lighting and air, and with the most beautiful plants; it is a piece of land somehow set apart from the rest of creation, "in the eastern regions." The earth was made good, but paradise has about it a special significance. It is known by Theophilus as God's "plantation." While this overall description could be said to slightly exceed the biblical account, Theophilus has set what he takes to be the appropriate stage for an exposition of the first part of his doctrine on man.

Theophilus now focuses his readers' attention on certain aspects of this stage, namely, the singular location of the trees called "life" and "knowledge." These two trees are in the midst of the garden and at the center of his dramatic rendition of man's history in paradise. The drama begins as follows:

> When God set man, as we have already said, in paradise to work it and guard it, he commanded him to eat of all the fruits, obviously including those of the tree of life; he commanded him not to taste the tree of knowledge alone. (2.24)

As we shall see in the next chapter, when Theophilus says that God commanded something or other, he is referring to the work of the logos. For it is the logos that functions as the voice of command to man in paradise. Theophilus first draws his readers' attention to the fact that man is not merely "permitted" to eat of all the fruit in the garden, but is "commanded" to do so. However, he quickly focuses on what is crucial in the biblical story, namely, the one notable dietary exception. Now someone could have asked the bishop, and perhaps Autolycus did, why is man forbidden to partake of the tree of knowledge when he is commanded to eat of all the other fruit in the garden—including the tree of life? Or, perhaps more to the point, why is death associated with the fruit of moral knowledge (what I will call, from this point on, "gnosis"[6])? Some of Theophilus' Greek readers, given their high regard for the acquisition of such gnosis, could have found this an odd dietary exclusion. Theophilus, of course, cannot rely on the scriptural text for a philosophical answer to the questions above. He must find an answer within his own anthropological speculations.

What Theophilus gives his readers in this quest to explain God's charge to Adam is a doctrine about who man actually is. Theophilus says of the first man:

> God transferred him out of the earth from which he was made into paradise, giving him *an opportunity for progress* (ἀφορμὴν προ-κοπῆς) so that by growing and becoming mature, and furthermore having been declared a god possessing immortality, he might also ascend into heaven. For man was created in an intermediate state, neither entirely mortal (θνητὸς ὁλοσχερῶς) nor entirely immortal

(ἀθάνατος τὸ καθόλου), but capable of either state (δεκτικὸς ἑκατέρων). (2.24)[7]

There are two issues being discussed by the bishop in this fascinating text; the first one is peripheral and the second is central to his teaching. First, why is man "transferred" out of the earth (where he is created in the opening story of Genesis) and into paradise (his home in the following story)? Theophilus' answer, to put it simply, is that God had great expectations for his created man, expectations which apparently could best be realized in a special environment. The second issue has to do with God's wanting to give man "an opportunity for progress."[8] The bishop believes Adam was placed in paradise to pursue a privileged "opportunity" and thus to fulfill his ultimate destiny. Or to put it another way, God gave man an advantage in his human quest for immortality and divinity by providing him with the sort of environment in which he could progress toward his goal.[9] The Greek word which Grant translates as "progress" in the quotation above is προκοπή; and according to G. Stählin, while this term often refers to "progress and prosperity in the physical and social sphere," it also has an "important use in the literary speech of Hellenism" denoting "the process of moral and spiritual development in man."[10] While Theophilus did not lay out many details regarding this original potential for human advancement, clearly he is speaking of a progress that is both growth and maturation toward a state in which man would be declared a god by God.[11] Furthermore, when man had garnered such a declaration, he could take the next logical step and "ascend into heaven." After all "heaven" is the place of God, a point he never directly makes but seems to affirm in his quotation of the Sibyl's poetry.[12] Theophilus himself usually speaks of heaven as a synonym for the sky. But there is no reason to doubt that Theophilus imagined a better place for man than even the original paradise. Man's destiny exceeded what this world had to offer. Thus, man was taken from earth and placed in paradise to enhance his potential for ascent to the immortal world of heaven.

So what is a human being? The previous passage contains the seeds of a definition in which man is suggested to be partly mortal and partly immortal. In other words, the reader is to infer, man is a mixture of mortality and immortality who can, nevertheless, regress to complete mortality or progress to complete immortality and divinity. Original man occupied, in Theophilus' doctrine, an "intermediate state," an existence between "death and non-death," or perhaps more precisely between "dying and non-dying." This is a somewhat convoluted, though technical, definition for which the bishop has laid little exegetical foundation. Nevertheless, as will be shown, he presents his doctrine in a consistent and cogent manner. In a passage, most of which was quoted earlier, Theophilus says of man's formation:

> The scripture teaches us, saying: "A spring went up from the earth and watered all the face of the earth, and God formed man, dust from the earth, and breathed the breath of life into his face, and man be-

came a living soul" (Genesis 2:6-7). This is why the soul is called
immortal by most people. (2.19)

This biblical passage may have led some of Theophilus' more scrupulous readers to assume that "created" man was not actually a "living soul," or at least not
until he was finally "formed."[13] It is difficult to tell exactly how Theophilus understands this notion of the soul's immortality. He seems to take it as not only a
popular belief but also as a scriptural assertion and, therefore, would not challenge it. On the basis of the texts we have observed so far, it seems Theophilus
believes in a two part process to man's origin. At man's creation a human body
was made. Shortly thereafter, at man's formation, that body was enlivened with
a soul. And furthermore, it seems Theophilus assumes that at the implantation of
the soul God made man, who was merely mortal, also immortal. In other words,
the bishop appears to be thinking like an anthropological dualist, where man is
made up of two parts, the soul which is the immortal part and the body which is
the mortal part. Man is a created and a formed being who is "neither *entirely*
mortal nor *entirely* immortal" (2.24).[14] In other words, we can say that he is in a
state of limbo between complete mortality and complete immortality.

As it turns out what is most important for Theophilus in his teaching regarding man's nature is that the man of paradise had a choice facing him which led
to either complete mortality or complete immortality. If he had chosen correctly
then he would have ascended automatically into heaven. There is no real counterpart to heaven mentioned in the bishop's writings. Theophilus nowhere speaks
of hell or even of some lower domain for those who choose wrongly. He does
speak occasionally of judgment, punishment and the wrath of God; but he is
ambiguous in regard to a place of final judgment.[15] The God of Theophilus has
created a body-soul human being that is capable of unifying his two parts in a
state of complete mortality or complete immortality. The man of paradise is capable of either state. There is for Theophilus an appropriate analogy for this
temporary human condition. He says: "Similarly the place paradise—as regards
beauty—was created intermediate between the world and heaven" (2.24). Theophilus was not saying that paradise was not a place in this world or on this earth,
but rather, as regards its beauty, it was exceptional.[16] While he used metaphorical language to locate paradise "between the world and heaven," he would also
locate man between mortality and immortality. Given what has been said up to
this point, how does Theophilus define the nature of the man of paradise? He
was a being made up of an ambiguous essence who was destined to make a serious choice about his future and, thus, how that ambiguity would be resolved.

According to Theophilus, what were the conditions under which the expectation of progression could be realized? Obviously man must nourish himself.
Man lived in paradise and he ate of the tree of life, which no doubt provided him
with special sustenance. Theophilus does not actually address the value of the
tree of life or the nature of its nutrients. But clearly he does not believe that man
would attain immortality of the body by merely consuming the fruit of life. For
him, such fruit only had value for sustaining the status quo, as man progressed

toward corporeal immortality.[17] However, Theophilus sees man's role in the garden as something more than that of a consumer. Man had a job in paradise, namely, he was "to work" and "to guard" the garden. This task, which is described in the very same terms in the Septuagint,[18] is generally understood as the tending of a garden. Theophilus, however, has a slightly more involved understanding of what is implied in the scriptural text, and so he takes the first of these terms and explains its meaning by using the second term. Theophilus says of man:

> The expression "to work" implies no other task than keeping the commandment of God, lest by disobedience he destroy himself, as he did through sin. (2.24)[19]

In this passage Theophilus explains the tending of paradise not as "tilling the ground," but as "keeping" or "observing" the commandment of God. Thus the divine charge "to work" is no longer related to the garden itself but to God's commandment.[20] In a sense the importance of caring for paradise has been superseded by the importance of caring for God's law. And so even here Theophilus is expanding upon his definition of who the man of paradise was. This man was also the creature whose job it was to keep God's law. Not to do so would be an act of self destruction, which was the path of sin that the first man actually took.[21]

What exactly was the law of the garden? The divine "command" in question, as Theophilus understands it, was twofold: to eat of the garden fruit, including the tree of life, but to exclude the fruit of the tree of knowledge. Before returning to the above question as to why the man of paradise is forbidden to partake of the tree of knowledge, which is his singular dietary exclusion, let us consider how Theophilus construes the tree of knowledge and the origin of death. In his words:

> The tree of knowledge was good and its fruit was good. For the tree did not contain death, as some suppose; this was the result of disobedience. For there was nothing in the fruit but knowledge, and knowledge is good if one uses it properly. (2.25)

Thus, it was the dereliction of man's work in paradise, the failure to keep of the command, that not only interrupted "progress," but also resulted in death.[22] Theophilus is insistent that the blame for human physical death not be placed on the quality of the fruit found on the tree of knowledge, that is, placed on gnosis itself. Theophilus does not want to be perceived as anti-intellectual. Knowledge is good, contrary to what some in his audience may have believed. But, who are those who would say this tree contained death? Given that the bishop does not identify anyone, this comment is probably a rhetorical defense against any reader disposed to shifting the burden of responsibility. Nevertheless, he is here consistent with his earlier claim, human disobedience is the culprit. It is disobedience that results in the state of human mortality for both body and soul.

Further foundation is needed before the question of dietary exclusion can be fully understood. Actually Theophilus' explanation regarding the problem of the tree of knowledge is rather complicated, and one must first understand something about Adam which the scripture has left unsaid. In addition to this, one must be informed about the plan of God for the man of paradise. The first of these concerns is addressed in the following passage where Theophilus claims:

> In his actual age (ἡλικίᾳ), Adam was as old as an infant (νήπιος); therefore he was not yet able to acquire knowledge properly. For at the present time when a child (παιδίον) is born it cannot eat bread at once, but first is fed with milk and then, with increasing age, it comes to solid food (στερεὰν τροφὴν). So it would have been with Adam. Therefore God was not jealous, as some suppose, in ordering him not to eat of knowledge. (2.25)

Well, there it is. Theophilus has made plain the nature of the first man and the problem with the tree of knowledge.[23] Apparently Adam's "age" was such that he could only be considered an "infant" or a "child" and, therefore, was not old enough to consume gnosis, let alone digest it.[24] Simply put, Adam was too young to process this kind of moral knowledge properly.

So why was such a tree in the garden in the first place? It seems reasonable to infer from Theophilus' exposition that he believed the fruit of the tree of knowledge was available in the garden so that it might be eaten by Adam at a time when his physiological and spiritual systems were more well developed, that is, after he had grown and could partake of "solid food."[25] The tree of knowledge was not an arbitrary plant in the garden. It would provide necessary nutrition for a mature person. But, before discussing the subject of human maturity further, the bishop is again concerned with his audience's potential for misunderstanding God's intentions. Theophilus' God is not motivated by "jealousy."[26] Nor is he parsimonious in his behavior. God is not hoarding gnosis, but parenting. This fact Theophilus will make exceedingly clear. So far, however, the reader is presented with an indelible image that would seem to adequately answer the earlier question regarding dietary exclusion.

If Autolycus was incredulous, Theophilus had in reserve two more arguments. Both of these explanations for God's withholding the fruit of knowledge still support Theophilus' original thesis that Adam, though situated in an intermediate state, had an "opportunity for progress." In his second explanation, Theophilus speaks of God's greater plan for the child, Adam. Here we are introduced to God's parental style in the education of his child. Theophilus says regarding the withholding of the fruit of gnosis:

> Furthermore, he wanted to test him, to see whether he would be obedient to his command. At the same time he wanted the man to remain simple and sincere for a longer time, remaining in infancy. For this is a holy duty not only before God but before men, to obey one's parents in simplicity and without malice. And if children must obey their

parents, how much more must they obey the God and father of the universe! (2.25)

The claim of divine testing and the suggestion of divine suppression (keeping man "simple and sincere" for a period of time) appear at first to be somewhat contrary to Theophilus' original thesis. If God was giving Adam an authentic opportunity to grow into the acquisition of moral knowledge, that is, to develop an adequate physical maturity so as to partake of gnosis, then why would he intentionally tempt a child, let alone desire that the child should remain in infancy? For Theophilus this test of obedience to the command of God regarding the tree of knowledge was the only appropriate tool for determining the maturation of Adam. Theophilus seems to believe that if Adam had remained obedient and left the tree of knowledge alone, as God had commanded, then at some later date God would have lifted the ban and Adam could have legitimately eaten the fruit of gnosis.

It is also the case, according to Theophilus, that there were two competing desires within the divine mind, one which wanted Adam to succeed, that is, to progress, and the second, which was just as parental as the first, that wanted to delay the sorrow at seeing a child grow and pass beyond the blush of innocence. Furthermore, this second divine desire has nothing to do with the actual suppression of Adam's potential by the imposition of an impossible test, but rather is suggestive of God's deep relationship with man. Theophilus does not want us to miss the importance of the obvious analogy he is drawing between God and Adam and parents and children. A divine parent's test of "simple and sincere" obedience is a fine pedagogical tool given that obedience "in simplicity and without malice" is a "holy duty." Apparently even the character of the obedience counts for something. Therefore, the bishop argued, God is not motivated by jealousy in his withholding of moral knowledge, but has man's best interests in mind as he planned and implemented a test or experiment which would demonstrate the man-child's stature and maturity.

Theophilus' third explanation for God's withholding gnosis is very quick to its point. In the bishops' words:

> Furthermore, it is shameful for infant children to have thoughts beyond their years; for as one grows in age in an orderly fashion, so one grows in ability to think. (2.25)

Here the bishop's initial concern is not with what the child can tolerate or the parent can teach, but with how the child reflects on himself. Theophilus believes that the child must achieve an adequate "age" not only to intellectually digest gnosis but to warrant and deserve it in the first place. Actually, in Theophilus' mind the possession of gnosis is only for grown-ups. No doubt the "orderly fashion" he is referring to here consists of the perpetual "keeping of the commandment of God" to shun the tree of knowledge, an activity that would allow for the normal emotional and spiritual development of the child. Will this lead to the lifting of the ban at some divinely established point? Theophilus seems to have believed it would. Earlier he said that with increasing age comes solid food: "So it would have been with Adam" (2.25).

Therefore, in summary, why was the tree of knowledge excluded from Adam's diet? First, the fruit of gnosis could not be properly digested by the infant Adam. Second, the fruit of gnosis was intended to be the lure or bait in an elaborate test of obedience which the infant Adam was expected to pass. Third, the fruit of gnosis would simply bring shame on one so young as Adam. The amount of space Theophilus devotes to the problem of the tree of knowledge suggests that he was engaged in considerable debate over the biblical text. The exegetical nature of his attempt to resolve the matter of gnosis suggests his intentions of making the scriptures accessible to an intellectual audience of Greek readers.

While Theophilus has explained and perhaps justified the original divine plan, that is, how the acquisition of gnosis was based on human progression, he must now interpret the biblical account of Adam's lost "opportunity for progress." Thus he reports:

> Again, when a law commands abstinence from something and someone does not obey, it is not the law which results in punishment but the disobedience and the transgression. For a father sometimes orders his own child to abstain from certain things, and when the child does not obey the paternal command he is beaten and receives chastisement because of his disobedience. The commands themselves are not the blows; the disobedience results in beatings for the disobedient one. So also for the first-formed man (πρωτοπλάστῳ), his disobedience resulted in his expulsion from paradise. It was not that the tree of knowledge contained anything evil, but that through disobedience man acquired pain, suffering, and sorrow, and finally fell victim to death. (2.25)

Essentially, what Theophilus has attempted to do throughout his exegesis of the Genesis creation story is to justify every complaint Autolycus might have had with the God of scripture. Theophilus' God was a parental figure who provided his child, here for the first time called "first-formed" man,[27] with all that he needed so that he might progress as expected, be declared a god and ascend into heaven. The accomplishment of such progression, however, would not be immediate, but would be a process described as "work." This work consisted of "keeping the commandment of God," which was, as we have seen, essentially avoiding the tree of knowledge until God judged Adam old enough to partake. Once Adam had arrived at an appropriate age and/or stature, Theophilus seems to assume, God would have deemed him mature and thus rewarded him with legitimate access to gnosis and, ultimately, immortality. What Theophilus teaches Autolycus is that it was Adam's "disobedience and transgression" which interrupted this scenario and not God's law, or what the bishop calls nomos.[28] Likewise, "punishment and chastisement" are the products of contemporary man's continual transgression and not God's nomos. In addition to this, Theophilus contends once again, that it was not gnosis that led to Adam's acquisition of pain, suffering, sorrow and eventually death, but human disobedience.

Thus, in conclusion, Theophilus has argued that Adam had a divinely ordained opportunity for progress, one which would have been characterized by growth and maturation, and ended in a declaration of divinity and ascension into heaven. But Adam breached his opportunity by his transgression. Not only is God's gnosis not to be blamed for Adam's lost opportunity, but neither is God's nomos. Only Adam himself is to be blamed. In his study of primal man, Theophilus sees himself as a defender of God's gnosis and his nomos. According to the bishop, man was originally a creature who could realize the sort of progression that would lead to a completely unified immortal body and soul. This expectation on the part of God, as the bishop argues, became an opportunity or program that included the timely and legitimate reception of gnosis by virtue of keeping nomos. Theophilus sees man as a creature who innately values gnosis. But, the bishop's point is that man must learn to value nomos as well if he is ever to enjoy gnosis legitimately. In fact the primary focus of the original program in paradise was not the reward of gnosis or immortality, but the doing of nomos.

Theophilus is not precise in his description of the elemental nature of man,[29] but he does provide occasional references to man's body (σῶμα), soul (ψυχή) and heart (καρδία).[30] He seems to have believed that the body, soul and heart account for the motions, actions and attitudes of man, respectively. Within the heart of the fallen man good and evil feelings are conceived and within his soul good and evil choices are made, the evil ones being the cause of the perpetual blindness in man to the truth of his origin. The bishop has nothing more to say about man's elemental nature. For him and his target audience such a theoretical subject was probably a moot point.

Nonetheless, man has two important key attributes. First, the bishop speaks of "the dignity of man" (τὸ ἀξίωμα τοῦ ἀνθρώπου) (2.18). Why is "dignity" attributed to man? Four reasons can be found in Theophilus' books: (1) God considered all the rest of his creation "incidental" compared to man (2.18). (2) Man was the "only work worthy of [God's] own hands" (2.18). (3) Man is God's "fabrication and image" (πλάσμα καὶ εἰκών) (1.4).[31] (4) The sun, moon and stars are for the "service and slavery of men" (1.4), while all plants and animals are "subordinated" as subjects and slaves to mankind (1.6, 2.18). These are the reasons the attribute of dignity legitimately belongs to man. This attribute goes to show that man was made to play the primary role in the created world and that role is as master and manager of the whole of the creation.

The second attribute of man goes to show that he was made to play the primary role in creation and history, namely, "freedom." The bishop says: "God made man to be free and self-controlled" (2.27).[32] While the context of this statement will be carefully discussed in the next section, consider the importance of this attribute of "freedom" or "self control" in Theophilus' doctrine of man. The bishop does not expand upon the sense of these words anywhere in his writings, leaving their obvious Hellenistic meanings to the understanding of Autolycus and his other readers.[33] Along with dignity, freedom separates man from the rest of creation. God created man free and thus autonomous in the task to determine himself. He could choose immortality through good behavior or mortality through evil conduct. The philosophical problems that derive from the belief in the coexistence of divine law and authentic human autonomy are not explored by Theophilus.

What can be inferred from Theophilus' discussion of man's nature is that he understood man to have been given all the tools necessary to be master of creation. But the bishop did not think focusing on man's nature was as important as focusing on his history. In fact his most significant anthropological claim in regard to human nature can be paraphrased: Man in his primal essence or in his paradise stage is a human being who functions in an intermediate state of existence, whose primary task is progression through the keeping of nomos. Man is in a very important sense a law keeper. The bishop emphasized primal man's free will, his immaturity, his unfinished state of being and his capacity for moral judgment. Man can choose obedience and its reward of a unified and immortal body and soul or he can choose disobedience and its penalty of a unified and mortal body and soul. However, as Theophilus understood God's expectation, once man had realized his full potential for immortality, which seems to have included the legitimate acquisition of gnosis, man would no longer be human, but divine. As for the place of paradise in this history, it was the training ground on which humanity in its childlike condition was to progress toward maturity and eventually achieve immortal and divine status.

An Occasion for Repentance

The question of Theophilus' doctrine of man has so far only been addressed in terms of Adam's unique opportunity for progress. The issue, however, cannot be left there. For Adam's failure to meet the expectation of the original divine plan raises a far more pertinent concern, namely, is there any hope for Adam's descendents? Is mankind forever bound by, and perhaps condemned to, mortality? Theophilus has been busy explaining God's original plan, including the divine right to forbid gnosis and to levy nomos. After all, God's paradise "experiment" has been a universal problem for theology, and so it is understandable that it should consume the bishop's attention in the early going.[34] However, having advanced his best arguments in that regard, he must move on to an even more serious set of problems. Theophilus has acknowledged fallen man's depravity and its consequences, but not yet presented his beliefs regarding the nature of fallen man's redemption. This latter task he is now prepared to do, yet still within the context of his Genesis exegesis. Because of disobedience, which led to Adam's acquisition of pain, suffering, sorrow and eventually death, God cast his child (children) out of paradise. Thus, as has already been pointed out, Theophilus' doctrine of man consists of two parts, the first detailing the experimental training ground of paradise and the second (given the Fall) rendering the prognosis for the banished man.

Before proceeding further, however, two remarks should be made about the nature and consequences of man's original disobedience or the primal sin. First, Theophilus appears to avoid a lengthy discussion regarding the role of Satan in the Fall of Adam. Theophilus certainly does not ignore Satan. But given that man deserves to carry the full weight for his transgression, Theophilus' Satan in *Ad Autolycum* is somewhat less consequential than one might expect.[35] Second, the bishop sees the consequences of human sin as extensive. Not only did the first sin change man's character, but it also changed the character of the animal kingdom. In other words, human sin has both human and non-human consequences. As the bishop reports:

> Wild animals are so called from their being hunted. They were not originally created evil or poisonous, for nothing was originally created evil by God; everything was good and very good. The sin of man made them evil, for when man transgressed they transgressed with him. If the master of the house does well, his servants necessarily live properly; if the master sins, his slaves sin with him. Just so, it turned out that man, the master, sinned and the slaves sinned with him. (2.17)

Other creatures than man are equally able to transgress God's law. While man's capacity for sin is apparently inherent in his nature, where does "animal sin" come from? According to Theophilus, primal man was the "master" of his habitat, which means among other things that his transgression was infectious to other creatures as well. While this idea of the corporate nature of sin may have seemed convoluted to Autolycus, it was scriptural truth for the bishop. Man is seen as the sole progenitor of all earthly evil.[36] The primal sin is treated by the bishop as the sole reason for the change in animal as well as human behavior and thus the calamity of creation. No outside force is ultimately responsible.

With this clarification of the origin and meaning of the primal sin, let us now consider the second part of Theophilus' doctrine of man. To begin with, the bishop formulates a provocative answer to a difficult question: How should we understand God's act of banishment? Theophilus says of this punishment:

> And in so doing, God conferred a great benefit upon man. He did not let him remain forever in a state of sin but, so to speak, with a kind of banishment he cast him out of paradise, so that through this punishment he might expiate his sin in a fixed period of time (τακτῷ κρόνῳ) and after chastisement (παιδευθείς) might later be recalled. (2.26)

This is another rather curious passage. Theophilus is here claiming that Adam's banishment was a punishment which conferred a "great benefit." This claim may have seemed absurd to the bishop's readers. They could easily have asserted that since this experiment failed leaving man bereft of any positive potential or expectation for his life, Theophilus' God was a perverted parent. However, according to the bishop's interpretation of the story, banishment is yet another, if not superior, opportunity. In fact, man's banishment was of a limited or qualified kind. Man was expelled from paradise, the bishop insists, only for a period of time and not for eternity. In Theophilus' language, a "fixed period of time" had been given to Adam so that "he might expiate his sin." Adam is to make compensation for his sin, which amounted to his transgression of what God had commanded. Adam had been expected to behave as a nomos keeper. But contrary to God's wishes he engaged in the premature consumption of gnosis.

But what, precisely, is the purpose of this "fixed period of time"? What is the nature of this new opportunity? Theophilus has begun to shift his attention from the context of Adam to the immediate condition of fallen humanity as a whole. The "fixed period of time" is the space of time allotted by God for *paideutheis* (παιδευθείς). While Grant has perfunctorily translated this Greek passive participle as "chastisement," the contextual setting of the term suggests a notion that is considerably more complicated and comprehensive than such a translation would offer.[37] One should not miss Theophilus' carefully nuanced idea by failing to take the substantive participle in its more usual sense. Liddell and Scott include in their first level of meanings "bringing up," "rearing," "training" and "educating" a child,[38] while G. Bertram offers a thorough history of a number of cognates—a history which emphasizes the "education," "cultivation," "enculturation" and "inculcation" of cultural patterns and values.[39] D. Fürst concurs.[40] Moreover, on closer examination, it appears that our pedagogically minded bishop is suggesting that fallen man has an opportunity to educate himself, an activity which is the counterpart to primal man's opportunity for progress (2.24).[41] Therefore, I would recommend that the term *paideutheis* be translated as "education."

However, while the participle *paideutheis* does not translate easily into a recognizable cultural concept, W. Jaeger has used a well known classical term in his patristic studies that seems more than adequate for what Theophilus appears to have in mind, namely, "paideia." Jaeger addresses the gravity of this term in the early Christian context most succinctly when he says "paideia is the gradual fulfillment of the divine providence."[42]

And so what is the upshot of Theophilus' thinking? Namely this: man is no longer to focus on progress but on paideia. As one might infer from Theophilus' discussion so far, man should seek to attain a sufficient maturity to deal with gnosis, and thus prove a better keeper of moral law or nomos. While maturity was originally a matter of God's determination, it is now the end result of a course in moral education. Theophilus, consistent with his self-perceived role as the instructor of Autolycus, believes mankind is in need of a remedial education or period of instruction in which to overcome deficiencies, grow more mature and thus worthy of higher knowledge than primal man possessed.[43] It could be said that Theophilus is laying out the particulars for achieving a Christian paideia. And what is the incentive for such an achievement? The reward is some sort of "recall" or summoning from banishment to what appears to be one's original state. Is the bishop claiming that man might later be permitted to reenter paradise and resume his progression toward immortal divinity?

How can Theophilus exegetically justify this sort of thinking? And what does the term "later" in the above phrase, "might later be recalled," actually assume? What is the time period envisioned for this revival? Just as modern scholarship has observed a subtle distinction between the creation and the Eden stories in the first chapters of Genesis,[44] Theophilus expertly points to an apparent redundancy in the second of these stories. The bishop's exegetical evidence for his interpretation of the paradise story is as follows:

> For this reason, when man was formed in this world it is described mysteriously in Genesis as if he had been placed in paradise twice; the first description was fulfilled when he was placed there, and the second is going to be fulfilled after the resurrection and judgment. (2.26)

Theophilus' reasoning is based on the Septuagint duplication of the verb "he placed" (ἔθετο) in Genesis 2:8 and 2:15, which suggests to him that God placed man in paradise twice. For Theophilus this apparent mystery consists of two different instances of God's actions toward man rather than an actual redundancy. The bishop also makes it very clear that his reading of the text implies that the first of the two divine "placements" was in antiquity, while the second is a matter of some future date. This future event is described as post "resurrection and judgment."[45] Thus, one can assume that the interval between antiquity and the future is in one sense what Theophilus has called the "fixed period of time," or what I propose we call his "period of paideia." In another, and more personally pertinent sense, this period of time can refer to each individual's life expectancy. As for the question above regarding the term "later," Theophilus wants his readers to know that they should be diligent with the present moment, for the period of paideia will come to an end with a selective recall to paradise.[46]

With this unusual eschatological reference, he begins an exposition of the second part of his doctrine of man. First, the bishop must explain the actual meaning and purpose of "death." Using a tightly constructed analogy to promote his exegesis of man's banishment from paradise, Theophilus says:

> Again, just as when some vessel has been fashioned and has some fault, it is resmelted or refashioned (ἀναπλάσσεται) so that it becomes new and perfect, so it happens to man through death; for he has virtually been shattered so that in the resurrection he may be found sound, I mean spotless and righteous and immortal. (2.26)

Theophilus seems to envision a second creation of the primal man or, to be more precise, a "refashioning" of an imperfect man, a man with some sort of "fault." Was primal man, who was created and formed by God, imperfect? What is the nature of man's fault? These appear to be problematic questions for Theophilus' audience. First, it is clear the bishop does not make any equation between this so-called fault and man's natural condition, that is, his intermediate state. Nor does the bishop suggest that fallen man was so thoroughly transformed by sin that he no longer possessed his original nature. However, the bishop's quartet of adjectives, "sound, spotless, righteous and immortal," does imply the resurrection of a different man than primal man or fallen man. For purposes of comparison one could refer to this "refashioned" man as "re-formed" man or simply the resurrected man.[47] The resurrected man no longer appears to be in an intermediate state, that is, suspended between potential mortality and potential immortality. By virtue of the resurrection, this passage seems to suggest, although it does not say so directly, that man (in both body and soul) is automatically possessed of the attribute of eternality, whether that be eternally mortal or eternally immortal.

Again the condition of intermediacy is not to be equated with man's fault. In actuality, the bishop is not interested in philosophizing about the nature of human faultiness and offers only a brief statement regarding its source. He simply notes, in no uncertain terms, that man is guilty of his own disobedience. What he does explore is the idea that because of the human fault or sin, fallen man must necessarily be re-formed. And further, this re-formed man will be a "new and perfect" man. And how, according to this passage, is such a man produced? The bishop's language initially suggests that it is "death" which produces this new and perfect man. However, the bishop does not hold the illogical notion that mortality is the cause of immortality. Rather, man's sin has placed him, or at least his corporeal existence (his body), in the precarious position of having to die. Man's body must be "shattered" and then melted down so as to be re-molded, that is "resurrected." Thus, it appears to be the resurrection which produces re-formed man. Death or mortality can be seen as a doorway to immortality. Nonetheless, it is only after the resurrection that one can become truly the immortal re-formed man.

Theophilus does not address at any length the nature of death or the afterlife. Such matters are theoretically intriguing for him but of less practical importance. Thus, Theophilus turns to his exegesis of man's banishment from paradise and proceeds to give his readers a more precise understanding of what I am calling the period of paideia. He says:

> God's calling and saying, "Where are you, Adam?"—God did this not as if he were ignorant but because he was patient and gave him an occasion (ἀφορμήν) for repentance and confession. (2.26)

Seizing upon an obvious problem first, Theophilus says God's search for Adam was not a matter of "ignorance," but of "patience." Furthermore, divine patience was actually an "occasion" for man to show his regret that he had disobeyed God. Thus, the period of paideia is here termed "an occasion for repentance and confession." This is, in Theophilus' scheme, the second stage in man's historical development (the first being the aforementioned "opportunity for progress"[48]). In his exegesis of the Cain and Abel story he again emphasizes this new development in human history, saying:

> But God, who is merciful and desired to provide for Cain, as he had
> for Adam, an opportunity for repentance and confession, said:
> "Where is your brother Abel?" (2.29)

For Theophilus this period of paideia is not just attributed to Adam but also to
Cain and, in the light of the passages which follow, to humanity as a whole.

While Theophilus does not use the term "confession" beyond these two instances, he discusses the meaning of "repentance" in several contexts.[49] A brief
look at two of these passages will help us understand his meaning. First, earlier
in chapter two, when he was analyzing the events of the fifth day of creation,
which consisted of the creation of the marine life, he said:

> Furthermore, those created from the waters were blessed by God so
> that this might serve as a pattern of men's future reception of repen-
> tance and remission of sins through water and a bath of regeneration
> (λουτροῦ παλιγγενεσίας), in the case of all who approach the truth
> (τῇ ἀληθείᾳ) and are reborn and receive a blessing from God. (2.16)

The bishop speaks of a "pattern" or "type" only in his analysis of the creation.
Earlier the dying moon was said to be a type of man and "then it is reborn and
waxes as a pattern of the future resurrection" (2.15). Now sea creatures or, better
yet, their watery genesis is a pattern that will be useful in describing how future
men will receive their "repentance and remission of sins." Future man's watery
genesis is a "rebirth" that takes place through a "bath of regeneration," which is
surely a reference to the New Testament concept of baptism.[50] God's plan for
Adam and Cain is extended to humanity as a whole. All men are expected to
make repentance and thus to "approach the truth,"[51] which is essential to rebirth.

Perhaps Theophilus' most important analysis of repentance, however, is
found in his *Hypomnema*, where, after laying out the content of what he calls the
"ten chapters" (3.9),[52] he turns to prophetic teaching. The bishop understands
prophecy as essentially a presentation of nomos:

> Now when the people transgressed the law which God had given
> them, because God is good and merciful and did not want to destroy
> them he not only gave the law but later sent prophets from among
> their brothers to teach and remind them of the content of the law and
> to convert them to repentance so that they would no longer sin. (3.11)

Immediately following this passage Theophilus quotes Isaiah (55:6-7; 31:6),
Ezekiel (18:21-3) and Jeremiah (6:9), all by name. Each of these prophets, in the
quotations he provides, insisted that the "lawless man" should convert. Consider
Ezekiel's actual words as quoted by the bishop:

> If the lawless man is converted from all the lawless deeds he has
> done and keeps my commandments and performs my ordinances, he
> will truly live and will not die. (3.11)

Of such biblical texts Theophilus says:

> There are many other passages, or rather innumerable other passages,
> in the holy scriptures concerning repentance, for God always wants
> the human race to turn away from all its sins. (3.11)

As was pointed out earlier, "keeping the commandment of God" is what is implied by "working" in the garden of paradise. These texts from the prophets
make it clear that this is the expectation of God for all of humanity and not just
Adam. Of course, what is most important here is to realize that Theophilus
teaches that conversion to repentance is in essence the keeping of nomos. Man
was banished from paradise where an opportunity for progress was available to
him. Now in a state of sin he is given, so it would seem, another chance. He now
possesses an opportunity for repentance.

In the bishop's language, this opportunity is a chance to "approach the truth"
and to learn "the content of the law." Conversion to repentance is a turning away
from the inclination to disobedience so thoroughly that it produces a "remission"
of sin and a "rebirth" into paradise. While God's original expectation for primal
man was progress based on the keeping of a particular commandment, there is
the suggestion in the bishop's discussions that God's new expectation for fallen
man is repentance based on the keeping of a considerably more extensive set of
commandments. The reason for this extensive set of commandments is not discussed by the bishop, but may be due to primal man's illegitimate acquisition of
gnosis.

While conversion is seen by Theophilus as a movement from penalty to reward, a reward that ultimately consists of immortality for both the body and the
soul, there apparently is still some ambiguity in Autolycus' mind regarding
Adam's original status which the bishop feels obliged to address. Once again he
poses the question he believes his readers may still find confusing: Was man by
nature mortal or immortal? The following passage is the bishop's last and best
attempt at answering this highly technical concern:

> But someone will say to us, "Was man created mortal (θνητός) by
> nature?" Not at all. "Was he then created immortal (ἀθάνατος)?" We
> do not say this either. But someone will say, "Was he then created as
> nothing at all (οὐδέν)?" We do not say this. In fact, man was neither
> mortal nor immortal by nature. For if God had made him immortal
> from the beginning, *he would have made him god*. Again, if he had
> made him mortal, it would seem that God was responsible for his
> death. God therefore made him neither immortal nor mortal but, as
> we have said before, capable of both (δεκτικὸν ἀμφοτέρων). (2.27)

This is a new phase in the textured discourse of Theophilus' doctrine of man. He
is compelled to offer a concise statement regarding the nature of primal man and
his post-paradise condition. In the bishop's opinion, man was not created wholly

mortal or wholly immortal, nor can he be said to be "nothing at all." The third element of this claim would seem to suggest Theophilus' unwillingness to consider the existence of a category other than mortality and immortality. While it would seem at first that the bishop has left himself in an untenable position, he believes he has one logically acceptable option left. Man as created by God was in some fashion "capable of both" mortality and immortality.[53] How did Theophilus arrive at this conclusion? The bishop believes that there are insurmountable problems with each of the two alternative theories, namely, that man was created mortal and that man was created immortal. First, if original man were made immortal he would be, for all practical purposes, a god. Apart from this statement, there is nothing in the bishop's thought to suggest that he might have a problem with the idea of God making a god. Nor does he seem to think Autolycus would object to this line of reasoning. Of greater concern to the bishop, however, is the problem found in the notion that God made man mortal. This would permit his opponents to claim that God was, therefore, "responsible" for man's death. Theophilus wants no causal connection between God and death. God is not guilty or responsible for death's manifestation nor for primal man's actions, no matter how young or innocent he may have been.[54]

Well, what exactly does the phrase "capable of both" mean? Theophilus, using language that would seem to address the contemporary man of his day, speaks of the options given to Adam in paradise. He says of Adam, that

> If he were to turn to the life of immortality by keeping the commandment of God, he would win immortality as a reward from him and *would become a god*; but if he turned to deeds of death, disobeying God, he would be responsible for his own death. (2.27).[55]

Thus the phrase, "capable of both," in conjunction with our earlier discussion, means that the nature of Adam's body and soul was actually to be determined by him or, to put it in more general terms, human choice was the essential factor in determining man's unified nature. Since God apparently created man without, but capable of, anthropological solidarity, it was man who was to decide which sort of solidarity would be achieved, and, thus, whether or not he would "become a god."

As was mentioned before, this notion of becoming a god seems peculiar given Theophilus' monotheistic teachings. One might ask, does the bishop believe in some sort of *theopoiesis*?[56] In both references to the notion of human divinization, Grant's translation appropriately uses the lower-cap "g" for the Greek word θεός. The bishop's idea of becoming a god could mean nothing more than a spiritual "at-one-ment" with deity, that is, to be in union or to be like-minded with God.[57] However, it is more likely that he is simply offering a different way of speaking about immortality. Whatever Theophilus had in mind by his use of this notion, one thing is clear, his writings do not treat it as a matter of controversy. Furthermore, there is nothing in the text suggesting that Autolycus would have challenged Theophilus' contention.

There is another instance of this sort of language in the bishop's work. In his exegesis of the creation-of-Eve story he reports: "For although God is one, error was already undertaking to implant a multitude of gods" (2.28). This "error" is associated with the "maleficent demon" called Satan. And Satan, in Genesis 3:6, said: "You shall become like gods!" Curiously, Theophilus does not seem to object to the substance of what Satan said; for in the bishop's teaching, gnosis (legitimately acquired) was part of the process of maturation toward divinity. Therefore, Satan's words actually substantiate the bishop's claim that man could become a god. What Theophilus does object to in Satan's statement to Eve, however, is the encouragement it includes to acquire gnosis illegitimately. For the bishop, Adam and Eve should have shown more restraint and patience. For through their "work" in paradise, that is, their keeping of the single command-ment, they would have received gnosis anyway. Theophilus might have been on less treacherous ground if he had followed Satan's literary lead and spoken only of man's becoming "like gods." But for him, immortality means much more than merely possessing gnosis.

Again, what is of central importance in Theophilus' statement is that God not be seen as the cause of man's wholly mortal state. Man is the culprit. Man turned to "the deeds of death" rather than pursue "the life of immortality." And the pursuit of the life of immortality for primal man was nothing other than "the keeping of the commandment of God."[58] But all of this is beside the point for the post-paradise human condition; for Adam chose the deeds of death and thus, to paraphrase Theophilus' own words, he is responsible for his own death. But how could primal man be legitimately held responsible when he was no more than an infant, certainly without the gnosis or the requisite knowledge to make wise judgments? Isn't this the weakness in Theophilus' argument? The bishop seems aware that his audience would exploit this point and so neatly noted: "For God made man to be free and self-controlled" (2.27). To acknowledge these attrib-utes of man, "freedom" and "self-control," is essential to Theophilus' doctrine. The claim that God created man free and thus autonomous in the task to deter-mine himself means that man had sufficient natural wisdom to make some moral choices, even though he was a child and without gnosis. Presumably primal man was able to distinguish between "right and wrong" but not necessarily between "good and evil" matters. Given this interpretation, the only conclusion Theophi-lus' readers should draw is that primal man was in no way deficient or disabled and therefore could have chosen either immortality through "right" behavior or mortality through "wrong" behavior.

So what is the prognosis for fallen man? Finally the bishop arrives at the heart of his teaching. He tells his readers in this key passage:

> What man acquired for himself through his neglect (ἀμελείας) and disobedience, [this thing] God now freely bestows upon him through love and mercy, when man obeys him. For as by disobedience man gained death for himself, so by obedience to the will of God whoever will can obtain eternal life for himself. For God gave us a law and

holy commandments; everyone who performs them can be saved and, attaining to the resurrection, can inherit imperishability. (2.27)

This is Theophilus' preeminent soteriological statement. The text, which begins with a reference to Adam, immediately shifts to mankind in general by addressing "whoever will," "us" and "everyone." Let us carefully consider this highly complicated passage. First, Theophilus has spoken of Adam's disobedience before, but what is Adam's "neglect" (ἀμέλεια)? The bishop is probably thinking of Adam's neglect of his "work," since, as he said earlier, this "implies no other task than keeping the commandment of God" (2.24). However, the only other context in which Theophilus uses some form of the Greek word ἀμέλεια is in the fourth chapter of his *Hypomnema,* where he is addressing Autolycus' continual doubt about "the word of truth." The bishop says, apparently comparing the studious habits of his listeners:

> I marvel especially in your case. In other matters you are diligent and investigate all subjects, but you listen to us with indifference (ἀμε-λέστερον). (3.4)

Perhaps neglect was added to the crime of disobedience simply to point out an apathy ("indifference") which the bishop observed in the ranks of his academic friends. Whatever may have been Theophilus' thinking regarding the full extent of the crime committed by primal man, he says here that "whoever will" can initiate his own salvation by abandoning disobedience and practicing obedience. Clearly the emphasis of this passage is not on "orthodoxy" but "orthopraxy." Moreover, it is not a nondescript obedience that Theophilus is talking about, but an obedience which is qualified by "the will of God," which is precisely the keeping of "the law and the commandments."

Earlier the bishop implied that eternal life and immortality were the products acquired only after the doorway of death, which was also a sign of condemnation, had been breached (2.26). But given the terms of the above statement, clearly Theophilus is of the opinion that man has the ability to obtain at least the rights to "imperishability" before experiencing physical death. Since, according to Theophilus' statement, it would seem obvious that man did not acquire imperishability through disobedience, but only by virtue of his obedience, then what actually is "this thing" that "God now freely bestows" because of obedience that man had already acquired in some measure through disobedience? While immortality seems a likely object of God's benevolence, it is unlikely that the bishop would speak of it as the product of man's disobedience. And while death is certainly the product of man's disobedience, it can hardly be the subject of primal man's desire or the object of God's benevolence. However, gnosis (knowledge of good and evil) was originally acquired through disobedience and was also referred to as the potential object of God's benevolence (2.25). But man could not make gnosis a regular part of his diet given his banishment from paradise. Thus it would seem that the bishop's point is this: that obedience to nomos, which is what God wills, leads to the free gift of gnosis. And with sufficient gnosis man will mature and eventually attain immortality and divinity. Thus, the bishop waxes poetic to say gnosis should be recognized as a divine gift that can in the manner of a reward be "won" through keeping nomos, a gift that ultimately nourishes the righteous man beyond mere god-likeness to godhood itself.

An Exposition on Human Destiny

The bishop makes several eschatological references from which he generates his exposition on human destiny. He briefly discusses the primary eschatological events of conflagration, restoration and judgment, and he defines the basic eschatological notions of punishment and immortality. These five Theophilian subjects are dealt with in this order after an analysis of the bishop's substantial teaching on the resurrection of man.

What does Theophilus say about the resurrection? His discussion of the resurrection (ἀνάστασις) begins in an apologetic context in the *Homilia*. He says to Autolycus:

> But you do not believe that the dead are raised. When the event takes place, you will believe whether you wish or not; your faith will be reckoned as unfaith unless you believe now. But why do you disbelieve? Do you not know that faith leads the way in all actions? (1.8)

The bishop is trying to persuade Autolycus into accepting his faith. Not because faith immediately leads to salvation, but rather because faith in the resurrection "leads the way in all actions," that is, prepares one for righteous living. The bishop resumes his discussion of the resurrection near the end of the book, where he says:

> But as for your denying that the dead are raised—for you may say, "Show me even one person raised from the dead, so that by seeing I may believe"—in the first place, what importance would your believing have after you have seen the event? In the second place, you actually believe that Heracles, who burned himself up, is alive and Asclepius, struck by lightening, was raised. And do you disbelieve what is said to you by God? Even if I were to show you a dead man raised and alive, you might perhaps disbelieve this. (1.13)

Theophilus will not argue the resurrection by citing examples of people who have come back from the dead. Examples would subvert the value of faith and would perhaps be futile anyway. Theophilus does not believe Autolycus is predisposed toward accepting such evidence from religions other than his own. However, he may be posturing. He may very well be uncomfortable with the idea of traditional examples of "resurrected men."[59] Nevertheless, his primary teaching in *Ad Autolycum* about the resurrection is that it is a future event which, when it happens, will affirm the faithful in their decision to believe in it.[60] So the bishop naturally turns to another argument, one which he believes is appealing to the pagan mind and one which does not necessitate physical proof. He says, consider the analogies which nature provides. In the bishops words:

> God has given you many indications for believing him. If you will, consider the termination of seasons and days and nights and how they die and rise again. And what of the resurrection of seeds and fruits, occurring for the benefit of mankind? One might mention that a grain of wheat or of other seeds when cast into the earth first dies and is destroyed, then is raised and becomes an ear. And does not the nature of trees and fruits yield seasonable fruits, by God's command, out of what is obscure and invisible? Furthermore, sometimes a sparrow or some other bird has swallowed a seed of an apple or a fig or something else and comes to some rocky hill or tomb and excretes it. Then that seed which had formerly been swallowed and had passed through such heat takes root and grows into a tree. All these things the wisdom of God works in order to demonstrate, even through these, that God is powerful enough to bring about the general resurrection (καθολικὴν ἀνάστασιν) of all men. (1.13)[61]

And further:

> If you wish to behold a still more marvellous sight, taking place to provide proof of resurrection not only from matters on earth but also from those in heaven, consider the monthly resurrection of the moon, how it wanes, dies, and rises again. Listen further: an example of resurrection takes place in yourself, even if you are ignorant of it, O man. Perhaps you once fell sick and lost flesh, strength, and appearance; but when you obtained mercy and healing from God, you recovered your body, appearance, and strength. Just as you did not know where your flesh went when it vanished, so you did not know whence it originated when it came back. But you will say: "From solids and liquids converted into blood." Certainly! But this too is the work of God, who formed them in this way, not of anyone else. (1.13)

These analogies, R. M. Grant has observed, seem a little bizarre and somewhat forced.[62] I would contend, however, that one needs to appreciate Theophilus' position. The bishop believes that the more analogies he can call forth the better he can convince. Whether Autolycus found any of these analogies convincing is not revealed by the bishop's rhetoric. Nevertheless it does seem plausible, given his particular analogies, that the bishop is arguing for a future bodily resurrection or the resurrection of the flesh. In his words, he imagines a resurrection of "body, appearance and strength."[63] In this connection the bishop asks his readers: "Then do you not believe that the God who made you can later make you over again" (1.8)? It should also be pointed out that the above texts address a "general resurrection" (καθολικὴ ἀνάστασις) of all human beings. However, the preeminent question he will later answer for Autolycus is resurrected to what?

The bishop raises the issue of resurrection again in the context of his exegesis on creation. Speaking of the divine work on the third day, Theophilus said:

> Though the earth became visible it was still unfurnished; then God formed it and adorned it with all sorts of herbs and seeds and plants. Further, consider their variety and their remarkable beauty and numbers, and the fact that through them the resurrection is signified, for a proof (δεῖγμα) of the future resurrection of all men. For what person who considers it will not marvel that a fig tree comes into existence from a fig seed, or that very great trees grow from other tiny seeds? (2.13-14)

Here it is clear that Theophilus sees the general resurrection as occurring at a "future" date, even if he believes in contemporary resurrections. Further, the growth of plants from seeds is to be understood as a "proof" of this future event. Grant translates the Greek word δεῖγμα as "proof," while M. Dods prefers "pattern."[64] However, the bishop may very well be thinking of his analogy as an actual "example" of the resurrection phenomenon. In fact, his rhetoric makes the analogy seem more than it really is. What the analogy signifies is simply that something new can grow out of something old.

A little later on the bishop admits that all his analogies are but "a pattern (δεῖγμα) and type of a great mystery" (2.15).[65] He says, in this regard:

> For the sun exists as a type of God and the moon as a type of man. As the sun greatly surpasses the moon in power and brightness, so God greatly surpasses mankind; and just as the sun always remains full and does not wane, so God always remains perfect and is full of all power, intelligence, wisdom, immortality, and all good things. But the moon wanes every month and virtually dies, for it exists as a type of man; then it is reborn and waxes as a pattern of the future resurrection. (2.15)

The sun is like God in that it never wanes but is always full. But the moon is like man in that it wanes to virtual death and waxes to new life. Thus again we have an example of the future resurrection of man.

The last references to the resurrection in Theophilus' works occur in a passage discussed earlier and so will not detain us long here. Responding to the question as to why man was cast out of paradise, the bishop says the event was really a "great benefit" to man (2.26). As we have seen it was not an act of eternal banishment, for some men would eventually be recalled after a period of education. And again, how does Theophilus defend this idea exegetically? The Genesis story, he contends, speaks of man being "placed in paradise twice" (2.26).[66] He says:

The first description was fulfilled when he was placed there, and the second is going to be fulfilled after the resurrection and judgment. Again, just as when some vessel has been fashioned and has some fault, it is resmelted or refashioned so that it becomes new and perfect, so it happens to man through death; for he has virtually been shattered so that in the resurrection he may be found sound, I mean spotless and righteous and immortal. (2.26)

This curious interpretation is centered on how man works out his own salvation. If man accomplishes his divinely given educational goals, the resurrection marks his favorable judgment and graduation. If he does not accomplish these goals, as we shall see shortly, the resurrection marks his condemnation and failure. What is sure in the bishop's doctrine is that every man will eventually experience the resurrection (cf. 1.13 and 2.27).

Before considering the destiny of man per se, notice how Theophilus understands the destiny of the world. In this regard the bishop briefly addresses both conflagration and restoration. Conflagration (ἐκπύρωσις) is only mentioned by Theophilus in a discussion of what the poets have to say about justice. He says of them: "and willing or unwilling they made declarations about the conflagration of the world (ἐκπυρώσεως κόσμου) in harmony with the prophets" (2.37). Concerning this conflagration, the bishop says that the prophets Malachi and Isaiah had much to say and so he quotes them.[67] However, neither of his quotations speaks about the destruction of the entire world by fire. In fact no Septuagint text actually supports this idea. What Malachi and Isaiah do address is the notion of fiery judgment for the ungodly and wicked.[68] Theophilus' ideas are consistent with those stated in II Peter 3:10, where it says:

> But the day of the Lord will come like a thief, and then the heavens will pass away with a loud noise, and the elements will be dissolved with fire, and the earth and the works that are upon it will be burned up.

This is the sort of conflagration the bishop seems to have in mind.

Likewise, the bishop speaks of restoration (ἀποκατάστασις) just once. In contrast to the Stoic notion of conflagration and restoration as "recurrent phenomena,"[69] the bishop contends that they both occur only one time. After the one conflagration there is the one restoration. But of what does this restoration consist? The bishop says:

> Wild animals . . . were not originally created evil or poisonous, for nothing was originally created evil by God; everything was good and very good. The sin of man made them evil, for when man transgressed they transgressed with him. If the master of the house does well, his servants necessarily live properly; if the master sins, his slaves sin with him. Just so, it turned out that man, the master, sinned and the slaves sinned with him. Whenever man again returns to his

natural state and so no longer does evil, they too will be restored
(ἀποκατασταθήσεται) to their original tameness. (2.17)

The loss of animal life is not an indigenous phenomenon of paradise, according
to Theophilus. It is an example of evil and the consequences of human sin, that
is, man's decision to disobey divine law. His master/servants analogy is intended
to suggest a significant connection between man and the animal kingdom. But
exactly how the moral decision of a superior would effect the morality of an
inferior, let alone what we would think of as an amoral animal, is not developed.
On this subject Theophilus only wants to make his rhetorical point and move on
quickly. And his point is this: Man will one day return to his "natural state," and
when this happens once again all that is wild will be tamed, domesticated, civilized and cultivated. Such is the extent of Theophilus' stated understanding of
the restoration of the world. However, the primary point to be drawn is that the
bishop believes this restoration is an actual earthly phenomenon—a return to
paradise.

  While his discussions of conflagration and restoration address the destiny of
the world, what of human destiny? On the one hand, with respect to the destiny
of the unrighteous man, Theophilus clearly believes in God's anger. The bishop
says of God: "If I call [God] fire, I speak of his wrath" (1.3). An incredulous and
perhaps derisive Autolycus is imagined to ask: "Is God angry" (1.3)? The response is forceful: "Certainly: he is angry with those who do evil deeds" (1.3).
The bishop speaks in the *Syngramma* (2.8, 26) about an actual eschatological
event in which God judges man, but he does not give his readers any details regarding that event. More often than not, his term "judgment" is associated with
divine wrath and punishment (2.14, 36-38). Theophilus appears to understand
this event only in terms of condemnation and penalty. While he offers no specific analysis or speculation on the nature of this penalty, he does accept the notion of a final and eternal punishment. Hades is mentioned three times in
Theophilus' books, once in a quotation from the Sibyl, which speaks of the
home of the demons (2.36), and twice in a quotation from Homer. Homer says:
"The soul, taking flight from the limbs, goes down to Hades," and also, "Bury
me so that swiftly I may pass the gates of Hades" (2.38). Theophilus quotes
Homer not so much to locate or provide a name for a place of eternal punishment, nor to corroborate his own teaching, but to demonstrate inconsistency in
his opponents' position:

> Even though the writers . . . said there was no judgment they admit-
> ted that there will be a judgment; those who denied the existence of
> sensation after death also admitted it. (2.38)

Perhaps the most explicit statement the bishop gives on the violation of
divine prohibitions, and the ensuing divinely ordained punishment, can be found
in the following text:

But to the unbelieving, who despise and disobey the truth but obey unrighteousness, when they are full of adulteries and fornications and homosexual acts and greed and lawless idolatry, there will come wrath and anger, tribulation and anguish, and finally eternal fire (πῦρ αἰώνιον) will overtake such men. (1.14)[70]

Theophilus supports this statement later when he points out that this "eternal fire" is confirmed by the Sibyl when she speaks to the recalcitrant, saying:

You do not wish to become sober and come to sober mind, Nor to know God as king, the all-seeing. Therefore a flame of burning fire is coming upon you; You will be burned in flames daily forever, Put to shame for your false useless idols. (2.36)

Beyond these few quotations and descriptions of the wicked one's fate, *Ad Autolycum* is silent. While the bishop does not offer a fully articulated position on eternal damnation, and certainly does not identify a specific place, such as hell, he clearly believes in some sort of unhappy ending for the unrighteous.

On the other hand, the destiny of the righteous man, or the man who improves himself during the period of *paideia,* is much different. Theophilus seems to affirm the Sibyl's claim when she says:

But those who worship God, the true and eternal, Receive life, for eternal time Dwelling in the luxuriant garden of paradise Eating sweet bread from the starry heaven. (2.36)[71]

In the bishop's mind at least the general sense of this prophecy is true and can be expressed plainly. He says of God:

For he who gave the mouth for speech and formed the ear for hearing and made eyes for vision will examine everything and will judge justly, rewarding each one in accordance with what he deserves. To those who with endurance seek imperishability through good works, he will give eternal life (ζωὴν αἰώνιον), joy, peace, rest, and the totality of good things which eye has not seen nor ear heard, nor have they entered the heart of man. (1.14)

This text affirms the fairness of God in judgment of all men and determination of their eternal destiny. For the righteous man it is a judgment of "eternal life" consisting of the "totality of good things"; but it is a judgment rendered in accordance with the persistent doing of "good works."

Given the bishop's discussion on the destiny of man, it appears that he believes in universal human eternality (ἀϊδιότης) but selective human immortality (ἀθανασία). Though without clear textual evidence, eternality belongs to both the righteous and the unrighteous (or lawless) in a qualified sense. The bishop speaks of eternal life and benefits, of eternal tortures and punishments, but he never speaks of eternal death. Nor does he ever speak of human pre-existence in any form. Presumably, for humanity, in contrast to God himself, there is no "from eternity," only "to eternity."[72] The term immortality, however, is carefully reserved by Theophilus for the future state of being, or the future domain, of the righteous man.

A more controversial expression of this claim for human immortality is that man can become God (γένηται θεός).[73] Here immortality is not simply the life-extending gift of God to man, but an even more substantive transformation verging on *theopoiesis* (θεοποίησις). While this unusual term is not found in *Ad Autolycum,* it would probably have been acceptable to the bishop. Even a conservative anti-Greek heresiologist like Hippolytus (ca. 170-236) seems to affirm this idea when he asserts, in his *Discourse on the Holy Theophany,* that the future of some men can be characterized as follows: "If, therefore, man has become immortal, he will also be God."[74] Athanasius (ca. 300-373), a century later, spoke explicitly of *theopoiesis,* but in the manner suggested by Irenaeus' earlier doctrine of recapitulation. Irenaeus (ca. 115-202) taught that through Christ, people are made incorruptible and that through redemption people will realize their divine destiny. Even Adam, said the bishop of Lyon, was "a child, and it was necessary that he should grow and so come to his perfection."[75] However, Adam failed, losing the "likeness" of God. It was Christ, as the new Adam, who progressed to complete maturity and thus restored the divine likeness to humanity. Borrowing the idea of "recapitulation" (ἀνακεφαλαίωσις) from the Apostle Paul,[76] Irenaeus makes it his own by expanding upon it. Christ, the incarnate son, became a second Adam reversing the wrong committed by the first Adam. In his words:

> When he became incarnate, and was made man, he recapitulated in himself the long line of human beings, and furnished us, in a brief, comprehensive manner, with salvation; so that what we had lost in Adam—namely, to be according to the image and likeness of God—that we might recover in Christ Jesus.[77] . . . [For] God recapitulated in himself the ancient formation of man, that he might kill sin, deprive death of its power, and vivify man.[78]

Thus Irenaeus concludes: "Our Lord Jesus Christ . . . [became] what we are, that he might bring us to be even what he is himself," that is, God.[79]

According to Athanasius, in the beginning Adam was endowed with God's logos, but then he lost it. Salvation can only be realized in the restoration of this lost logos to mankind—and this is the point of the incarnation. Hence, Athanasius can say of the work of Christ:

> For he was made man that we might be made God (θεοποιηθῶμεν); and he manifested himself by a body that we might receive the idea of the unseen Father, and he endured the insolence of men that we might inherit immortality.[80]

For Athanasius, participation in Christ as the archetypal logos is *theopoiesis.* This theological precision is outside the scope of both Theophilus' doctrines of man and the logos. Nevertheless, becoming immortal as a definition of deification is a common notion to both Theophilus and Athanasius, and, therefore, not so transgressive as one might take it to be. But for Athanasius deification has to do with mystical participation in the logos who is Christ, while for Theophilus it is achieved through obedience to nomos. How common Theophilus' expression actually was in second-century Antioch is uncertain, and while it is unlikely that he understood that expression to be controversial, he does articulate man's soteriological graduation to immortality as deification.

In summary, several eschatological references are essential to Theophilus' doctrine on man. While conflagration and restoration appear to be post-resurrection events, the universal judgment is the defining moment of human destiny. The divine judgment of all people determines eternal punishment for some and eternal reward for others. With respect to eternal reward, the human goals of restoration and immortality are achieved by a law-oriented life. Moreover, conversion to Theophilian Christianity is not a single act at all, but the beginning of a righteous life that includes the persistent doing of good works and thus will lead eventually to a qualified deification.

Theophilus' Theory of Man

What ideas are implied in Theophilus' teachings on man? What vision of man does he promote in his doctrine? In other words, what elements make up his anthropological theory of man? He tells us that after man had been banished from paradise, he broke the law, which was no more than a single command of God not to include gnosis in his diet. Thus, primal man had deformed his character and that of the creation for which he was responsible. The meaning of man's existence, in Theophilian terms, seems to have been equivalent to his original vocation. Man was expected to seize his God-given opportunity for progress. Adam and Eve were so made and formed that they could grow and mature beyond their child-like state, that is, beyond the very real condition of intermediacy (neither entirely mortal nor immortal), and incline themselves toward immortality—reaching for the goal of deification. But disobedience (or the pre-mature consumption of gnosis) made it impossible for man to fulfill his original vocation. Primal man was removed from the place (paradise) in which that vocation was possible given the nourishment of the tree of life (the sustenance for continual corporeal existence until sufficient physical and/or spiritual maturity to consume gnosis). Deprived of the fruit from the tree of life and the tree of knowledge, man became entrenched in mortality, or a state of dying.

From these details, and others mentioned above, it appears that Theophilus believes man to consist of both a mortal body and an immortal soul. The mortal body of primal man could grow and at some point become immortal, thus united in nature with its soul. This physical and spiritual growth could take place natu-

rally in the context of paradise given the presence of the tree of life with its indefinite supply of vivifying nutrients. Given this scenario, man's progression
was not "on the clock," so to speak. Man's growth and progression were determined by his capacity to keep a commandment to refrain from consuming the
fruit of the tree of the knowledge of good and evil until he had gained permission to eat of it. But primal man's impatience got the better of him and he lost
access to the tree of life. This loss of access seems to have meant that while the
soul's immortal status would remain operative until physical death, the body's
potential for immortality had been seriously compromised. Now the human body
will undergo physical death and resurrection, and man, as a unification of body
and soul, must face the prospect of eternal mortality.

The primal sin, however, had not tapped God's capacity to show love and
mercy. So fallen man was permitted to reclaim his vocational goals; but, in his
post-paradise world, they were of necessity revised. In the post-paradise world,
man would have a new and much tougher working environment. In other words,
given that it was inevitable that man's body and soul would encounter solidarity
of nature after his death and resurrection, if man wanted to achieve immortality,
the conditions for such an achievement could no longer take place in an environment designed for an indefinite period of progression. "Work," which had
consisted of simply a one-commandment law, would now be a "way of life"
(πολιτεία) built on a law of many commandments. The new situation in which
man found himself is not one of progressive maturation, but of progressive salvation. Although God had established the conditions for salvation, it is man himself who must make reparation for his sin and correct his behavior and thus work
out his own salvation. In the end, the man who does so will return to his natural
state, be "recalled" to his original paradise condition, however that is to be defined, and reassume his original goal and destiny. Primal man's original stint in
paradise could be called an indefinite period of maturation, and perhaps the
bishop envisioned the post-resurrection man once again given access to the tree
of life and reinstated in his original vocation of maturing to immortal status.
Nevertheless, man's occasion for repentance is an opportunity for complete recovery from the repercussions of sin. In a sense one could say this recovery is
actually a rehabilitation of man during a period of paideia. The specific opportunity that Theophilus holds out to Autolycus is to study the prophetic message,
and then to keep the law prescribed. As he explicitly says: "One must . . . become a student of the legislation of God" (3.17).[81]

Notice that in the anthropological doctrine of *Ad Autolycum,* there is no accounting for the role of the historical Jesus or the Christ of faith. The dominant
event of human history does not appear to be the "good news" of Jesus' birth nor
the merit-making act of Jesus' death on the cross, but the benevolent act of God
in providing man with a second chance and a revived vocation. While I believe a
good case can be made for Theophilus' intentional avoidance of Jesus, clearly
there is a paper-thin role for Jesus as savior in *Ad Autolycum 's* protreptic doctrine on man. As for divine "grace" (χάρις), Theophilus is careful not to juxtapose it with human responsibility. Therefore, having acknowledged that "grace

preserves" man during disobedience (3.15) and "grace leads" man to obedience (3.23),[82] the bishop's focus is always on human responsibility.

This chapter has shown that, according to Theophilus, contemporary man is still to function as a nomos keeper. Theophilus' doctrine on man is here closely connected to his soteriology. The original human vocation of progress toward immortality was circumvented by the human response to the original command of God. Primal man disobeyed God's primal nomos and was expelled from paradise. Fallen man would have to renew this nomos-keeping vocation if he were to re-enter paradise. However, while both his original vocation and the conditions of progress toward maturity and eventually immortality had changed in the post-paradise world, his body-and-soul nature had remained the same. The following is a schematic of the Theophilian dispensations of man based on the bishop's theory in *Ad Autolycum* regarding human nature and development:

THEOPHILIAN DISPENSATIONS OF MAN[83]

	Paradise	Fixed Period of Time	Resurrection
Human Nature	• Primal Man = Mortal Body + Immortal Soul	• Fallen Man = Mortal Body + Immortal Soul	• Righteous Man = Immortal Body + Immortal Soul • Lawless Man = Mortal Body + Mortal Soul
Human Development	• The opportunity for progress or the period of progression toward maturation	• The occasion for repentance or the period of education toward salvation	• Righteous Man is recalled to paradise to experience eternal life and immortality. • Lawless Man will remain in the world to experience eternal punishment and mortality.

The program for salvation must be completed within what Theophilus called the "fixed period of time (τακτὸς χρόνος)" or what I call his period of education toward salvation—that is, a definite time period in which to learn and practice repentance. Theophilus appears to believe that repentance is a process in which man works out his own salvation through nomos keeping, that is, the keeping of the credal and moral commandments contained in the Septuagint and the New Testament. Actually, the "great benefit" attached to man's "acquiring pain, suffering, sorrow and finally death," is this opportunity for repentance, which is seen by the bishop as a time of education and growth that will come to a positive end for the righteous with the resurrection, judgment and restoration. Salvation is won through the nomos-keeping activity of each individual person, so again it is correct to say that in Theophilus' protreptic system in *Ad Autolycum* each person works out his own salvation. In other words, while paradise was created for man and then lost by man, it can be regained by man himself. The salvific economy of human nomos keeping will eventually lead to immortality and deification. With this doctrine on man now established, let us consider a slightly more complicated matter, a second protreptic doctrine which can be unearthed from these documents, namely, Theophilus' teaching on the agents of God.

Notes

1. This doctrine is classically called anthropology. The other two doctrines deal with divine agency and salvation, but might be called logology and nomology given Theophilus' special descriptions.

2. Theophilus is reading LXX 1:27—καὶ ἐποίησεν ὁ θεὸς τὸν ἄνθρωπον, and 2:7—καὶ ἔπλασεν ὁ θεὸς τὸν ἄνθρωπον, and calling his readers' attention to a potential problem.

3. Genesis 2:7ff.

4. According to H. Bietenhard, in C. Brown's *Dictionary of New Testament Theology* (Grand Rapids: Zondervan, 1986), volume 2, 761: "In later Judaism there were many varied speculations about the paradise of Genesis 2 and 3. It was assumed that it was created before time, or on the third day of creation, and that in consequence of Adam's sin it was removed and hidden either at the extreme edges of the earth, on a high mountain or in heaven. It is located in the third heaven (AMos. 37:5 and Sl. Enoch 8:1)." Paradise is mentioned in the New Testament in Luke 23:43, II Corinthians 12:3 and Revelation 2:7. Paul speaks of a man who was "caught up to the third heaven" or "caught up into paradise."

5. Liddell and Scott, 1412a, give a brief range of meanings for ἡ πλάσις like "moulding" or "conformation of an infant." Given that a passage will be mentioned shortly in which Theophilus describes the original man of paradise as an "infant," it is plausible that the bishop saw the distinction between the "creation" of man and the "formation" of man as being a biblical recognition of two kinds of divine action in the beginning of human history, first a recognition of man being "conceived" and second of man being "born" or made adaptable to a new environment. *The Epistle of Barnabas* 6.9 also speaks of ἡ πλάσις τοῦ Ἀδάμ. But the context in *Barnabas* makes it clear that the subject is the one and only creation of man.

6. This Greek Theophilian term, γνῶσις, is here used as an abbreviation for the capacity to distinguish what is morally "good and evil" in contrast to the capacity to distinguish what is morally "right and wrong." While Theophilus is not explicit about the difference, it must be inferred from the fact that he understands original man to possess the moral capacity to choose to do what is obedient. As we shall see, man possesses certain attributes by nature, one of which makes it possible for him to apprehend the difference between obedience and disobedience. For Theophilus the nutrients of the fruit of the tree of knowledge clearly supply a different kind of moral insight, knowledge not only of what is right and wrong, but perhaps knowledge of why something is right or wrong. As for the use of the term gnosis in the wider context of moral discourse and as a specific genre, see W. A. Meeks' discussion of "Gnomic Discourse" in *The Origins of Christian Morality* (New Haven: Yale University Press, 1993), 71-79. In contrast with lists of vices

and virtues, Meeks speaks of "the collected maxims, moral aphorisms, clever similitudes, and rules of thumb that were also evidently a major part of early Christian's moral discourse." He offers an explanation of this material: "The Greeks called such sayings *gnomai,* the Latins *sententiae.* Collections of such wise moral sayings, sometimes culled from various poets and philosophers of the past, sometimes adapted for a particular school of thought, were much in vogue in the Hellenistic age. Many of the *gnomai monostichoi,* the 'one-liners,' gathered from the the the comic poet Menander have survived. So have the *kyriai doxai,* 'Principal Doctrines,' of Epicurus, another unnamed collection of Epicurus's gnomes known from the library that preserves it as *Gnomologium vaticanum,* and many of the sayings of Pythagoras that, Iamblichus tells us, novices wishing to join the Pythagorean communities had to memorize." Moreover, "collections of gnomes were also used for more advanced education—the Stoic philosopher Chrysippus, for example, is said to have made a collection to reinforce his own lectures and for use by students . . . [while] the sayings of Pythagoras and those of Epicurus, many in gnomic form, were used in the instruction of converts to their respective schools of philosophy."

7. R. M. Grant's translation is slightly modified here, though its sense is preserved.

8. This term, ἀφορμη (opportunity), usually conveys in most contexts a "starting point." However, the term was occasionally used to refer to funds or capital for business ventures.

9. Why was paradise built? What is its purpose? Why is man placed there? Answers to those questions are only hinted at by Theophilus. He seems to treat paradise the way a modern person would a laboratory in which an experiment is to be conducted.

10. G. Stählin, "Προκοπή" in G. Kittel's *Theological Dictionary of the New Testament* (Grand Rapids: Eerdmans, 1968), volume 6, 705.

11. This provocative idea of man's potential for divinity, an issue raised by Theophilus in only one other passage, will be discussed shortly.

12. "For what flesh can see with eyes the heavenly and true immortal God, who dwells in heaven" (2.36)?

13. Theophilus could also be interpreted as suggesting that created man was only a disembodied spirit until he was formed of the dust of the ground and then filled with the divine soul. The bishop speaks of the soul (ψυχή) numerous times throughout his books, but never offers a sustained philosophical explanation. This passage in 2.19 is the only one in which he gives any explanation about its nature. He does become a critic of Plato's presentation of the soul (3.7) because the philosopher is inconsistent on whether he thinks it is immortal or not. Although I see nothing in Theophilus' thought in *Ad Autolycum* that would lead to any conclusions regarding how he understood the status of the human fetus, if he equated creation with conception and formation with birth, I wonder if he would have equated personhood only with birth?

14. The two commonly used Greek adverbs, ὁλοσχερῶς and καθόλου, respectively, do not appear to represent a semantic distinction for the bishop.

15. 2.8, 14, 26, 37, 38; 3.9, 12.

16. See 2.24, where the bishop guards against this potential confusion by quoting Genesis as to the location of Eden in the east, saying that he wanted "to show that paradise is *of* earth and was planted *on* the earth."

17. What other assumption can be drawn from his language? In Revelation 2:7 we read that "the spirit says to the churches: To him who conquers I will grant to eat of the tree of life, which is in the paradise of God." According to H. Bietenhard, in C. Brown's *Dictionary,* 763, "[This] passage may be compared with Test. Lev. 18:11; Eth. Enoch 24:4; 25:4f. which suggests that as early as the 2nd. century B.C. the tree of life was thought of in connection with the temple at Jerusalem. . . . The thought takes up that of

Genesis 3, where after eating of the tree of the knowledge of good and evil, man is barred from the tree of life. Those who overcome the trials and temptations of this world . . . are promised not only restoration of what Adam lost but access to life in a way which Adam never had." Bietenhard makes his case on the basis of Revelation 22:1f. and 14 which "gives a final vision of the tree of life in its final vision of paradise (though it does not use the word) in terms of the new Jerusalem." This New Testament passage says: "Then he showed me the river of the water of life, bright as crystal, flowing from the throne of God and of the Lamb through the middle of the street of the city; also on either side of the river, the tree of life with its twelve kinds of fruit, yielding its fruit each month; and the leaves of the tree were for the healing of the nations. . . . Blessed are those who wash their robes, that they may have the right to the tree of life and that they may enter the city by the gates."

18. That is, ἐργάζεσθαι and φυλάσσειν.

19. There is in Theophilus' language a shift from the plain sense of φυλάσσειν (to watch, to guard and to secure) to the metaphorical sense (to keep, to maintain or to observe).

20. H. Bietenhard, in C. Brown's *Dictionary,* 761, says of certain pseudepigrapha teachings: "In the renewed creation paradise will again emerge from its concealment. God or the messiah will bring it, as the dwelling-place of the righteous and blessed, to the renewed earth, to Palestine, in the neighborhood of Jerusalem. Taught by God himself, the righteous will study the Torah in paradise, and God will prepare for them the messianic meal. Above all, they may enjoy the fruit of the tree of life."

21. Theophilus mentions the word "sin" (ἁμαρτία) some fourteen times in all three of his books (1.2; 2.14, 17, 24, 26, 28, 35; 3.11, 13, 15, being the primary texts).

22. The term "death" (θάνατος) is used 24 times (14 in the second book). While in each instance Theophilus is clearly speaking about the end of physical life, the notion of spiritual death does not seem alien to his thoughts in several contexts (2.25, 27, 29 and the quotation from the Sibyl, "death-dealing poison," in 2.36). However, when he speaks of "the sensation after death" (2.38), "the reward after death" (3.2) and even "the death of the lawless man" (3.11), the bishop is dealing with physical mortality.

23. Regarding the infancy of the primal parents cf. Irenaeus, *Demonstration* 12 and 96 and *Against Heresies* 4.39-40, but especially 3.22.4, where we read that Adam and Eve "had no understanding of the procreation of children: for it was necessary that they should first come to adult age." See G. Ruiz, "L'enfance d'Adam selon saint Irénée," *Bulletin de Littérature Ecclésiastique* 89 (1988), 97-111.

24. The Greek word ἡλικία, meaning age or stature, is discussed in a similar vein in a couple of New Testament texts. See Ephesians 4:13-14, where the author claims that in the community certain tasks must be fulfilled "until we all attain to the unity of the faith and of the knowledge of the son of God, to mature manhood, to the measure of the stature (ἡλικίας) of the fullness of Christ; so that we may no longer be children (νήπιοι)." In Luke 2:52 the term ἡλικία is used of Jesus: "And Jesus increased (προέκοπτεν) in wisdom and in stature (ἡλικίᾳ), and in favor with God and man." In the first text it is the individual members of the community of Christians who must achieve a greater maturity and stature, one that resembles the "fullness of Christ," while the second text merely points out that Jesus did achieve such progress (προκοπή). This New Testament language is also that of Theophilus.

25. This image is popular in the New Testament as well. See I Corinthians 3:1-2, where the author says: "But I, brethren, could not address you as spiritual men, but as men of the flesh, as babes (νηπίοις) in Christ. I fed you with milk, not solid food (βρῶμα); for you were not ready for it; and even yet you are not ready." See also He-

brews 5:12-14, where the author seems to suggest a connection between this image and the tree of knowledge, by saying: "For though by this time you ought to be teachers, you need some one to teach you again the first principles of God's word. You need milk, not solid food (στερεᾶς τροφῆς); for every one who lives on milk is unskilled in the word of righteousness, for he is a child (νήπιος). But solid food is for the mature (τελείων), for those who have their faculties trained by practice to distinguish good from evil." While the first text, which addresses levels of Pauline teaching, is less clear about the nature of "solid food" (βρῶμα), the second text is precise and puts "solid food" (στερεὰ τροφή) in a context that would have appealed to Theophilus if he had read it. Theophilus uses the language of the author of Hebrews, namely, that στερεὰ τροφή is not for one who is a νήπιος but a τέλειος.

26. Perhaps Theophilus intends a polemical comment against the pagan gods and their jealous ways.

27. Theophilus' term πρωτόπλαστος (first-formed) is used only three times in his extant books, here in 2.25 and twice in 3.23 (where he was attempting to lay out the true chronology of human history, which began with Adam). This rare term is used of Adam also in Wisdom 7:1 and 10:1. But Theophilus uses the term to speak of Adam as the first man in paradise rather than the first created man. Adam was created and then "formed" so as to participate in the drama of paradise. From this point on I will call the first-formed man or the man of paradise, "primal man," so as to distinguish him from the post-paradise man or the man of banishment, whom I will call "fallen man." A third distinction for Theophilus is "resurrected man."

28. "Nomos" is the term used throughout my book for both God's primal command in the garden and the moral commands in the post-paradise world.

29. While he probably could have, and may have, produced the anthropological precision of an ecclesiastical theology—cf. Justin's *Dialogue with Trypho* 4-5; Irenaeus' *AH* 2.19, 29, 33-34 and Tertullian's learned treatise on the soul—such precision exceeded his protreptic needs in *Ad Autolycum*.

30. See especially 1.2, 5, 7, which suggests that Theophilus believed in an anthropological "triunity."

31. Whereas we might expect the biblical language of "image and likeness," his use of πλάσμα is intriguing. As H. Braun, in *TDNT,* vol. 6, 255, points out, "πλάσμα is commonly used for the product of the artisan . . . or the construct of the imagination . . . [but occurring] in the Hellenistic period for body in dualistic antithesis to ψυχή." Perhaps he wishes to suggest to his readers that this distinction is a Christian one as well. Most probably Theophilus' meaning here is related to his usage of the adjective πρωτόπλαστος in his Genesis commentary.

32. Ἐλεύθερον γὰρ καὶ αὐτεξούσιον ἐποίησεν ὁ θεὸς τὸν ἄνθρωπον. My translation. For some reason R. M. Grant overlooked this statement and accidentally left it out of his translation.

33. The question of determinism and free will are deeply rooted in classical religion and philosophy. While some elements of both Platonism and Stoicism taught free will, there are significant strains of fatalism widely spread throughout the Greco-Roman world. See Cicero's *On Fate,* Ps.-Plutarch's *On Fate* and Alexander of Aphrodisias' *On Fate,* for several examples of how serious the topic of fate had become for philosophical inquiry. In second-century Christianity, the subjects of human responsibility and accountability were explored by Justin the Martyr (*1 Apology* 29; 10; 12 and 43), but not with the same intensity as we will find in Theophilus.

34. This problem is usually discussed in terms of an inquiry known as theodicy. See J. L. Crenshaw *Theodicy in the Old Testament* (Philadelphia: Fortress, 1983); Crenshaw

and S. Sandmel *The Divine Helmsman: Studies on God's Control of Human Events* (New York: KTAV, 1980); R. Gordis *The Book of God and Man* (Chicago: University of Chicago Press, 1965); Gordis "A Cruel God or None—Is There No Other Choice?" in *Judaism* 21 (1972), 277-84; and especially J. Barr, "The Authority of Scripture: The Book of Genesis and the Origin of Evil in Jewish and Christian Tradition," *Christian Authority: Essays in Honor of Henry Chadwick,* edited by G. R. Evans (Oxford: Oxford University Press, 1988), 59-75.

35. Satan is mentioned only twice (2.28, 29), but not outside the context of the Genesis story. Satan is called "the maleficent demon" (ὁ κακοποιὸς δαίμων) who is "still at work in those men who are possessed by him." He is not only called a demon, but also a "dragon" (*δράκων*) because he "escaped" (ἀποδεδρακέναι) from God. According to Theophilus, Satan was originally an angel. The bishop concludes by saying he could expand upon the subject, but it is dealt with sufficiently elsewhere. He does not explain whose book he has in mind here, his or someone else's. The bishop speaks of demons several times (1.10; 2.6, especially 8; and 3.2), but without any description. Theophilus claims that δαιμόνια or δαίμονες filled people with pride and misinformation, but never speaks of them as the origin of evil. He has relatively little to say about demons or Satan compared to Ignatius (*Trallians* 8, 10; *Romans* 5, 8; *Ephesians* 17 and also *The Martyrdom of Polycarp* 17) or Hermas (*Mandates* 7, 9, 12.2, 6) or Justin the Martyr (*Dialogue with Trypho* 100, 125 and several place in his *Apologies*) or Tatian (*Oratio Ad Graecos* 8, 9, 12, 14-16 and 19) or Athenagoras (*Legatio* 26-27) or the Pseudo-Clementines (*Recognitions* 2.44-45, 5.17, 9.4 and *Homilies* 10.10-14, 19.9 and 12). While Irenaeus speaks of Satan or the Devil as a fallen angel (*Demonstrations* 16-17), he is also described as the power behind the Antichrist (*AH* 5.21.1) and he plays a much more significant part in human misdeeds than Theophilus has admitted in *Ad Autolycum* (*AH* 3.8.2, 3.18.6, 3.23.1, 5.21.2-3, 5.22.1-3 and 5.24.1). Nevertheless, it is as true for Theophilus as it is for these other Christianities, and even Enochian Judaism, in contrast to Hellenistic and Rabbinic Judaisms, that Adam's sin and human responsibility are correlated with a strong belief in the evil role of Satan. See the important study of the Theophilian Satan in N. Zeegers-Vander Vorst, "Satan, Eve et le serpent chez Théophile d'Antioche," *Vigiliae Christianae* 35 (1981), 152-69.

36. Actually Theophilus calls the first woman "Eve" in 2.28, ὁ ἀρχηγὸς ἁμαρτίας ("the pioneer of sin"). However, one would be hard put to find a developed hamartiology in the bishop's work. While Theophilus does not use the language of "original sin," he certainly believes the effects of the primal sin are operative in the contemporary world. He sees no logical difficulty between primal sin and divine providence. The Fall is due to an abuse of free will. He does not believe that a defective choice presupposes a defective nature. As will become obvious in the Theophilian quotations to follow, he does seem to believe that humanity shared in some fashion in Adam's actual disobedience, but there is little evidence as to whether he also believed in inherited guilt or physical transmission of sinfulness. He might have favored, as did Irenaeus (*AH* 3.18.7), a mystical solidarity with Adam over against any notion of a genetic fault that could impair individual freedom. For an overview of early Christian teachings on the "Fall" and "Original Sin" see M. Blowers' articles in *EEC,* 342-44 and 669-71, respectively.

37. Theophilus typically uses two other terms, ἐπιτιμία and κόλασις, to refer to punishment or chastisement (see especially 2.25, 26, 38). It is only here in 2.26 that the bishop uses the term παιδευθείς.

38. Liddell and Scott, 1286a-87b. For corroboration see Arndt and Gingrich, 608a-9a.

39. G. Bertram, "Παιδεύω," G. Kittel, *Theological Dictionary,* volume 5, 604, says that even in the LXX, where the meanings are often associated with the idea of penalty,

this set of terms "can also take on a more intellectualized sense, and stand for 'culture', in the sense of the possession of wisdom, knowledge, and discernment."

40. D. Fürst, "Παιδεύω," G. Kittel, *Theological Dictionary,* volume 3, 776, reports that the LXX occurrences of παιδεύω (used 84 times) and παιδεία (103 times) "are found especially often in Proverbs (vb. 12 times; noun 29 times), in the Psalms (vb. 13 times; noun 5 times), and in Sirach (vb. 15 times; noun 35 times), and rarely outside the prophetic and Wisdom literature." Further, 777, "in the wisdom of Proverbs there is a gradual change from the process of discipline to the effect of it, viz. 'instruction', which has to be learned (Proverbs 1:2), bought and kept (Proverbs 23:23). . . . [But] the educational aim of God is to lead his people to the realization that they owe their existence to the saving will of Yahweh alone, and therefore owe obedience to their divine instructor (Deuteronomy 8:1-6)."

41. Man's physical growth and maturity has now become "academic." While simple patience had been enough in the first phase of man's history, now man would be expected to demonstrate greater scholarship and moral fiber. As will shortly be made clear from the bishop's own language, man now became a full-time student.

42. W. Jaeger, *Early Christianity and Greek Paideia* (Cambridge, MA: Harvard University Press, 1965). He says of the term that it represented in the Greek-speaking word "an ideal of human existence to which every educated man and woman and every civilized nation had aspired ever since the ideal was launched by the century that produced Plato and Isocrates" (133). However, Jaeger says of the specific Christian valence "the true *paideia* is the Christian religion itself, but Christianity in its theological form as . . . Christian gnosis, for it is obvious that the interpretation of Christianity as gnosis per se implies that it is the divine *paideia*" (62). Furthermore, "the merging of the Christian religion with the Greek intellectual heritage made people realize that both traditions had much in common when they were viewed from the higher vantage point of the Greek idea of *paideia* or education, which offered a unique general denominator for both" (62).

43. Ultimately this is an education provided by God, whom the bishop called "an instructor of the godly" (παιδευτὴς τῶν θεοσεβῶν) in 1.3.

44. E. A. Speiser, *Genesis,* The Anchor Bible (Garden City, NY: Doubleday, 1985), 18-19, points out that this distinction has spawned "an enormous literature," one study of which he mentions is over 600 pages long. He says of these two stories, often read as a single story, "the account [from 2:4b-3:24] deals with the origin of life on earth, as contrasted with the preceding statement about the origin of the universe as a whole. The contrast is immediately apparent from the respective initial sentences. The first account starts out with the creation of 'heaven and earth' (1:1). The [Eden] narrative begins with the making of 'earth and heaven' (2:4b). The difference is by no means accidental. In the [first] instance the center of the stage was heaven, and man was but an item in a cosmic sequence of majestic acts. [In the second] the earth is paramount and man the center of interest. . . . This far-reaching divergence in basic philosophy would alone be sufficient to warn the reader that two separate sources appear to be involved, one heaven-centered and the other earth-centered. The dichotomy is further supported by differences in phraseology (e.g., 'create' : 'make') and in references to the Deity ('God' : 'God Yahweh'). . . . Yet despite the difference in approach, emphasis, and hence also in authorship, the fact remains that the subject matter is ultimately the same in both versions."

45. This is the only passage in Theophilus' three books where these two words occur in tandem as two parts of a singular event. He speaks often of God's present and future judgment (2.8, 14, 26, 31, 36, 37, 38; 3.9, 12) and of the future resurrection (1.13, 14; 2.14, 15, 26, 27).

46. There may be some ambiguity regarding the resurrection to eternal punishment in Theophilus' thought, but these two passages (both quoted above, from 2.26) could be interpreted to suggest a purgatorial state in which character improvement for all people is possible. However, more often than not, Theophilus does not sound like a soteriological universalist, where all humanity achieves immortality.

47. R. M. Grant has translated the Greek word ἀνάπλαστος as "refashioned." But we can infer a Theophilian parallel between this word and πρωτόπλαστος (in 2.25 and later in 3.23) as "first-formed" man.

48. This Greek word, ἀφορμή, translated by R. M. Grant as "occasion," is the same one used earlier in 2.24 and translated "opportunity."

49. 2.16, 26, 29; 3.11, 19.

50. See Titus 3:5, where this same phrase, "bath of regeneration," is used, but coupled not with "water" as in Theophilus, but with "renewal in the holy spirit": διὰ λουτροῦ παλιγγενεσίας καὶ ἀνακαινώσεως πνεύματος ἁγίου. The reason for this conjunction becomes clear when the next verse from Titus is considered. What holy spirit is the author of Titus referring to? The one οὗ ἐξέχεεν ἐφ᾽ ἡμᾶς πλουσίως διὰ Ἰησοῦ χριστοῦ τοῦ σωτῆρος ἡμῶν (3:6–"which he poured out upon us richly through Jesus Christ our savior."). For Theophilus, the historical Jesus or the Christ of faith nowhere appears to be the source of salvation. Strictly speaking, in *Ad Autolycum* baptism is related to the initiatory act of anointing itself and not to the imitation of Jesus.

51. The Greek term ἀλήθεια is used 38 times in Theophilus' three books; in some chapters it is dealt with extensively (1.1, 18; 2.1, 8, 12, 14, 15, 16, 22, 23, 33, 34, 35, 38; 3.1, 2, 3, 4, 12, 15, 17, 21, 23, 26, 30).

52. The *Deka Kephalaia* (δέκα κεφάλαια) is of considerable importance to Theophilus, as we shall see in chapter five of this book.

53. Earlier in 2.24, Theophilus had said that Adam was "capable of either (δεκτικὸς ἑκατέρων)" of these two states of being. It is unclear whether or not Theophilus intends any semantic difference by the use of these terms, "each" or "both." He probably does not, even though the potentially troublesome adverbs ὁλοσχερῶς and καθόλου ("entirely") are missing and perhaps avoided in the present text (2.27). Clearly he does not seem to hold to the illogical position that man is capable of being wholly mortal and immortal simultaneously. The concept of two exclusive natures simultaneously in one person belongs ultimately to Pope Leo and the Council of Chalcedon (451) and not to Theophilus.

54. As 2.17 seems to suggest, man was the progenitor of all earthly evil, thus sin and death.

55. The Greek word ἀθανασία is employed twice in Theophilus' books, here and in 2.15. The only other time Theophilus actually uses the abstract concept of "immortality" is in 2.24, where he employs the Greek word ἀϊδιότης. He seems to have no semantic or contextual reason for this shift in language.

56. The bishop never uses the Greek word θεοποίησις but his language is conducive to the notion.

57. There is biblical precedent for this usage in Psalm 82:6, and in its reference in John 10:34-36, where we read, "You are gods (θεοί ἐστε)." Theophilus does not quote these texts, but is probably aware of them. He is not making any concessions to polytheism in his reference to human divinization. His monotheistic credentials are well established in *Ad Autolycum* (see 2.4, 6, 8, 28, 34, 35, 36, 38; 3.2, 7, 9, 12).

58. Cf. Matthew 19:17, where Jesus says to the rich young man, τήρει τὰς ἐντολάς. In 2.24, Theophilus had said Adam and Eve were φυλάσσειν τὴν ἐντολὴν τοῦ θεοῦ. Theophilus' use of the New Testament verb τηρέω in the 2.27 passage translated above.

59. Theophilus is not interested here in a discussion of the resurrected Jesus or the meaning of such an event (cf. John 11:24-25, Romans 6:5-11 and I Corinthians 15:12-19). Nor does he speak of an "exalted son of man" such as Daniel 7:14 (cf. Mark 14:62 and Revelation 1:7). Moreover, Theophilus does not seem to be aware of non-canonical traditions which provide details on the resurrection of Jesus (cf. *The Gospel of Peter* 9-14 and *The Ascension of Isaiah* 3.16-18), or provide comparisons between Christ, Lazarus and the believer (cf. Irenaeus' *AH* 5.7.1-2 and 5.13.1).

60. See especially 2.13-14. According to Josephus, *The Jewish War* 18.11-22, the idea of the resurrection was a sectarian belief which the Sadducees rejected, but the Pharisees promoted (cf. Mark 12:18-27).

61. Cf. this argument with those in *I Clement* 24-26 and Tertullian's *The Resurrection of the Flesh* 11-13.

62. R. M. Grant, *Greek Apologists of the Second Century* (Philadelphia: The Westminster Press, 1988), 173-74.

63. C. W. Bynum, *The Resurrection of the Body in Western Christianity, 200-1336* (New York: Columbia University Press, 1995), 30-31, comments on the bishop's efforts as moving "toward understanding survival as material continuity" by employing the science of his day. She claims: "When he deploys the standard set of organic metaphors, found in I Clement [23-26 and 38], he changes them so as to convey a sense that a material element persists; in his account, true biological change becomes inexplicable." Cf. *II Clement* 8.4-6; Athenagoras' *Legatio* 36; Justin's *I Apology* 18-19; Tatian's *Oratio Ad Greacos* 5.3-6.1 and Tertullian's *The Resurrection of the Flesh* 14-17. These texts argue that the body is included in the Genesis notion of the "image of God" and that the body which committed good and evil must share in reward and punishment. Theophilus, however, does not use this notion in his exposition. Nor does he explain the whereabouts of the soul after man's corporeal death.

64. M. Dods, "Theophilus of Antioch To Autolycus," *ANF,* volume 2, p, 100.

65. Notice Grant's shift in his translation of δεῖγμα.

66. Genesis 2:8 and 15.

67. In 2.38 he quotes Malachi 3:19 and Isaiah 30:28 and 30.

68. Most scholars interpret the lake of fire in the New Testament text, Revelation 19:20, the same way.

69. R. M. Grant, "Theophilus of Antioch to Autolycus," *Harvard Theological Review* 40 (1947), 253-54. See C. Brown, *Dictionary,* volume 1, 654 on ἐκπύρωσις and volume 3, p.146 on ἀποκατάστασις.

70. Cf. with the longer list of vices in 1.2 (ostensibly directed at Autolycus, but clearly meant to describe the cultural weakness of all of the bishop's opponents), and the New Testament lists in Romans 2:8f. and I Peter 4:3.

71. Cf. Aboth 5.20 in H. Danby, *The Mishnah* (New York: Oxford University Press, 1987), 458, which says: "The shameless are for Gehenna and the shamefast for the garden of Eden." Also, see Targum Neofiti, Genesis 3:25, cited in G. Boccaccini's "The Preexistence of the Torah: A Commonplace in Second Temple Judaism, or a Later Rabbinic Development?" *Henoch* 17 (1995), 329-49. The idea that paradise is reanimated for the righteous is a longstanding theme in Jewish thought. See the index listing "Paradise for righteous ones" in James H. Charlesworth's *The Old Testament Pseudepigrapha,* 2 volumes (Garden City, NY: Doubleday, 1983), volume 2, 982.

72. See especially 2.36. Theophilus does not seem to think of eternity, at least not when he uses it to qualify humanity, as a state unconditioned by time.

73. See discussions in 2.24, 27.

74. Hippolytus' *Discourse* 8—Εἰ ἀθάνατος, ἔσται καὶ θεός. R. M. Grant, "Theophilus of Antioch to Autolycus," 253. Cf. the translation in *ANF,* volume 5, 237. A. C. Coxe, who provides notes for the *ANF* text, is obviously disturbed by this statement from Hippolytus and suggests that the bishop was referencing 2 Peter 1:4, where it states: "in order that through these things you might become participants of the divine nature (ἵνα διὰ τούτων γένησθε θείας κοινωνοὶ φύσεως)."

75. Irenaeus' *Demonstration,* 12, cited in *EEC,* 117 and also in J. Smith, *St. Irenaeus: Proof of the Apostolic Preaching,* Ancient Christian Writers 16 (New York: Newman Press, 1952), 56. Both Irenaeus and Theophilus share this idea of Adam's original infancy in paradise.

76. Ephesians 1:10—"As a plan for the fullness of time, to unite (ἀνακεφαλαιώσασθαι) all things in him, things in heaven and thing on earth."

77. Irenaeus, *AH* 3.18.1.

78. Irenaeus, *AH* 3.18.7.

79. Irenaeus' *AH,* book 5, preface. Cf. Ignatius of Antioch, *Ephesians* 20.2, who claimed that immortality is equivalent to life "in Jesus Christ." Irenaeus, *AH* 5.1.1, says that immortality is "participation" (κοινωνία) with God. Also, consider the several early Christian discussions of *theosis* (θέωσις), "a sharing in the very being and nature of God," documented in J. Pelikan, *Christianity and Classical Culture: The Metamorphosis of Natural Theology in the Christian Encounter with Hellenism* (New Haven: Yale University Press, 1993), 281-86, 317-18 and 332-33.

80. Athanasius, *De Incarnatione Verbi Dei* 54.3. See M. Wiles, *The Making of Christian Doctrine* (Cambridge: Cambridge University Press, 1967), 107-8, where he says that Athanasius and the Fathers of the church in general were teaching "gods by grace" (θεοὶ κατὰ χάριν) and not "God by nature" (θεὸς κατὰ φύσιν). Wiles writes: "The dominant concept of salvation in this context was that of being 'made partakers of the divine nature' (2 Peter 1.4)—in a word, of divinization: 'Because of his immeasurable love he became what we are, that we might be made divine.' But when they spoke in these terms the Fathers did not intend the parallelism to be taken with full seriousness. The Word, who was fully God, did not become fully man that he might make us full men become fully God. In speaking of man's divinization the Fathers intended to convey that men should become gods only in a secondary sense—'gods by grace' was the phrase they used; it was never believed that they would become what the Word was—namely, 'God by nature.' "

81. Δεῖ . . . μαθητὴν γενέσθαι τῆς νομοθεσίας τοῦ θεοῦ.

82. These are the only two usages of χάρις in the bishop's writings.

83. The language employed here is primarily from 1.14 and 2.24-27.

Chapter 4

The Agents of God

Theophilus wrote *Ad Autolycum* to persuade his readers to become Christians. For this reason I have called these three books protretic literature, and its teachings, protreptic theology. The words of Theophilus make their appeal for an understanding of the Christian God and the history of his work in the world in terms of divine wisdom (sophia), divine spirit (pneuma) and, most emphatically, divine word (logos).[1] Therefore, it will be useful to carefully analyze how the bishop employs such terms in these documents. With an introduction to his rhetoric of divine agency and a look at the distribution of these terms (sophia, pneuma and logos) throughout *Ad Autolycum,* we can begin this analysis. This chapter concludes—after an explanation of the origin of the logos and the sophia,[2] and a summary of the work of all three agents of God—with a schematic presentation of my understanding of the Theophilian theory of divine agency.

The Rhetoric of Divine Agency

Theophilus' *Ad Autolycum* does not address the subject of angels. According to R. M. Grant, it is sophia, pneuma and logos who are his essential "intermediaries" between God and the world.[3] Grant is of the opinion that Theophilus uses these terms to refer to something more than just abstract personifications of God's activity in the world, thus warranting their description as intermediaries. While Theophilus does treat them as agents of God, he does not call them intermediaries or attribute to them the full ontological status of personhood. So, what do these terms represent in Theophilus' theological system? In most contexts the sophia, the pneuma and the logos appear to be treated as "hypostatized entities." W. O. E. Oesterly and G. H. Box define "hypostasis (ὑπόστασις)" in what I take to be a primitive Christian sense, as "a quasi-personification of certain attributes proper to God, occupying an intermediate position between personalities and abstract beings."[4] Theophilus does not use the term hypostasis, although his language would more often than not seem to fit Oesterly and Box's definition. In a few instances, Theophilus employs the sophia, the pneuma and the logos to explain God's nature, attributing to him the qualities of divine wisdom, spirit and reason. However, these Greek terms usually have to do with divine action in the world. It is important to notice that Theophilus is not writing philosophical theology per se; and therefore, he does not distinguish what appears to be two separate usages, one describing these terms as representing attributes of God and a second as divine agency. This apparent ambiguity makes it difficult for the modern interpreter to state the bishop's doctrine with precision. What is incontrovertible is that these terms and the divine activity they represent are fundamental to Theophilus' understanding of his religion. While I find the technical terms "intermediary" and "hypostasis" too suggestive of an ontological status that might be inappropriate for Theophilus' meaning, the discussions in this book will loosely define Theophilus' sophia, pneuma and logos as divinity acting in this world in terms of specific personified agents of God. In talking about these divine agents, I do not think he took them to be real self-sustaining entities, that is, angels or demigods. Rather, I think it is much more likely that he saw them as literary fictions useful in describing God's power, God's revelation of himself and God's actions in the world, that is, as personified agents with anthropomorphic characteristics. While I think the notion of personification is fair to his rhetoric in *Ad Autolycum,* I would not exclude the possibility that he understood the figures of the sophia, the pneuma and the logos to be something more than that.[5]

According to Theophilus, how does God generate these agents? How do they function in the world? What is their relationship to each other? Moreover, if they are personifications, what specifically do they personify? The bishop has several things to say about each of them that would answer these questions. Again, his comments are less systematic than one might like. The bishop is pragmatic in *Ad Autolycum* and what he has to say about such agents is tied to his purpose in convincing Autolycus of his need for the Christian God and the Christian way of life. If this point is missed, then the reader of this collection of documents may find himself exaggerating this Theophilian doctrine in the misguided hope of more fully conceptualizing the bishop's ecclesiastical theology. Again, conceptualization is difficult given the protreptic character of this theology. Having said this it would be worth our while to look at two examples of his protreptic rhetoric, namely, the so-called trinitarian discussions of *Ad Autolycum.* The two questions we should ask ourselves as we study these two texts are whether they present us with hypostatized entities and are they actually trinitarian church teachings.

If God is wholly transcendent, then how does he create, let alone govern, the world? This problem calls for some intensive work on the part of Theophilus. God in some mysterious fashion apparently extends his being into the field of cosmic existence without violating his transcendence. Given that Theophilus saw Autolycus as a theological neophyte, he did not want to burden him with excessive technical descriptions. Furthermore, the bishop did not want his descriptions to exceed his immediate exegetical needs, which presumably were governed by the questions of his potential convert. Therefore, when it came to the particular question of divine extension into the cosmos, the bishop employed anthropomorphic rhetoric and the common image of God as a man with strong hands. God's mind conceived of a project, but it took his hands to bring the concept to reality. And so, the bishop fosters an image of God extending his hands out of heaven and into the cosmos to manufacture a world.[6] This image is built, as we shall see, by combining two important Jewish traditions, that is, the "Wisdom tradition" with the "Word tradition."

Theophilus' doctrine of the hands of God is developed primarily in a passage from the *Syngramma* where he discusses the creation of man. But before looking at that passage, let us consider an earlier discussion regarding the so-called "trinity" of Theophilus. J. Quasten claimed that "Theophilus is the first to use the word τριάς (trinitas) for the union of the three divine persons in God."[7] J. N. D. Kelly concurred, saying Theophilus "was the first to apply the term 'triad' to the Godhead."[8] D. F. Wright supports these earlier assessments when he says of Theophilus (and some other theologians of his day):

> Theophilus was the first Christian writer to use the Greek word *trias* in this context . . . [and], although Christian theology now for the first time talked explicitly about "three" divine beings, . . . stress fell on a plurality within the Godhead.[9]

However, I think that all of this trinitarian language is derived from the modern historian's anticipation of later theological developments and, therefore, is anachronistic when directed towards Theophilus. Theophilus does not speak of plurality within the so-called Godhead, let alone present a primitive or alternative form of the trinity.

The passage in question is found in Theophilus' exegesis of the fourth day of creation, where he begins by making some rather startling comparisons. The bishop says:

> On the fourth day the luminaries came into existence . . . . And these things contain a pattern and type of a great mystery. For the sun exists as a type of God and the moon as a type of man. As the sun greatly surpasses the moon in power and brightness, so God greatly surpasses mankind; and just as the sun always remains full and does not wane, so God always remains perfect and is full of all power, intelligence, wisdom, immortality, and all good things. But the moon wanes every month and virtually dies, for it exists as a type of man; then it is reborn and waxes as a pattern of the future resurrection. (2.15)[10]

And then, it is said, he formulates his "trinity."

> Similarly the three days prior to the luminaries are types of the triad (τῆς τριάδος) of God and his logos and his sophia. In the fourth place is man, who is in need of light—so that there might be God, logos,

> sophia, man. For this reason the luminaries came into existence on
> the fourth day. (2.15)

Is Theophilus really intending in this passage to develop a theological trinitarian notion of the Godhead? Whether he intended to do so or not is of little consequence for many modern scholars who have felt compelled to award him the dubious title of inventor of the Trinity. And why would they do this? Because he is the first Christian to use the term *trias* in the context of divinity. However, a careful reading of the text shows Theophilus' goals were more practical and less theologically innovative.

The key to understanding this passage by Theophilus is the lacuna in the first quotation in the preceding paragraph, which I created for the sake of argument. This is material that some scholars simply overlook. After his opening sentence, "On the fourth day the luminaries came into existence," Theophilus explains why God created what he did on specific days:

> Since God has foreknowledge, he understood the nonsense of the
> foolish philosophers who were going to say that the things produced
> on earth come from the stars, so that they might set God aside. In or-
> der therefore that the truth might be demonstrated, plants and seeds
> came into existence before the stars. For what comes into existence
> later cannot cause what is prior to it. (2.15)

Theophilus is trying to convince Autolycus that the actual creation order is itself a foil to paganism. He is defending divine cosmic activity by maintaining that, contrary to philosophical speculation, the natural order of vegetational reliance on solar light does not necessarily exclude God as creator when one is made privy to the creational order. In fact, he claims, the revelation of the creational order was designed to demonstrate God's involvement with the world. While his circular argument is susceptible to criticism, it is an attempt to convince his readers that "what comes into existence later cannot cause what is prior to it." His concern is not with plants and stars, but he uses the biblical creation order to deal with a much more important concern, namely, the Hellenistic claim that man is the measure of all things. While he does not make this concern explicit, it can be inferred from his argument.

The bishop is not arguing the nature of the "Godhead." Using the language of analogy, he says the sun can be a type of God because the sun is greater than the moon, a type of man. If Theophilus had known some lunar physics, he might have added that God does not reflect man but man reflects the light of God. Further, man exists as the brightness of the moon is relative to its reflective power. The moon waxes and wanes but the sun always remains full. The point is simple: God is prior to man. Theophilus continues with his analogy and contends that the first three days of creation are to be compared to God, his logos and his sophia. According to the creation story, first there was light and second a firmament and third the earth. His analogy is useful in that it gets him to the fourth day, not that it explains God's nature. In fact, he is not really interested with any potential lessons to be found in this analogy. It is the fourth day that provides the lesson he wishes to teach. On the fourth day the luminaries come into existence: the sun, the moon and the stars. In an important sense these luminaries are in their totality a type of man, for just as they needed light to produce their brightness so man needed God. It is not so much the *triad* that interests Theophilus as the *tetrad.*

Perhaps there is some confusion in Theophilus' choice of words or his diction that would lead the reader to focus on the *triad.* While he uses the noun τριάς (τριάδος) for his threesome, he does not use the parallel τετράς (τετράδος) for his foursome. Rather he speaks only of the fourth member of his foursome, and therefore uses the appropriate form of the adjective, τέταρτος. But the context makes it clear that he is actually addressing the subjects of a threesome (τριάς) and a foursome (τετράς). Further, it is the subject of the foursome from which the reader is to learn the primary lesson.[11]

Now let us return to the earlier discussion of the hands of God. When it comes to the creation of the fourth element of the *tetrad,* man, the previous two elements, the logos and the sophia, play a coordinated and cooperative role. The bishop says:

> When God said, "Let us make man after our image and likeness," he first reveals the dignity of man. For after making everything else by a word, God considered all this as incidental (πάρεργα); he regarded the making of man as the only work worthy of his own hands. Furthermore, God is found saying "Let us make man after *the* image and likeness" as if he needed assistance; but he said "Let us make" to none other than his own logos and his own sophia. (2.18)

Here in this key passage Theophilus builds an elaborate image on a biblical foundation. He wants to make contemporary sense out of the ancient creation-of-man story. God said, according to the Septuagint, "Let us make man according to our image and likeness."[12] In his first quotation of this passage in the above text, Theophilus retains the Septuagint pronoun, "our," in reference to the terms, image and likeness. In the second instance, he deletes the pronoun calling specific attention to the phrase "Let us make."[13] Theophilus is concerned to identify the "us" in this phrase. Who is God talking to as he prepares for the next stage in his creation? Theophilus says he is talking to the logos and the sophia. How are we to understand these figures? First, we should notice that Theophilus is struggling with the text to make sure his readers understand that, despite the language of the biblical story, the "us" was not intended to suggest God was asking "anyone" for help.

Then to whom was God talking? Second, we should notice that the bishop wonderfully imagines God anthropomorphically as a man looking down at his own two hands, speaking to them as extensions of himself, and telling them of the job that now confronts them. It is a job which will take both of them working in concert. But, surely all creation needed both the logos (the right hand?) and the sophia (the left hand?) working together? Apparently not. Theophilus saw that in the creation story God had used only impersonal imperatives (Genesis 1:3-25—"Let there be") to initiate the activities of the first day through the first part of the sixth day.[14] However, during the second part of the sixth day, when God was about to engage in the making of man, he employed for the first time the first-person plural imperative (Genesis 1:26—"Let us make").[15] God appears to be soliciting the activity of another. But, Theophilus wants to be clear that God is talking to none other than himself or more precisely to his own hands. For the sake of the image, and presumably the preservation of the traditionally established names of the agents of creation, Theophilus identifies these fictional divine hands as the logos and the sophia. According to the bishop's interpretation of these events, the logos needed no help in constructing what is subordinate. However, it seems that man is the supreme accomplishment of the creation, and perhaps a more complicated phenomenon to produce as well. Everything else is "incidental (πάρεργος)" to the creation of man. God deemed the dignity of man as warranting the active participation of both the logos and the sophia. To put it another way, all of creation, with the exception of man, could be produced in a single-handed fashion—that is to say, by a word (logos). Nevertheless, with the production of man, God chose to dig in with both hands. Despite his vivid projection of this image, the bishop is not calling his readers' attention to the work of demigods, but rather to the significance of God's real involvement with the creation of the world and especially with the creation of man. The bishop's language and extended metaphor shows that he is more interested in pedagogical rhetoric than in theological system building.

When Theophilus thinks of God's providential care of the world, he says that it wholly resides within the hand of God.[16] It is clear from Theophilus' work that he wants to dabble with the theme of the hand(s) of God. Consider two examples. First, at one point the bishop wants to demonstrate to Autolycus the utter worthlessness of the Greek god called Zeus Tragedian. For Theophilus, this god's story is self-evident proof of his illegitimacy; and so the bishop asked, rhetorically, "Why should I relate . . . that the Zeus called Tragedian, after burning his own hand, as they say, is now worshipped among the Romans as a god?" (3.8). After all, how can Zeus perform divine work without his hand? And second, in contrast to the worship of idols and heavenly bodies, Theophilus quotes Hosea (2.35), where it says:

> This is your God, who made firm the heaven and founded the earth,
> whose hands showed forth the whole host of heaven, and he did not
> show them to you so that you should follow them. (Hosea 13:4)

While these passages demonstrate Theophilus' curiosity with the theme of the hand(s) of God, he does not really embellish the image by speculating on God's two separate and identifiable hands.[17] Even the obvious question invoked by his rhetoric—namely, does each hand have a definable task?—is left unexplored.

Thus, in conclusion, Theophilus promotes a religion of monotheism in the context of a protreptic theology. He is not trinitarian or intentionally the initiator of trinitarian ideas. Most emphatically Theophilus says: "We acknowledge a god, but only one" (3.9). God is the one and only creator and governor of the cosmos. God made the world and he keeps it going. Next to God's oneness, however, it is important to understand that Theophilus' God is completely transcendent. Theophilus offers his readers no essay on God's love for his creation or even God's emotional attachment to it. But God's otherness is stressed and explored in sufficient depth for Theophilus' purposes (1.3). God is so utterly removed from his creation that human articulation is compromised by the sheer inability to conceptualize divinity. Thus, God is not only ineffable but also nearly incomprehensible. Nevertheless, we are not totally devoid of insight into divinity. We may speak of God's attributes and use appellations for God. Moreover, as appropriate for the pedagogy of the unlearned, Theophilus is also comfortable in using the analogical language of personification. Thus, God may be imagined as having two hands—the logos and the sophia (2.18). God's logos hand was certainly more than adequate for the creation of the world in general, but one aspect of the creation moved God to employ both of his hands. With the logos and the sophia together God formed man. Once again, one should not read any trinitarian dogma into Theophilus' thought regarding the hands of God. Some scholars have done so in their casual analysis of the passage in which Theophilus exegetes the creation story and uses the Greek term *trias* in the context of God, the logos and the sophia (2.15). However, Theophilus' use of the term *trias* is rather arbitrary, referring to the first three days of creation as a type for the work of God and his two hands. Theophilus extends the typology to include the first four days of creation, which become a type for God, the logos, the sophia and man. Theophilus is arguing the practical point that God not only mentally conceived of the creation, but, by extending both of his hands into the cosmos, was physically involved with it. Further, without his logos hand and his sophia hand, there would be no man, just as without three days there would be no fourth. Such teachings and theological rhetoric were designed to draw Autolycus away from his paganism long enough to at least consider what the bishop's religion had to offer.

Having considered these two examples of the bishop's protreptic rhetoric, and before engaging further specific texts from which I will formulate the bishop's doctrine of divine agency, let me say a few words regarding the frequency of Theophilus' references to his three primary agents. First, the Greek word σοφία (sophia) is mentioned twenty-seven times in Theophilus' three books. R. M. Grant translates the Greek word as "sophia" fifteen times suggesting its status as an agent of God, and as "wisdom" twelve times implying attributive status. However, in six of the latter, the term is translated with an initial capital letter as "Wisdom," and in each of these instances, I can see no good reason for avoiding its obvious meaning as an agent (2.9, 12, 22, 35, 38).[18] Second, the Greek word πνεῦμα (pneuma) is mentioned thirty times in Theophilus' three books. While all of these instances of the term pneuma could be said to represent divine agency, I will be calling special attention to the bishop's usage of the pneuma qualified by the adjectives holy (2.9, 30, 33; 3.17, 23), divine (2.33), pure (2.8, 33) and unique (2.13), which occur only eight times.[19] Third, the Greek word λόγος (logos), which is slightly more complicated, is mentioned thirty-seven times. Twenty-seven instances of the term were translated as "logos" in contexts that are obviously addressing an agent of God. Six instances were translated "word," three of which occurred in the phrase "word of truth" (2.14, 3.1, 4), two were qualified by the adjectives holy and divine (3.13, 14, respectively),[20] and one occurred in a context which maintained that everything had been created "by a word" (2.18). The remaining four instances of the term occur in the phrase translated "our message," and only in the *Hypomnema* (3.4, 29). The frequency of all three terms in the context of divine agency can be compared in the following chart:

FREQUENCY OF DIVINE AGENCY IN *AD AUTOLYCUM*

Divine Agents	*Homilia*	*Syngramma*	*Hypomnema*
Sophia	7	13	1
Pneuma	8	19	3
(qualified)		(6)	(2)
Logos	4	22	3
Totals	19	54	7

This frequency chart allows us to make several observations. First, notice the preponderance of these terms in the context of the theology of the *Syngramma*. This is perfectly understandable. His exegetical task in this book demands the sort of technical language that would needlessly complicate the apologetics of the *Homilia* and the historical and ethical discussions of the *Hypomnema*. Second, observe his preference for the sophia and the pneuma over the logos in the apologetic context of the *Homilia*. This is harder to account for, but may reflect both the bishop's intent to base the defense of his religion on an appeal to wisdom and spirituality and to resist using the logos outside the more technical theological discussions of the *Syngramma*.[21] Third, while these terms are less frequent in the historical and ethical context of the *Hypomnema*, there is a modest preference for both the pneuma and the logos over the sophia in the bishop's third book. That preference for the pneuma and the logos in the *Hypomnema*, as well as in the *Syngramma*, parallels the higher reliance on specific New Testament materials in these two books. With this information as background, let us begin with an analysis of the key passages where Theophilus speaks of the agents he calls the sophia and the pneuma, and speculate on their relationship independent of the logos.

The Sophia and the Pneuma of God

The term sophia, in its usage as an agent, is seldom treated independently of the pneuma or the logos in Theophilus' works, but when it is one can distinguish several minor usages and a primary usage. The bishop's initial reference to the sophia comes in the context of a rhetorical description of God by the use of several appellations and attributes. The bishop says: "If I call him sophia, I speak of his offspring (γέννημα)" (1.3). What does he mean by God's "offspring"? While, in another context, Theophilus attempts a precise explanation of how the sophia became God's offspring, neither here nor anywhere else in his books does he explain why the sophia should be understood as God's offspring. The bishop does press the point that "the form of God is ineffable and inexpressible" (1.3), that is to say, God is beyond visual description, and thus the reader must consider him in abstract terms. The term sophia, as a universal appellation for wisdom, seems an appropriate expression of the divine. Further, the bishop apparently assumes that the notion of sophia as offspring is one that Autolycus would have known or could have intuited. Perhaps, as a curious observer of Theophilus' sacred scriptures, Autolycus was privy to the fact that this notion was popular in Wisdom literature. In Proverbs 8:22-25, the sophia says:

> The Lord made me the beginning of his ways for his works. He established me before time was in the beginning, before he made the earth, even before he made the depths; before the fountains of water came forth, before the mountains were settled, and before all hills, he begets me (γεννᾷ με).

Such passages from Proverbs are likely sources of the bishop's own thought and rhetoric.[22] A little later in the *Homilia* we read that God's "sophia is most powerful" (1.7). And what is his authority for this claim? In this same passage, he makes a strong allusion to a Septuagint text from Proverbs as his proof:

> God by sophia founded the earth; he prepared the heavens by intelligence; by knowledge the abysses were broken up and the clouds poured forth dews. (Proverbs 3:19)

The sophia is therefore God's powerful offspring who was involved with creation. These texts from Proverbs are usually read by modern scholars as metaphors for how God works in this world, and the sophia is usually understood to be a poetic personification of that divine activity.[23] In fact, there are two more agents in the above text, namely, the "intelligence" who prepares and the "knowledge" who breaks up and pours forth. While Theophilus appears to be interpreting these texts as describing the work of God using personified figures, he is obviously interested in extending the metaphoric language for the sophia and portraying her as an agent of God with her own independent existence as God's offspring.

Therefore, what role does the sophia play in the creation story as understood by Theophilus? To maintain that the sophia founded the earth seems to suggest an involvement with the entire creation. There is a passage in the *Homilia* where Theophilus asks Autolycus to observe all of God's works. Then the bishop adds:

> Consider . . . the orderly course of the stars . . . with the morning star rising and giving notice of the coming of the perfect luminary, the conjunction of the Pleiades and Orion, Arcturus, and the chorus of the other stars in the orbit of heaven, to all of which the manifold sophia of God gave individual names. (1.6)[24]

The same phrase, "the manifold sophia of God," is used in Ephesians 3:10 as a passive element that is revealed through the active presence of the church.[25] That is to say, the Ephesians text does not treat the term sophia as a designation for an agent but as an attribute of God revealed through the community's activity in the world. But in Theophilus' statement he seems to envision the manifold sophia as an actual figure who is functioning specifically as the onomatologist of the heavenly bodies.

Theophilus speaks of the manifold sophia of God in his *Syngramma* as well, but this time in reference to the creation of sea life. He says:

> On the fifth day were created the animals from the waters; through these, as in them, is demonstrated the manifold wisdom of God. For who could enumerate their numbers and their varied progeny? (2.16)

Grant's decision to translate the Greek σοφία as "wisdom" in this passage suggests that he takes the term to refer only to an attribute of God.[26] However, given the previous text above, the likely answer to the rhetorical question in this passage (and antecedent to the interrogative pronoun) is God's agent the sophia. I believe it is implied here that the sophia is the personified agent of God who "enumerates" the species of sea creatures. Interestingly, in neither of these Theophilian passages is the sophia technically a creative force, but rather an intelligence who brings order to the universe and can inform regarding names and numbers.

As these two passages regarding her raison d'être show, the sophia is involved not only with cosmic matters but also with the micromanagement of the earth. In a third passage embellishing this latter function of the sophia, Theophilus points out that there are "many indications" which would lead one to affirm the doctrine of the resurrection of the dead. He begins by saying:

> God has given you many indications for believing him. If you will, consider the termination of seasons and days and nights and how they die and rise again. And what of the resurrection of seeds and fruits, occurring for the benefit of mankind? One might mention that a grain of wheat or of other seeds when cast into the earth first dies and is destroyed, then is raised and becomes an ear. And does not the nature

of trees and fruits yield seasonable fruits, by God's command, out of what is obscure and invisible? (1.13)

But what do these wondrous events have to do with the sophia? According to Theophilus, all these indications (or, what Grant calls, "parables of nature"[27]) are constructions rendered by the sophia. Theophilus continues:

> All these things the sophia of God works in order to demonstrate, even through these, that God is powerful enough to bring about the general resurrection of all men. (1.13)

It is the sophia herself who prepares these proofs as a witness to the power of God to perform mass resurrection. Here, the figure of the sophia is Theophilus' personified agent of God's intellect demonstrating the sort of truth that is beneficial to human conversion. Therefore, so far, it would seem that the sophia is involved with managing both heaven and earth, and convicting the human mind.

Theophilus has considerably more to say regarding the sophia's role in the inspiration of the prophets. He says:

> The men of God, who were possessed by a holy spirit and became prophets and were inspired and instructed by God himself, were taught by God and became holy and righteous. For this reason they were judged worthy to receive the reward of becoming instruments of God and containing [sophia] from him. (2.9)[28]

In this passage the sophia could be defined as a divine attribute. But she is rewarded to certain men and thus functions as a passive agent of God in their lives. His discussion of the sophia and her role in prophecy is an important subject for him and he appears to have formulated several underlying technical propositions. First, Theophilus would say that a person who is receptive to the instruction of God and thus seeks to be righteous is a man who may be rewarded. Second, Theophilus claims that such a man is a person worthy of becoming an "instrument" of God, that is, a spokesperson for God—a prophet. Finally, Theophilus adds detail to the making of the instrument or the prophet. For him such men were "possessed" by the pneuma (that is, divinely inspired) and "contained" the sophia (that is, divinely instructed), a process that led to their becoming "holy and righteous."

In the above passage from the *Syngramma*, God is, technically speaking, the active teacher. The sophia is presented, therefore, as an agent of the divine wisdom and as the knowledge required to make someone a prophet. In fact, the sophia is the internal agent while the pneuma is perhaps the external agent of divine activity on earth. The sophia is possessed but the pneuma possesses. In his later *Hypomnema,* there is a passage where the bishop seems more inclined to regard the sophia's function in the world as that of an instructor. After discussing how Christians have conducted themselves in society, Theophilus issues a formulaic list of the sources of morality. He says:

> Truth controls, grace preserves, peace protects; holy logos leads,
> sophia teaches, life controls. (3.15)

This is a fascinating statement that at first appears unevenly constructed. The
sophia is treated as an active agent of instruction, and the logos is a leader. But
truth, grace, peace and life are all equally active agents in this piece of rhetoric.
Therefore, it again appears that the bishop is intensely involved with poetic personification as a tool for presenting God's work in the world.

Now, what precisely did the sophia "teach" the men of God to prophesy?
Theophilus believes that:

> Through [the sophia] they spoke about the creation of the world and
> about everything else; for they also prophesied about pestilences and
> famines and wars. There were not just one or two of them but more
> at various times and seasons among the Hebrews, as well as the Sibyl
> among the Greeks. (2.9)

The sophia's work is extensive and sensitive. However, her work is not unique
to the Hebrew scriptures. The sophia appears to be involved with the truth wherever it is found, and thus even in certain prophecies of the Greeks.[29] The content
of some of this prophecy is information regarding natural and human disasters.
But foremost in the mind of Theophilus is the information to be gained from the
sophia about the creation of the cosmos. Autolycus may have asked what evidence of the sophia's work Theophilus would put forth to sustain his continual
trust in the reliability of this sophia? Theophilus tells his readers that the prophets were "consistent":

> All of them were consistent (σύμφωνα εἰρήκασιν) with one another
> and with themselves, and they described events which had previously
> occurred, events in their own time, and events which are now being
> fulfilled in our times. For this reason we are persuaded that their pre-
> dictions of coming events will prove correct, just as the former
> events took place exactly. (2.9)

It is the "symphonic" nature of all prophetic witnesses whose predictions prove
correct that impresses Theophilus and leads him to endorse the reliable work of
the sophia.

Theophilus points out in another passage from the *Syngramma,* that some so-
called prophets did not access the same divine data and were not as reliable.
However, in this passage it is not the sophia who was the presumed teacher of
the true prophets, but the pneuma:

> The Egyptian prophets and Chaldaeans and the other writers should
> have made accurate declarations concerning the creation of the world
> and the making of man and the later events, if they really spoke by a
> divine and pure spirit and if the utterances made through them were

true. They should have announced not only past or present events but also those which were going to come upon the world. (2.33)

The pseudo-prophets could not make reliable declarations because they, unlike the inspired prophets, were not possessed by "a divine and pure" pneuma. With this introduction to the pneuma, what specifically does Theophilus have to say regarding its function in the world?

In addition to the above texts, there are several other important passages on the pneuma that should be considered. The bishop's initial reference to the pneuma comes in the same passage where we found the first mention of the sophia. The bishop says: "If I call him spirit, I speak of his breath (ἀναπνοή)" (1.3). What does Theophilus mean by God's "breath"? In a passage discussing the invisibility of God, the bishop says:

> As a pomegranate, with a rind surrounding it, has inside many cells and cases, separated by membranes, and has many seeds dwelling in it, so the whole creation is surrounded by the spirit of God and the surrounding spirit, along with the creation, is enclosed by the hand of God. (1.5)

The pneuma is apparently understood to be the protecting agent of God over the whole of the creation. However, it also functions as a veil hiding the actual hand of God that encloses the creation. Taken with another passage the role of the pneuma in the creation context becomes much clearer. He says in this text:

> This is my God, the Lord of the universe . . . [who] gave a spirit to nourish [creation]. His breath (πνοή) gives life to everything; if he held back his spirit by himself everything would fail. (1.7)

The pneuma as God's "breath" initially gave life to the creation and then nourishment essential to its survival.[30] Beyond this general description of the pneuma's function in creation, the bishop speculates on the procedure for instilling life into the cosmos. He says:

> The "spirit borne over the water" was the one given by God to give life to the creation, like the soul in man, when he mingled tenuous (λεπτόν) elements together, for the spirit is tenuous (λεπτόν) and the water is tenuous (λεπτόν), so that the spirit might nourish the water and the water with the spirit might nourish the creation by penetrating it from all sides. The unique spirit occupied the place of light and was situated between the water and the heaven so that, so to speak, the darkness might not communicate with the heaven, which was nearer to God, before God said: "Let there be light." (2.13)

The bishop is interpreting Genesis 1:2, which says that the pneuma moved over the waters, as a technical explanation of the life-giving phenomenon. The life force is imagined as a reaction that occurs when "delicate," "refined" or "subtle" chemicals are mixed together.[31] God's breath, like the wind, had separated the darkness of earth from the inherent light of heaven. But before it was replaced by the created lights, this breath had mingled with the water of the earth producing a synthetic substance that penetrated the earth animating it with creatures. Theophilus believes this process to be the origin of the human soul as well as all of life.[32] This explanation of the creation may have been appealing to Autolycus' Hellenistic mind. The pneuma, according to these passages, plays a major role in the creation of earthly life.

It is in the role of the pneuma as medium of revelation, however, that Theophilus has most to say. After the bishop's discussion of Cain and Seth and before his discussion of the deluge, he digresses for a moment to say:

> For those who desire and love learning, it is easy to make a description of all the generations from the holy scriptures. (2.30)

And why is this so? The bishop continues:

> All these things are taught us by the holy spirit [who] spoke through Moses and the other prophets; so that these books which belong to us, the worshippers of God, are proved to be writings not only more ancient but also more true than all historians and poets. (2.30)

While the historical accuracy of these documents is insured by the mediating activity of the pneuma, it is not the pneuma's revelatory power in the mind of the prophets on which Theophilus focuses, but its pedagogical force in the lives of those who are receptive, namely, the members of his Christian community.

The idea of the pneuma as the teacher of the Christian community is even more pronounced in the following passage. The bishop boldly asserts:

> For this reason it is plain that all the rest were in error and that only the Christians have held the truth—we who are instructed by the holy spirit who spoke in the holy prophets and foretold everything. Furthermore, you must devotedly search the things of God, I mean those spoken through the prophets, so that by comparing what is said by us with what is said by the others you will be able to discover the truth. (2.33-34)

Theophilus concludes from his own analysis of the history and prophecy of the Greeks that they were, for the most part, in error. And then he adds a most startling claim: "Only the Christians have held the truth." Notice, he does not say only the Christians and the Hebrews have held the truth. Therefore, Theophilus could be of the mind that his Christianity is the contemporary extension of the Hebrew religion. Or, he might be suggesting by his language that it is only the Christians who are "instructed" by the pneuma, while the "holy prophets" are merely "possessed" by it as the conduits of truth. If he were maintaining the latter, then he would most likely have concluded that Christians are taught by the pneuma while the pneuma only spoke through Moses and the other prophets.

Thus, Christians would have "held" the truth while the Hebrew prophets were instruments who "contained" the wisdom of God. Perhaps in Theophilus' mind, these prophets were unaware of the subtleties and full importance of what they prophesied and so were not necessarily in complete command of their subject. The teacher is the pneuma who instructs students capable of understanding the full import of this instruction, namely, the contemporary Christians.[33] However one might interpret his claim regarding the Christians' exclusive possession of the truth, and there is considerable support for the idea that he saw Christianity as an extension of the Hebrew religion (as we shall see in the next chapter), the bishop is clearly saying that Christians are good students and their teachings can withstand the criticism of the skeptic—like Autolycus, for example. All one has to do is simply study the prophetic word in the scriptures to see if the contemporary Christian position parallels what is read. Theophilus is confident that the results of this experiment will support his claim.

There are two other similar passages in Theophilus' *Ad Autolycum* where the subject of the pneuma is addressed. In both the activity of the pneuma is appealed to as the ultimate reason for the accuracy of the Christian documents. In the first of these texts, the bishop responds to the claim that those historians who relied on diviners and seers for their information produced reliable histories. Before denying this claim, he says:

> How much more, then, shall we know the truth, since we learn it from the holy prophets, who were filled with the holy spirit of God? For this reason all the prophets spoke harmoniously and in agreement with one another when they predicted what was going to happen to the whole world. The very outcome of the previously predicted and fulfilled events can teach those who love learning—or rather, love truth—that their proclamations are really true, those which were made concerning the times and seasons before the deluge and the number of years from the creation of the world up to the present. (3.17)

The Christians are in full possession of the truth. How did they come by this truth? The holy prophets provided it. How did these prophets come by it? They were filled with the pneuma. This fact accounts for their harmonious agreement in their predictions, and their predictions can be tested by contemporary knowledge of the events they predicted. So, if they are capable of predicting the future accurately, Theophilus argues, how much more reliable we must presume them to be when detailing past events. In either case, it is this pneuma who has actually provided the information to the prophets and ultimately to the Christians.

While it is unclear whether Theophilus' argument was sufficiently cogent for a skeptic like Autolycus, it is clear that the bishop made this appeal to the pneuma, as the medium of true revelation, the presuppositional foundation of his historical method. At the beginning of his biblical chronology, he says:

> In order for us to give a more accurate demonstration of periods and
> times, by God's help—not only recording the events after the deluge
> but also those before the deluge, so that we can state the total number
> of all the years as well as possible—we now proceed to do so, going
> back to the first beginning of the creation of the world, which Moses
> the minister (θεράπων) of God described through the holy spirit.
> (3.23)

Theophilus believes that an accurate chronology of the pre-deluge years is possible and demonstrable given the description provided by Moses, a man who
was no less than "the minister of God." Where did Theophilus get this Mosaic
title? The Greek word θεράπων (minister or servant) is common in the Septuagint, but only used once in the New Testament (Hebrews 3:5).[34] In this single
New Testament instance of the term, an argument is made for the superiority of
Jesus the son over Moses the servant. The title "minister of God" is also given to
Moses in the Septuagint text from Exodus 4:10 and raised again in the same
context in Wisdom 10:16-21. In the Exodus passage Moses complains, as God is
commissioning him at the burning bush, that he does not possess the necessary
eloquence for the job described. God makes it clear that he need not worry, for
he will receive divine instruction when the time comes. In the Wisdom passage,
the specific source of this divine instruction to Moses is revealed. The text reports:

> [The sophia] entered into the soul of the servant of the Lord
> (θεράποντος κυρίου), and withstood dreadful kings [with] wonders
> and signs . . . [she] opened the mouth of the dumb, and made the
> tongues of them that cannot speak eloquent. (Wisdom 10:16, 21)

This Wisdom text is a likely source for Theophilus' use of the Mosaic title "the
minister of God," especially since its notion of the sophia does not run counter
to his own usage of that term. The sophia of this text is a substantial force as an
instructor.

Having analyzed the key passages where Theophilus speaks of the sophia
and the pneuma, it seems to me that the post-paradise activity of the bishop's
sophia is similar to that of the bishop's pneuma. If this similarity were intentional blending, where would Theophilus get such an idea? The pneuma is associated with the sophia in Isaiah 11:2, where it is said of the "rod out of the root
of Jesse":

> And the spirit of God shall rest upon him, the spirit of [sophia] and
> understanding, the spirit of counsel and strength, the spirit of knowl-
> edge and godliness shall fill him.

According to this hymn, the pneuma is a repository of several attributes of God,
one of which is the sophia. In I Enoch 49:3 it is said of the "elect one":

In him dwells the spirit of [sophia], the spirit which gives thoughtful-
ness, the spirit of knowledge and strength, and the spirit of those who
have fallen asleep in righteousness.

According to this text, it is actually the spirit of sophia, who possesses various
attributes, that dwells in the figure called the Elect One. However, it is in another Wisdom text that the closest parallel to Theophilus' blending of these con-
cepts can be found, namely, Wisdom 1:5-6a. We read there:

For the holy spirit of discipline (παιδείας) will flee deceit, and re-
move from thoughts that are without understanding, and will not
abide when unrighteousness cometh in. For [sophia] is a loving spirit.

D. Winston, in his discussion of this Wisdom text, calls the pneuma of *paideia,*
"that divine tutor,"[35] stressing its educational work. It is possible that the sophia
and the pneuma, both of whom play a significant educational role in his first two
books, are occasionally used as the bishop's personification of the scriptures.
With their roles in creation fulfilled, both the sophia and the pneuma became the
force behind the enlightenment of man. Furthermore, the bishop is confident that
an honest evaluation of the teachings of the sophia and the pneuma will yield the
conclusion he has drawn, namely, that Christian scriptures contain the truth.
With this survey of Theophilus' description of the sophia and the pneuma concluded, let us now consider the greater detail he offers regarding the divine logos.

The Primacy of the Logos of God

Theophilus' teaching about the logos is considerably more involved than his
teachings on the sophia or the pneuma. When Theophilus uses the term logos, he
is always in the midst of an extensive technical teaching about God's person and
creative activity or about the source of Christian morality. As we shall see, in
contrast to the terms sophia and pneuma, the bishop reserves the logos for a
higher level of discussion. Theophilus' teaching about the logos in *Ad Autolycum* is designed to tell the uninformed Autolycus what he needs to know about
the Christian God and the Christian faith in order to make an informed decision
for Christianity or, at the very least, avoid misrepresentation of Christian teaching and perhaps become "a real lover of learning."[36] In Theophilus' words:

Although we have many things to say about our way of life and the
ordinances of the God and fashioner of the whole creation, we consider that we have now made sufficient mention of them that you too
may know them from what you have read thus far, so that as you
have hitherto been a lover of learning, you may become (a real) one.
(3.15)

This sentence concludes an important discussion about Christian conduct in which the logos plays an essential role. To use the common term logos in a context that would obviously be controversial for most of his non-Christian Greek readers, suggests that Theophilus believed it would be an attractive tool in winning converts, or at least in building a bridge between the two communities. In other words, the bishop does not have to explain the usual sense of the logos to Autolycus who no doubt was sufficiently educated in philosophical and theological terminology. In fact, given the primacy of the logos in Theophilus' books, one could say his central protreptic tool is this multi-dimensional term.[37]

This section is a review and examination of each instance of Theophilus' use of the term logos as personified agent. The bishop speaks of the logos as an agent of God in all three of his books. As was pointed out above, he addresses the concept four times in the *Homilia,* twenty-two times in the *Syngramma* and three times in the *Hypomnema.* It is important to see that Theophilus' conception of the logos is not presented systematically or complete in any one of these books, but is actually developed over the course of all three. Therefore, our primary concern in this substantial section is to demonstrate that development. It is with the speculation of the *Homilia,* the commentary of the *Syngramma* and the formulas of the *Hypomnema* that such development can be documented. In the fourth section of this chapter, the several theses that emerge here regarding the generation and function of the logos will be briefly outlined.

The Speculation of the *Homilia*

In the *Homilia,* Theophilus first uses the term logos as one of the names or appellations of God: "If I call him logos, I speak of his beginning (ἀρχήν)" (1.3). What does Theophilus mean by the word ἀρχή (beginning) in this descriptive sentence? This text occurs within a creed-like passage that speaks of seven divine attributes and thirteen divine appellations. Upon first encounter, this passage strikes the reader as an awesome display of insight into the nature of divinity—which was probably Theophilus' intent. But given its rhetorical character, the text is simply too sparse for a substantial analysis. What is important to keep in mind, however, is that the logos and the "beginning" form a conjunction in Theophilus' mind.

In the second usage of the logos in the *Homilia,* Theophilus offers considerably more information. The bishop believes that Autolycus, though he is morally and intellectually blind at present, could eventually "see" the Christian God. This optimism comes at the end of a discussion arguing God's "invisibility" to the human eye. So how is it possible to see God if he is invisible? Theophilus claims that God can be seen or at least recognized through his works, and so he introduces his presentation of those works with the words: "This is my God, the Lord of the universe" (1.7). But it soon dawns on the bishop that his adversary needs additional information regarding his illness and its cure, as well as encouragement to break its grip on his spiritual life. Thus, Theophilus says to Autolycus:

> You speak of [God], O man; you breathe his breath (pneuma); you do not know him. This has happened to you because of the blindness (τύφλωσιν) of your soul and [blindness of (πήρωσιν)] your heart, but if you will you can be cured. Deliver yourself to the physician, and he will couch (παρακεντήσει) the eyes of your soul and heart. Who is the physician (ὁ ἰατρός)? He is God, who heals and gives life (ζωοποιῶν) through logos and sophia. (1.7)

According to Theophilus, Autolycus is blind in his soul and heart. But this disease can be cured by letting the physician heal him. God is ultimately the "physician,"[38] but the logos and the sophia are presented as his effective agents of the healing process. How does Theophilus envision the actual work of these agents? In this connection, there are several significant points to be made about this passage. First, the Greek verb ζωοποιέω (give life), a term that seems better associated with the creative or generative act than with the healing arts, is used here.[39] Theophilus does not want Autolycus to miss the significance of his plight. The work of these divine agents is not meant merely to satisfy his curiosity about God, but to provide Autolycus with spiritual health in the form of conversion and eventual salvation. Second, this passage gives specifics about both the disease and the cure. The Greek verb παρακεντέω (couch) is a technical term for a surgical procedure that involves the use of a scalpel-like instrument for the removal of a cataract from the eye.[40] What is the nature of these blinding cataracts? While Grant's translation observes no subtlety in the bishop's language, Theophilus actually describes the blindness in two different ways. Theophilus tells Autolycus that he has "a blinding (τύφλωσις) of the soul," which may implicate the patient in causing his own disease.[41] But the bishop is not so unsympathetic as this might suggest. Almost as a second thought, Theophilus adds that Autolycus' disease is also to be understood as "a blindness (πήρωσις) of the heart," a more natural sounding disorder or affliction for which the patient may be perceived as a victim.[42] Thus, Autolycus is confronted with both the psychological and physical aspects of his condition. He is suffering from a self-inflicted disease. He is a "guilty victim" whose situation can only improve by taking responsibility.

However one might describe the nature of the disease, and this is the third point of the passage, the patient can take responsibility by seeking out the only physician who has the cure for his condition. Toward this end, Theophilus asks Autolycus: "What sick man can be cured unless he first entrusts himself to the physician" (1.8)? And what of the cure? The bishop again asks: "Do you not know, that faith leads the way in all actions" (1.8)?[43] Thus, in the bishop's concluding statement to this passage, whatever the logos and the sophia may represent in Theophilus' analogy, the scalpels of God's skilled hands or God's hands which skillfully manipulate the scalpels, it is still the restorative procedure itself that is important. It is a procedure that begins most naturally with trust or faith.

Theophilus has made a case for understanding conversion from paganism to Christianity as a cure for blindness of faith, a cure rendered by a transcendent God who is yet immanent in his logos and sophia. He has not yet, however, explained how this divine agency works.

Having exhausted the medical analogy, he turns to a more conventional understanding of these agents. Not only are the logos and the sophia personified agents of healing, but also they are personified agents of the creation itself. The bishop says, from a passage partially quoted earlier:

> God made everything through logos and sophia, for by his logos the heavens were made firm and by his spirit all their power. His sophia is most powerful: God by sophia founded the earth; he prepared the heavens by intelligence; by knowledge the abysses were broken up and the clouds poured forth dews. (1.7)

As Grant points out in his interposals to this text, Theophilus is here using a couple of passages from the Septuagint, namely, Psalm 32:6 and Proverbs 3:19-20.[44] By his juxtaposition of these biblical texts, Theophilus seems to be distinguishing the actual work of divine agents. How many does he envision in this passage? There are probably only two agents: the logos and the sophia. Theophilus does transpose the biblical "breath of God's mouth," from Psalm 32:6, with "his pneuma." However, the terms "spirit," "intelligence," and "knowledge" appear to parallel each other, and, therefore, the latter two do not seem to be examples of other independent agents, at least not in this context. The logos is here responsible for the heavenly half of the creation while the sophia is the founder of the earth. Having established the presumption of faith in achieving spiritual sight, Theophilus adds that "if you know these things, O man, and live in purity, holiness, and righteousness, you can see God" (1.7). It is interesting to notice that Theophilus does not claim that the "cure," or one's salvation, rest simply on the knowledge of God passed on to Autolycus, but includes ethics—a developed notion of proper behavior. Once again, Theophilus is concerned not only with "orthodoxy" but also, and primarily, with "orthopraxy."

But as was recorded above, Theophilus firmly believes that "faith leads the way in all actions"(1.8). And so he concludes:

> But before all, faith and the fear of God must take the lead in your heart; then you will understand these things. When you put off what is mortal and put on imperishability, then you will rightly see God. For God raises up your flesh immortal with your soul; after becoming immortal you will then see the immortal, if you believe in him now. Then you will know that you unjustly spoke against him. (1.7)[45]

Here, with his conclusion to a discussion about God's invisibility, the bishop has formulated an invitation to convert. But notice how he has arrived at this invitation. He tells his readers that if one is acquainted with the right things, and practices the right things, they can "see God" and "understand these things."

Autolycus may see God in some sense through the recognition of God's works, but more is required for him to move beyond his misrepresentation of who God really is. Autolycus must come to possess real faith and the "fear of God" now in the present life, and then, when death ensues ("putting off what is mortal"), the believer's flesh and soul will become "imperishable" and "immortal," and he will see "the immortal" (ὁ ἀθάνατος).[46] The insistence of the word "now" is important to Theophilus, for he repeats it when he later says to Autolycus, "Your faith will be reckoned as unfaith unless you believe now" (1.8). Once death has come the opportunity will have passed.

With the above texts, Theophilus has concluded his task of expounding upon the necessary conditions for "visualizing" the invisible God. He has done so by clearly spelling out the substance of conversion, which is what he ultimately means by "seeing God." To accomplish this task he mentions the work that God achieves through the logos and the sophia. What we learn about the logos in the *Homilia* is significant. The logos, in this book, is an appellation for God that is to be understood as having an independent existence. That is to say, Theophilus appears to treat the logos as an individual agent personifying God's work of healing as well as that of creating. However, as intriguing as this notion in the *Homilia* is, the *Syngramma* has designed a far more sophisticated conception of the logos. Nevertheless, one should keep in mind that the *Homilia* is Theophilus' attempt at an apologetic and his concern here is with the defense of his faith and the conversion of Autolycus, while the *Syngramma* is preeminently concerned with this man's education in the Christian religion.

The Commentary of the *Syngramma*

Theophilus' notion of the logos in his *Homilia* was probably adequate for his purposes there, namely, to defend the Christian faith against misrepresentation and to convince his readers of its value as a better way of life. The *Homilia* was a setting forth of Theophilus' *theosebeia,* that is, his religion (2.1). The *Syngramma,* on the other hand, is a treatise with a more complicated presentation of the logos. The *Syngramma* falls into two distinguishable parts, a polemic (2-9 and 33-38) and an exegetical treatment of the early chapters of Genesis (10-32). Theophilus' exegetical work is a sort of mini-commentary that probably existed independent of the *Syngramma* as a whole. Also, the commentary was certainly a later work than his *Homilia* given its apparent development of terms like the logos. In other words, the bishop's presentation of the theological logos in the *Homilia* is a plausible foundation for his usage of the term in the biblical commentary of the *Syngramma,* and with his first book he has, so to speak, brought Autolycus up to terminological speed.

Theophilus opens the initial section of his commentary on the creation with prolegomena, and it is within this introductory material that we encounter his first major discussion of the logos. He says of the Hebrew prophets:

In the first place, in complete harmony they taught us that he made everything out of the non-existent. For there was nothing coeval with God; he was his own locus; he lacked nothing; he existed before the ages. (2.10)

Nevertheless, God wanted to create a world. Why? Why would God who "lacked nothing" want to create a man? Theophilus claims, after emphasizing God's self-sufficiency, that:

[God] wished to make man so that he might be known by him; for him, then, he prepared the world. For he who is created has needs, but he who is uncreated lacks nothing. (2.10)

This answer to the "why" of creation seems internally contradictory. If God lacked nothing, then why did he desire something—to be known by man? Theophilus does not engage Autolycus in a discussion of divine psychology, but quickly points out that this desire to create man meant that God would have to create an environment for him because "he who is created has needs." Actually, Theophilus' introductory comments are designed to shift Autolycus' attention from the troubling "why" to the more manageable "how" of creation.

The most important factor in explaining the "how" of creation is God's logos. The following passage is the first of two which treats the generation of this logos. Theophilus says:

Therefore God, having his own logos innate in his own bowels (ἐνδιάθετον ἐν τοῖς ἰδίοις σπλάγχνοις), generated (ἐγέννησεν) him together with his own sophia, vomiting (ἐξερευξάμενος) him forth before everything else. (2.10)

Theophilus' exegesis of Genesis has a number of intriguing elements, but this passage is universally considered one of his most innovative ideas.[47] Theophilus tells us that originally the logos resided within God's "bowels," that is, the viscera or inward parts. This Greek term, σπλάγχνα, is also used to refer to the heart, lungs or liver, as well as womb.[48] The internal organ this term was intended to represent is not made explicit by the bishop. What is explicitly said is that the logos was first "innate" (ἐνδιάθετος) within God, and then God "generated" (ἐγέννησεν) him by a process, which Grant translates as "vomiting" (ἐξερευξάμενος). How is the origin of the logos (and the sophia) to be understood in this brief description? Is the logos presented here as an aspect of God's existence or an actual entity contained in God's body? As for the graphic image of disgorgement or regurgitation, of what value is it to the bishop's discussion at this point? On one level, Theophilus' language can be understood in a physical sense. But it can also be understood figuratively or in a metaphorical sense. Furthermore, with respect to the physical level, it is not altogether obvious from this language which "cavity" he is imagining as the source of the logos, that is to ask, are we dealing with an oral or vaginal delivery of God's agent? What is

Theophilus' dominant metaphor? The bishop will shortly offer his readers a reconstruction of this image, which I think resolves the issue.[49] But for now, let me suggest that he appears to be blending the language of the Septuagint text of Psalm 109:3 with that of Psalm 44:1 for this metaphorical construction.[50]

While it would be better to draw our conclusions about his understanding of the origin of the logos after observing his later reconstructed image, consider at least this much: Perhaps this image is designed to personify God's thought which originates in the divine mind and is at some point uttered as the spoken word (making the logos no longer innate reason but uttered speech). This is a straightforward interpretation. But, Theophilus appears to be dealing with something more than merely uttered words. As the bishop will show, for him this generated logos is also a creative force as an agent of God. What he wishes to reveal in explicit and memorable language is the fact that there was a divine determination to create something. For the bishop, creation was not an arbitrary, let alone an accidental, event.

Why must the generation of the logos be a prerequisite, as Theophilus says in the above text, for "everything else"? The bishop's answer is as follows:

> [God] used this logos as his servant (ὑπουργὸν) in the things created by him, and through him he made all things. (2.10)[51]

The pronoun in the phrase "the things created by him" could refer to God himself. But given the following phrase, "through him [God] made all things," the bishop is probably claiming that the "serviceable logos" (ὑπουργὸς λόγος) was God's chosen agent for the task of actually making the world. Theophilus continues his discussion of the logos, saying:

> He is called beginning (ἀρχη) because he leads and dominates everything fashioned through him. It was [the logos], spirit of God and beginning and sophia and power of the most high, who came down into the prophets and spoke through them about the creation of the world and all the rest. For the prophets did not exist when the world came into existence; there were the sophia of God which is in him and his holy logos who is always present with him. For this reason he speaks thus through Solomon the prophet: "When he prepared the heaven I was with him, and when he made strong the foundations of the earth I was with him, binding them fast." (2.10)[52]

In the imagery of this passage, Theophilus perceives cosmic forces, which were innate within God, at work in some identifiable ways. He now expounds upon his earlier claim in the *Homilia* (1.3), where he introduced the logos as the ἀρχή (beginning). It seems the logos "leads and dominates" in the creation event. Mapping out exactly and theologically how the logos functions in this manner is less important to the bishop than that he offers a reasonable, although modest, explanation of this highly provocative Greek term, ἀρχή. The logos also plays the role of informant to the prophets on the details of creation. This role, however, is attributed to the logos in the guise of several different figures: the spirit of God, the beginning, the sophia and the power of the most high. While he appears to be blending all of these figures and the traditions they represent into that of the logos, he does highlight the sophia.

The sophia is said to be "in" God and the logos is said to be "with" God. Does this distinction have any significance for Theophilus? Perhaps. But as we observed in the earlier passage from this same chapter, the logos was innate "in" God too, before being generated "with" the sophia. Therefore, one cannot take the bishop's language to be saying that the logos is simply the sophia externalized. In the *Syngramma* the expression that the logos was "with" God seems to be for Theophilus the same as saying the logos was "in" God. The bishop is not here concerned with the grammatical propriety of his prepositions. So, what is he doing here with these figures of the sophia and the logos? The bishop, in his interpretation of Genesis 1:1, is juxtaposing the sophia tradition of Proverbs 8:22-30 with the logos tradition of the Prologue to John's Gospel, and thereby leading his readers into a synthesis of the two. How does he accomplish this task? First, he appropriates the initial phrase from the Gospel statement: "In the beginning was the logos and the logos was with God" (John 1:1).[53] For Theophilus the Gospel phrase "in the beginning was the logos" means that the logos *is* the beginning. Second, he reads the Johannine logos into Proverbs 8:22-30. Now, the logos becomes the speaker and subject of this Wisdom text, replacing the sophia. Thus, I believe the bishop, in his own mind, had revised this passage to read:

> The Lord made me [logos] the beginning (ἀπχὴν) of his ways for his works. He established me [logos] before time was in the beginning. . . . When he [God] prepared the heaven, I [logos] was present with him . . . . And daily I [logos] rejoiced in his presence continually.

Where the sophia had spoken in the first-person, the logos now speaks. This new reading of Proverbs does not mean that the sophia has been preempted from the biblical text, only that Proverbs is no longer seen as a wisdom tradition, exclusively. Thus, the background for Theophilus' exegesis of Genesis 1:1 is Proverbs 8 blended with the Prologue to John's Gospel. The ambiguity created by this process is slowly worked out as the bishop moves from his prolegomena to the commentary itself.

Theophilus begins his interpretation of Genesis 1:1 with a rather peculiar argument:

> And Moses, who lived many years before Solomon—or rather, the logos of God speaking through him as an instrument—says: "[By] the beginning [created God] heaven and earth" (Ἐν ἀρχῇ ἐποίησεν ὁ θεὸς τὸν οὐρανὸν καὶ τὴν γῆν). First he mentioned beginning and creation, and only then did he introduce God, for it is not right to mention God idly and in vain. For the divine sophia knew in advance that some persons were going to speak nonsense and make mention

of a multitude of non-existent gods. Therefore, in order for the real
God to be known through his works, and to show that *by* his logos
God made heaven and earth and what is in them, he said: "[By] the
beginning [created God] heaven and earth." (2.10)[54]

Theophilus opens his commentary on Genesis with an introduction to the real
author of this biblical book. The real author is not Moses but the logos of God,
who used Moses as an "instrument." Theophilus, with a peculiar observation, is
taken by the fact that the text addresses "the beginning" first and "the creating"
second, and only then does it speak of God.[55] What does this obvious fact mean?
Theophilus formulates a two-part answer to what he takes to be an important
question: Why does Genesis begin in the way it does?

First, perhaps drawing on the third of the ten commandments, the bishop
says God's name should not be used "idly and in vain" (Exodus 20:7)[56] and such
would be the case if the word order of the text was: (1) Beginning, (2) God and
(3) Creating. How so? Because, in Theophilus' mind, some readers might take
"beginning" to grammatically modify God and thus presume the creator to be
one particular god among many, namely, the "beginning god" or the "logos
god." If I correctly understand his concern, it seems a bit fussy. Nevertheless,
the bishop claims that the author of Genesis was not being paranoid, given the
historical fact, as he puts it, of the human tendency toward polytheistic "nonsense." Therefore, Genesis grammatically begins the way it does to prevent the
distortion of the enemy, and perhaps a theological accident by a novice.

Second, Genesis begins with the activity of the "beginning," which is to say
God created by his logos. As was pointed out earlier, Theophilus believes that
one of the logos' names was "beginning." Thus, the preposition in the phrase "in
the beginning" is not to be understood as an expression of time but of instrumen-
tality.[57] Therefore, the opening phrase from Genesis should be translated, "by the
beginning," and thus interpreted to mean, "by the logos." In other words, the
author of Genesis deliberately mentions God only after the logos and the creation to make the point that the one God is only known by observing his logos'
work, an observation that should prove the truth of Theophilus' religion. From
this first major discussion of the logos in the *Syngramma,* the bishop has prepared his readers for the technical usage of the logos as a special agent throughout this book.

Before considering Theophilus' second discussion of the logos in the *Syngramma,* it is important to notice how he closes the above discussion. He says:

> These are the first teachings which the divine scripture gives. It indi-
> cates that the matter from which God made and fashioned the world
> was in a way created, having been made by God. (2.10)

Though far from being emphatic and unambiguous the bishop has here restated
his belief in *creatio ex nihilo.* Earlier he argued that the sovereignty of God demanded this idea.

> What would be remarkable if God made the world out of pre-existent
> matter (ὑποκειμένης ὕλης)? . . . [The] power of God is revealed by
> his making whatever he wishes out of the non-existent (οὐκ ὄντων),
> just as the ability to give life and motion belongs to no one but God
> alone. (2.4)[58]

Having expounded upon the logos' creation of the basic primal material,
Theophilus returns to the story of Genesis.

> Light (φῶς) is the beginning of the creation, since the light reveals the
> things being set in order. Therefore it says: "And God said, Let there
> be light. And there was light, and God saw the light, that it was
> good." Made good, that is to say, for man. (2.11)

Is Theophilus suggesting that because the logos is the beginning and the beginning is the light that, therefore, the logos is the light? After all, it is the light that
"reveals the things being set in order," and the logos has already been associated
with revelation. To answer this question, consider how Theophilus develops the
idea. After his quotation of the first few verses from Genesis, Theophilus offers
his "exegesis and plan (οἰκονομίαν) of the Hexaëmeros" (2.12). There he
claims:

> "In the beginning God made heaven." That is to say that through the
> beginning heaven was created . . . . The unique spirit occupied the
> place of light . . . . Therefore the command of God (ἡ διάταξις τοῦ
> θεοῦ), his logos, shining like a lamp in a closed room, illuminated
> the region under heaven, making light separately from the world . . . .
> God by his logos made the water come together into one assembly
> and made visible the dry land which was previously invisible. (2.13)

What does Theophilus teach in this passage? The logos has power to move water. But perhaps more importantly, the logos is a revealer who provides light and
may therefore be called the light in certain biblical texts. The logos is known by
yet another name in Theophilus' interpretation of the Genesis story, that is, "the
command of God," or the διάταξις, who shines "like a lamp" and is an illuminator. The logos, as the personification of God's creative power, is also deeply
involved in the revelation of this work. And so the bishop uses the appropriate
language of "light," "shining," "lamp," "illumination," and the making of something "visible" that had been "invisible." This variety of language shows the
wide-ranging nature of Theophilus' logos speculation.

Because we have already considered the third and fourth instances of the logos in Theophilus' *Syngramma*,[59] we must now discuss what one may consider
Theophilus' most important logos passage. This text is part of his exegesis on
the history of man in paradise. In response to Autolycus' question—"You say
that God must not be confined in a place; how then do you say that he walks in
paradise?" (2.22) — the bishop replies:

> Indeed the God and Father of the universe is unconfined and is not present in a place, for there is no place of his rest. But his logos, through whom he made all things, who is his power and [sophia], assuming the role of the Father and Lord of the universe, was present in paradise in the role of God and conversed with Adam.

Answering Autolycus' question, which he takes to be a paraphrase of the divine question posed by Isaiah 66:1 ("And of what kind is to be the place of my rest?"), Theophilus affirms God's omnipresence.[60] But notice that he does so using the tool of personified agency. The bishop re-introduces to his readers the logos "through whom [God] made all things." They are told, however, that this logos is the same as God's "power and wisdom." In First Corinthians 1:24, a passage that Theophilus must have been aware of, one encounters this same juxtaposition of attributes, and yet this time it is Christ who is said to be the power and the wisdom.[61] The bishop then goes on to say that the logos was authorized to create after "assuming the role of the Father and Lord of the universe." That is to say, the logos is the specific generator and ruler of the cosmos. And furthermore, Theophilus claims that this same cosmic logos was present in paradise "in the role of God" and was "conversing with Adam." Whatever may have been his peculiar understanding of the power and the wisdom of God, in this passage, the logos is functioning as creator and governor of the universe and interlocutor with the first man.

Having concisely identified the logos as the cosmic creative force, the immanent sovereign principle and the divine dialogical partner of man, he now expands his description with a rather unexpected twist. Theophilus says:

> For the divine scripture itself teaches us that Adam said that he "heard the voice." What is the "voice (φωνή)" but the logos of God, who is also his son?—not as the poets and mythographers describe sons of gods begotten of sexual union, but as the truth describes the logos, always innate in the heart of God (ἐνδιάθετον ἐν καρδίᾳ θεοῦ). (2.22)

Now the reader is asked to understand that the logos, in this role of God in paradise, is God's "voice." Theophilus is here calling attention to the logos as a disembodied voice,[62] perhaps the same voice that commanded Adam, saying, from every tree in paradise, but for one, you may eat food.[63]

However, as the question that initiated this discussion implies, Autolycus was more concerned with the idea that God "walked" than that he "talked." The specific problem that Autolycus raises, namely, that of an omnipresent and a localized deity,[64] is actually created by his reading of the story about the fall of man. In the Septuagint, Theophilus' skeptic read:

> And they heard the voice of the Lord God, *who* was walking in paradise at evening, and Adam and his wife hid from the face of God in the midst of the trees of paradise. And the Lord God called Adam and said to him, where are you, Adam? And he said to him, I heard

your voice in paradise and I was afraid because I am naked, and I hid.[65]

Now Autolycus seems to be asking, how can God, who is by definition omnipresent, be localized? Or to put it another way, if God is not localized, how can he walk in a particular locality? Theophilus addresses Autolycus' philosophical problem by pointing out that a careful reading of the biblical text shows that it was not God at all who walked in paradise. The antecedent of the relative pronoun ("who") underlined in the biblical text above is not technically the Lord God but his voice, who is none other than the previously introduced logos. And further, this logos as voice is also called God's son. This is the first and only time Theophilus speaks of his God as having a son, and he makes it absolutely clear to his readers that the term is used not to describe a relationship derived from "sexual union,"[66] but only to suggest the logos' authority derived from his intimacy with God. I would venture to say that the bishop expanded his personified image so as to better account for how God the omnipresent spirit walked in paradise. While the term logos (word) would supply an appropriate notion for God's talking, the term son (an actual physical presence) would enhance the image of God's walking. With this substitution of logos-son for God himself, in the garden of paradise, Theophilus believes he has solved the philosophical problem of omnipresence and localization and thus seizes the occasion to shift Autolycus' attention back to his earlier discussion of the logos.

Perhaps fearing the kinship metaphor, and yet committed to finding an acceptable expression for the consistency his theology demands, he returns to an earlier notion upon which I think he improves. Previously Theophilus had said that the logos was "innate in [God's] own *bowels*" (2.10). Here he claims that the logos is "always innate in the *heart* of God" (2.22). However, what is important in these two separate accounts is not the obvious change from "bowels" (σπλάγχνα) to "heart" (καρδία), but rather Theophilus' consistency in maintaining that the logos originated from within God. In the former text the emphasis was on the logos as generated by God and thus the reader could reflect on divine presence in the world, while in the latter text the emphasis is on the logos as related to God and thus the reader could reflect on divine affection for the world. The bishop wishes to be precise about the meaning of the word ἐνδιάθετος (innate). Therefore, continuing the quotation above, he says that "before anything came into existence [God] had this [logos] as his counsellor (σύμβουλον), his own mind and intelligence" (2.22). The term "innate" in this context seems to include the idea that God was intellectually at-one with his logos, and so the logos is given the further appropriate appellations of "counsellor," "mind" and "intelligence." Of these three, "counsellor" is probably the least expected and most revealing of the functional purpose behind the intimacy and authority of the logos.[67]

There are several phrases in the Septuagint that the bishop may well have read in this connection. The first one is found in the following verse from Isaiah 9:6a, where it says:

> For a child is born to us, and a son is given to us, whose government
> is upon his shoulder: and his name is called the messenger of great
> counsel (μεγάλης βουλῆς ἄγγελος).

This "angel of great counsel" is an intriguing figure, and though an unlikely literary antecedent, it may fit the bishop's conceptual context.[68] However, a better literary antecedent can be proposed. I believe Theophilus is offering a rhetorical response to the rhetorical question posed by Isaiah 40:13, deriving his answer from Jeremiah 23:18. Consider these two texts in juxtaposition:

Isaiah 40:13	**Jeremiah 23:18**
a) "Who has known the mind of the Lord?	a) "Who has stood in the counsel of the Lord,
b) and who has been his counsellor,[69]	b) and seen his [logos]?[70]
c) to instruct him?"	c) who has hearkened, and heard?"

Theophilus may have deleted the "c" phrase of the Isaiah text,[71] and replaced it with the "b" phrase of the Jeremiah text. Thus, with these minor adjustments, the bishop could have formulated his biblical response: The logos is God's counsellor and mind.

But if the logos as God's counsellor is always innate in God's mind or heart, how is it that he comes to be an independent agent of God? Theophilus imagines the following scenario:

> When God wished to make what he had planned to make, he generated (ἐγέννησεν) this logos, making him external (προφορικόν), as the firstborn of all creation. He did not deprive himself of the logos but generated the logos and constantly converses with his logos. (2.22)

The bishop introduces his readers to the concept of the "external logos" for the first time. There is no "vomiting-him-forth" explanation (2.10) or physical imagery describing how the logos became an independent agent. There is no sharing of the cosmic stage with the sophia in this account of the logos' origin. And in this story the logos is called "the firstborn of all creation," a Septuagint and New Testament phrase that is unique in the books of Theophilus, and thus accounting for the earlier title, "the beginning."[72] But, why does Theophilus say that God did not "deprive" himself of the logos and "constantly converses" with the logos? On the surface, it would seem that God no longer possessed the logos if the logos was external from him. But this notion of the complete separation of the logos could not be tolerated by the bishop, for then the logos might be perceived as having his own mind and thus fail to legitimately represent God.[73] For Theophilus, "generation" is not equivalent to "deprivation," at least not in the context of personified divinity. The logos' intimacy with God cannot be violated in any fashion even though the logos must also have an independent status. When Theophilus says that the logos is always innate in the heart of God, this is to be taken figuratively to mean the logos is constantly conversing with God. God and the logos must be of one mind and so they communicate without ceasing.

As confirmation of his claim, Theophilus cites the gospel writer John and quotes the first and third verses of his work.

> Hence the holy scriptures and all those inspired by the spirit teach us, and one of them, John, says, "In the beginning was the logos, and the logos was with God." He shows that originally God was alone and the logos was in him. Then he says, "And the logos was God; everything was made through him, and apart from him nothing was made." Since the logos is God and derived his nature from God, whenever the Father of the universe wills to do so he sends him into some place where he is present and is heard and seen. He is sent by God and is present in a place. (2.22)

This is Theophilus' only documented reference to a New Testament passage and here he includes it among the "holy scriptures" and the writings "inspired by the pneuma." Thus, what John says is of the highest authority for the bishop. In contrast to an earlier discussion that also involved Wisdom traditions (2.10), he is not here fixated on the term "beginning." But rather he is focused on his argument. How is it that God did not deprive himself of the logos when he generated the logos? The bishop's answer is that the logos is none other than God himself, which for him is tantamount to saying that the logos derived his nature from God. The language of sonship and firstborn suggests that the dominant metaphor in his earlier explanation of the logos' generation was that of birth rather than of illness.[74] For better or worse, logically speaking, this is Theophilus' explanation of the origin of the logos.

How independent is the logos, metaphorically speaking? Theophilus says, in the above text, that "whenever the Father of the universe wills to do so he sends [the logos] into some place where he is present and is heard and seen" (2.22). This phrase "Father of the universe" is used six times by Theophilus, and all in the *Syngramma* (2.4, 22, 25, 34). The bishop likes to use a wide variety of terms to refer to divine providence, thus he calls God the maker, creator, fashioner, Lord, locus, pilot, and master of the universe. But why does Theophilus call God "Father"? Earlier Theophilus gave us his reason when he said God is "Father because he is before the universe" (1.4). Thus, we can infer that the reason Theophilus calls the logos "son" is because he is the first born of the universe. The logos had been called a "servant," reflective of his work in the universe on behalf of his master (2.10). But here the logos is a son who is sent into the universe as a representative of his father, to be "heard and seen" in his own right. Again, the bishop's language has moved from merely describing divine presence in the world to appreciating divine affection for the world.

What we have learned about the logos in the *Syngramma* is considerably more substantial than what the *Homilia* had to offer. In the *Syngramma* the logos receives far greater attention as an agent of God. Moreover, the logos is treated as having a separate identity from the transcendent God. The logos is, in one instance at least, called the son and identified as a representative of a transcendent father. The logos is also called the beginning and servant, functioning as the light who reveals, and the voice who counsels and commands. However, the logos' primary function is to converse with both God and humanity. The logos functions for all practical purposes as a go-between, informing man regarding the mind of God. Now that our review of the *Syngramma* is completed, one should conclude that Theophilus' logos notion is his dominant tool for personifying God's work in the world, that is, divine work expressed primarily in terms of creative power and revealed wisdom.

The Formulas of the *Hypomnema*

If Theophilus' readers found the logos of the *Syngramma* too abstract or technical, his presentation in the *Hypomnema* may have appeared more practical, and thus clarified some issues for them. In Theophilus' third book we are introduced to a heavily qualified and somewhat more tangible notion of the logos. The *Hypomnema* speaks of "the logos of truth" (3.1, 4), "the holy logos" who teaches (3.13) and leads (3.15), and "the divine logos" who both orders and instructs us (3.14). In all but one of these instances, R. M. Grant has translated the Greek term "logos" as "word" because the context is suggestive of scripture.

The one exception is found in Theophilus' discussion of Christian conduct, which concludes with highly rhetorical claims: "God is acknowledged; truth controls, grace preserves, peace protects; holy logos leads, sophia teaches, life controls, God reigns" (3.15). While this list is only a part of a larger statement, by abstracting it one can observe a couple of features leading to the conclusion that Theophilus is treating the logos and the sophia as human values or ideals. First, while he is probably making allusions to the holy scripture, in this context he is explicitly speaking about the divine reason needed to lead, and the divine wisdom needed to teach, the community of believers. However, truth, grace, peace and life, along with reason and wisdom, are also the values of the wider human community. Theophilus' rhetoric is designed to appeal to Autolycus' highest ideals. So, if Autolycus actually wants to experience these ideals, he can encounter them—controlling, preserving, protecting, leading and teaching—in the bishop's church. Second, this list of terms is bracketed by references to the God who is acknowledged and who reigns. In such an arrangement of terms Theophilus may be extending a subtle invitation to Autolycus to acknowledge the bishop's God as reigning over his life, and thus to join the community which fully enjoys these ideals. Nevertheless, given that Theophilus has made a commitment to treating the logos and the sophia as personified figures, Grant's translation is not unexpected or inappropriate.

Moreover, there is a precedent in Theophilus' thinking for calling the logos figure a leader (and also a teacher). According to the bishop:

> The divine [logos] gives us orders about subordination to principali-
> ties and powers and prayer for them, so that we may lead a quiet and
> tranquil life; and it teaches us to render all things to all men, honour
> to whom honour is due, fear to whom fear, tribute to whom tribute;
> to owe no man anything except to love all. (3.14)[75]

Consider the language in this passage. First, the bishop says, "the divine logos orders us." In a passage from the *Syngramma* quoted earlier, the logos was called "the command of God," a phrase referring to the "let there be" of creation (2.13). A little later God's "command" to Adam in the garden of Eden was re-ferred to as the "voice" of God, which was also said to be God's logos (2.22). Thus, it is not much of a leap from this language to the idea of the logos as a leader. There is also the obvious connection between the "voice" of the garden and the logos as teacher. According to the text above the divine logos "teaches us," which is also to say it imparts information to us. The only question that re-mains to be answered is what kind of information does the logos impart?

In the *Hypomnema* Theophilus introduces his readers to a new voice, namely, "the gospel voice." The context is a discussion on ethics, which begins with the words:

> Concerning chastity the holy [logos] teaches us not to sin either in
> deed or even in thought, not to imagine any evil in our heart. . . . The
> gospel voice provides a stricter teaching about purity. (3.13)

Theophilus appears to be contrasting the holy logos and the gospel voice, but they both are teaching the same thing, that is, chastity. The holy logos is repre-sented by several texts from Proverbs (4:25, 6:27-9),[76] while the gospel voice is represented by several texts from Matthew (5:28, 32).[77] However, the purpose of the bishop's exercise was to demonstrate that the holy logos has evolved into the gospel voice. While the gospel voice is not identified in any other way, but is most likely a reference to the essential ethical teachings of the New Testament Gospels, clearly it is a provocative term in the light of Theophilus' earlier thoughts on the work of the paradise voice. The bishop's thought probably did not remain static over the course of his career. Neither did his theological teach-ing regarding the logos in the course of *Ad Autolycum*. His logos evolved from the context of the voice of paradise to the voice of the Gospel, from the ethics of Proverbs to the stricter ethics of Matthew. But more on this in the next chapter, where we will analyze his teaching on the significance of the moral law itself.

Theophilus' Theory of Divine Agents

With this review and examination of how Theophilus developed his doctrine on the agents of God over the course of his three books, it is clear that the bishop chose not to offer a systematic presentation. In fact, each of his discussions appears to take a somewhat different slant on these figures, promoting a sense of ambiguity regarding their identity. He seems to be rethinking the issues involved every time he responds to specific questions from his audience. Without a doubt, Theophilus is a pragmatic and resourceful bishop. He shows a kind of quixotic rawness in the *Homilia* when confronted by a highly intellectual alter ego in Autolycus. In the *Syngramma,* Theophilus is more circumspect and yet even more innovative when he needs answers to the difficult questions raised by the skeptic's reading of the creation story. He clearly is more relaxed in the *Hypomnema.* It is in this third encounter with Autolycus that he attempts to resolve outstanding issues and to rely on the power of the scriptures to convert his former adversary turned curious protégé.

All three books taken together demonstrate his pragmatism in answering only what is put before him and his resourcefulness to meet that need with carefully formulated innovations. But in spite of the differences and the growth in sophistication within the three books, is it possible to say that *Ad Autolycum* possesses a single mature position that could legitimately be called a doctrine? Given that he nowhere recants earlier teachings, though he does seem to revise some, it is safe to say that such a doctrine of agency could be reconstructed. His abstracted position falls naturally into two parts, which when taken together tell his readers why these three agents (the sophia, the pneuma and the logos) are important to his religious rhetoric. The first part of this doctrinal statement speaks of the unique generation of the sophia and the logos. The second part deals with the functions of all three agents. In the conclusion to this chapter, I will briefly suggest a possible explanation for the ambiguity in the imagery of his rhetoric.

As we have seen, the two key passages which layout Theophilus' thought regarding the generation of the sophia and the logos are both found in the *Syngramma,* and represent a rather consistent image with a few divergent details. In the first passage (2.10) we are introduced to the twin conceptions of the sophia (σοφία) and the logos (λόγος) as originally innate in God's splanchna (σπλάγχνα), but expelled before the creation. In the second passage (2.22) the logos alone is innate in God's kardia (καρδία), but in order for the creation to take place the logos had to become external. On the surface the two most obvious differences between these two accounts of the generation of God's agents, presented schematically below, are the references to God's splanchna in the first and kardia in the second, and to both agents in the first and only one in the second.

THEOPHILUS' TWO ACCOUNTS OF THE GENERATION
OF DIVINE AGENTS

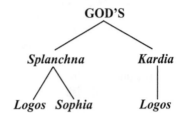

Why Theophilus should have employed two significantly different Greek terms, splanchna and kardia, in such a sensitive teaching may rest on his intentions in each context. The context of the first passage on generation is a careful exegesis of the first two verses of Genesis. In this exegesis, Theophilus is interested in informing his readers regarding the mechanics behind the generation of these personified agents of God's creative work. Without such information, his audience would not be able to make the transition from a transcendent God to a divinely conceived creation. The context of the second passage on generation is an obnoxious question by Autolycus regarding the localization of God implied by the Genesis verse that says God was present in paradise. Here the bishop tailors his response so that his teaching on generation is limited to what is sufficient to explain divine presence.

So why does generation proceed from splanchna in the first passage and from kardia in the second? And we might ask, in this connection, why is generation perceived as expulsion in the first and only as externalization in the second? A third question must also be considered, picking up on the second obvious difference mentioned above, why is the sophia included in the first generation passage and excluded in the second? How does the context of each passage help explain these divergent details? First, the passage in which Theophilus interprets Genesis 1:1 should be seen as his primary text regarding generation. It is here that the bishop emphasizes that the specific earthly work of the transcendent God can be understood only through a discussion of the activities of his personified agents. Given that there are philosophical traditions which can explain how this is possible, that are both accessible to him and plausible to his audience, he uses them. He needed to explain the separation of these divine agents from the transcendent God and so committed himself to a graphic image of the mechanics of generation. Although unable to provide him with all the language his rhetoric demanded, it was the Wisdom tradition (with texts like Proverbs 8) that satisfied his limited philosophical requirements. Using this tradition he could not easily dispense with its primary agent, the sophia, even if he wanted to do so.

However, when Theophilus came to Autolycus' question regarding God's omnipresence, and Genesis' apparent localization of deity, all the bishop really needed to do was to remind his friend of the earlier exegesis. God is himself not localized in the cosmos, but his personified agents are localized in the role of deity. Given this explanation the bishop's overwhelming need is to emphasize continuity between God and his agents. While it is important to understand their separation and independence in order to satisfy any lingering philosophical doubt regarding the reality of divine work in the world, it is even more significant to realize that this imagined physical separation does not imply spiritual or intellectual separation. Thus, the graphic image is not required in the second presentation of generation, while the reference to the continual relationship between at least one of the agents and the divine kardia is useful in order to highlight intimacy and authority. The same can be said for the familial language of the second passage, namely, father and son. So while the imagery of the belly or the womb expelling these agents is more than adequate to promote the idea of separation from transcendency, the imagery of the external agent proceeding from the divine heart modifies the notion of separation so as to maintain the continuity of intimacy and authority. Theophilus' rhetoric is fighting for Autolycus' mind on every point.

A more troubling aspect of this second passage is its failure to include the sophia. Whereas Theophilus apparently needed the Wisdom tradition in his exegesis of the creation story, he did not need it in his explanation of God's presence in the garden.[78] God as the logos was said to be walking in the garden in the form of a voice. While the bishop seems to ignore the absurdity of a voice walking in the garden, he focuses on the fact that it talks to man. Given that the logos as "word" fits in better than the sophia as "wisdom," the Word tradition (as found in a text like the Prologue to John's Gospel) satisfied his rhetorical needs. Having made this contextual case for the exclusion of the sophia in the second statement on generation, one should not disregard the clear priority of the logos in Theophilus' last two books. Thus I would venture to suggest an additional reason for the absence of the sophia in the second statement, namely, that the bishop is in the process of phasing out the sophia tradition and replacing it with the more New Testament-oriented logos tradition.

However, from the bishop's perspective, with these two accounts of the generation of the immanent agents, the problems of separation from and continuity with the transcendent God were admirably solved. So, what is to be concluded regarding Theophilus' mature teaching about the generation of these two agents? The sophia and the logos were both innate in God, and they are the personifications of God localized and at work in the world. For Theophilus God cannot be localized but his agents can be. To be localized they must be made external, a process that can be mechanically imagined as God giving birth. Thus the sophia is called the offspring (γέννημα) of God and the logos the beginning (ἀρχή) of the creation. Surprisingly, what Theophilus asks his readers to imagine about the generation of these two agents in no way seems to violate his monotheistic position. They were designed to make the mystery that is God accessible to his Greek audience without compromising his biblical understanding.

The generation of the sophia and the logos is usually perceived as Theophilus' most unique contribution to second-century theology, but one should not underestimate his contribution regarding the function of these agents. It is in this regard that he has the most to say. How do the sophia and the logos, as well as the pneuma, function in the world? This question is for Theophilus little more than a revision of the query, how does God function in the world? The sophia, the logos and the pneuma are legitimate names for God in the context of any discussion regarding his providence. As names for God, the sophia is said to be God's offspring, the pneuma is God's breath and the logos is God's beginning. While one might infer that Theophilus thought of both the sophia and the logos as the anthropomorphic hands of God at work in the creation, he explicitly speaks of the logos as God's servant and son. On the one hand, the logos as the anthropomorphic servant or son of God is said to have created something out of nothing, and thus is also called the firstborn of creation. But the logos is more than a creator of matter. He is also the creator of diversity. As such, the logos is called the command of God. One specific and central command is "Let there be light." However, the logos is not only to be regarded as the force behind the creation of the light, but the light itself. For the logos is to shine like a lamp, illuminating the world. This illumination is a metaphor for the physical work of the logos in moving water and exposing dry land, that is to say, making dry land visible. On the other hand, while the pneuma is said to have given life to every-thing that was made and is still surrounding the creation with continual nourish-ment, the bishop speaks in more anthropomorphic terms of the sophia as the powerful figure that founded the creation, that named the stars and that enumer-ated the animals. I take Theophilus to mean that, unlike the logos, who was the "command" of the creation, the sophia was the actual "conception" of the crea-tion, who also brought order to its diversity. But the sophia's greatest work in the creation process is when she is called upon to assist in the special creation of man. When all else could be created by a word, a mere command, it took both the logos and the sophia together to manufacture a human. So much for the teachings of Theophilus on the function of these personified agents in the crea-tion story.

Given that only the logos is said to play a role in the drama of paradise, let us consider the post-creation activity of this agent first. The logos not only created the heavens and the earth but, as was said above, he was their illumination. And yet, this illumination is also very real in the work of the logos as a revealer of truth to humanity. To be a proper revealer the logos must be in communication with two worlds at the same time. The logos is the counsellor of God and thus knows God's inner thoughts—God's mind. The logos is no ordinary counsellor, but is intimately connected with God and thus is said to be his son, thereby es-tablishing a familial relationship of father and son, although Theophilus does not make too much of this. For him this image is meant to convey an important point, namely, that the logos is always present with God in that he is in constant conversation with him. Thus, this image emphasizes intimacy and authority. On the other side of the equation the logos converses with man too, initially with Adam in paradise. As such the logos is said to be the voice of God in the world. When God's voice is heard it is the logos who is speaking. As the voice, Theophilus implies that the logos is playing a very specific role outside of paradise as well. He was present with Adam in the garden, walking and talking with him. But beyond the garden walls the logos encountered Adam and others, making them instruments of his illuminating work. The logos revealed the truth by speaking through the prophets, especially through Moses the lawgiver and Solomon the man of wisdom. This truth is primarily that which heals the spiritual blindness of people and thus the logos is an eloquent agent of this healing process. This is, no doubt, accomplished through the logos' activity as a moral leader. The logos shows people how "not to sin either in deed and even in thought." This ethic is known as the stricter teaching of the gospel voice, which is said to be "our message" and "our way of life" promoted by the "living voice." Thus, we can infer that the leadership work of the logos continues in Theophilus' parish. Perhaps even in Theophilus' person.

The sophia is not mentioned in the context of paradise, but is briefly addressed as a role player in the post-paradise world. The sophia is a teacher who accomplishes her task by being possessed by her students and thus informing them regarding creation. These students of God's creation are better known as prophets who speak not only about the past but also about the future of the creation, and they do so in a consistent fashion when containing the sophia. But the sophia is also involved with the intellectual project that takes place in the receptive human heart, that is, the demonstration of the truth of the resurrection of all men. For Theophilus, the sophia's post-paradise activity, which includes this contemporary enlightenment, is very important. However, her work tends to blend in with the post-paradise activity of both the logos, as describe above, and the pneuma to be considered now.

The pneuma, who is holy, divine, pure and unique, is said to have possessed and filled the prophets of the true God, and to have instructed the Christians in the truth. What the bishop has said or implied about the logos with respect to Moses and himself, he says of the pneuma as well. The pneuma is an agent who actually spoke through Moses and now teaches Theophilus and the members of his parish. In fact, the only reason Christians are in exclusive possession of the whole truth is because they are personally instructed by the pneuma. Given that Theophilus does not address the pneuma as mystically engaging Christians, one can infer that the pneuma was thought to use scripture as its private tool in these teachings. After all, this tool was created by the activity of the pneuma in filling the prophetic writers with the knowledge they needed. As Theophilus' commitment to the sophia tradition appears to wane in his second and third books, his attraction to the pneumatic tradition seems to increase. I would venture to guess that the sophia, for all practical purposes in the second-century Antiochene Christian community, has in the functional sense evolved into the pneuma. Theophilus has and ought to receive higher points for his rhetoric than his precise formulation of theology. Nevertheless, the bishop might have been willing to argue in an ecclesiastical setting that while the continuing work of the logos is the wisdom of the external word of scripture that leads the Christian community, the continuing work of the pneuma is the internal force of enlightenment that instructs this community.

So what is to be concluded regarding Theophilus' mature teaching in *Ad Autolycum* about the function of the sophia (ἡ σοφία), the pneuma (τὸ πνεῦμα) and the logos (ὁ λόγος)? Consider the following schematic, with its formulations of the dispensational functionality of Theophilus' three major personified agents of God's work in the creation, in paradise and in the post-paradise world.

THE FUNCTIONS OF THEOPHILUS' DIVINE AGENTS

	Sophia	Pneuma	Logos
Creation	• Wisdom of God • Power of creation • Foundation • Namers of stars • Enumerator of animals • Hand of God in the formation of man	• Breath of God • Life of creation • Nourishment • Protecting spirit surrounding all of creation	• Word of God • Command of creation • Light • Servant • Hand of God in the creation of all that exists
Paradise			• Voice that was heard • Firstborn Son that was seen • Counsellor to God and man
Post-Paradise	• Prophets contain the Sophia, who also demonstrates through nature the truth of the resurrection	• Prophets are possessed and filled by the Pneuma so that all humanity might be instructed in the truth	• Prophets are the instruments of the Logos, who provides ethical leadership for the world

The sophia is the force that conceived the creation and gave it basic meaning. The sophia's role in the post-paradise context can be characterized as primarily divine enlightenment made available to all men regarding their resurrection, but particularly to the Hebrew prophets regarding the creation story. The pneuma is the force that breathed life into the creation and continues to surround it with nourishment. The pneuma's role in the post-paradise context was to possess and fill the Hebrew prophets and through them to instruct humanity by proclaiming the truth which is promoted in the Christian community. The logos is the force that first commanded the creation to come into existence and then illuminated its presence. The logos' role in paradise as the voice that was heard and the firstborn son that was seen was based on the logos' intimacy with God and his authority over humanity given his position, vis-à-vis God, as a divine counsellor. The role of the logos in the post-paradise context can probably be characterized as the ethical voice which made instruments of the Hebrew prophets and became stricter in the Gospel writings, but is yet living in the contemporary voice of Christian teachers. In this later role the logos is both the individual's source of spiritual healing and the community's source of exclusive truth. Something of the sort was probably the theoretical foundation for Theophilus' speculations on divine agency and his interpretations of the scriptures.

As would have been obvious to any of his readers, Theophilus has drawn ambiguous portraits of these three agents. Their functionality appears more often than not to overlap. However, it also seems that while his commitment to the sophia tradition appears to be fading near the end of his second book, his appreciation for the pneumatic and logos traditions grows stronger. If this is an accurate observation then one could suggest that the logos and the pneuma both inherit certain conceptual meanings from the sophia tradition. Whatever may be true of Theophilus' understanding of these three agents, in terms of his contemporary community's needs, a community that he is desperately trying to convince Autolycus to join, the theological function of the sophia, the pneuma and the logos come to nearly the same thing. They are tools of personification employed to explain the mystery of God's presence and work in the world.

Whatever Theophilus has said regarding these three personified agents of God, their generation and their function, must somehow be understood or at least appreciated within the framework of his monotheism. In all that he has written, not once did he mention that he thought it was important for Autolycus to see these agents as intermediaries with ontological status. The full personhood, servanthood or sonship of the logos (his primary agent) would probably have seemed inappropriate to Theophilus, for it is the logos' inseparable intimacy with God that is ultimately determinative of his authority to speak to humanity. But, the theologian must be able to talk about God as functioning in the world in a localized fashion without sacrificing his beliefs in either divine transcendence or omnipresence. For Theophilus, God's agents can be present, seen and heard, whereas God as transcendent must not be reduced to the mundane. The academic and theological tradition to which Theophilus is privy has only one tool for explaining divine providence, and that tool is the personification of agents like the sophia, the pneuma and the logos. Theophilus is pragmatically committed to this tool, but it ought not to be exaggerated so as to supersede the reality of God's oneness, or compromise, as we shall see, the status of law keeping as an effective means of salvation. Thus, he does not permit his teaching on these agents to violate his theological monotheism or his soteriological nomism. Once again let me say, I believe Theophilus' teaching was designed to draw Autolycus away from his paganism long enough to consider the bishop's religion. Using intriguing imagery to explain potential roadblocks to conversion, Theophilus offers his readers an attractive invitation to his faith. While one could take the logos mentioned in *Ad Autolycum* to be a substitution, surrogate, metonymy or euphemism for Jesus or the pre-existent Christ figure, the protreptic language of Theophilus in this collection of books does not help the reader make this identification. Theophilus' *Ad Autolycum* does not present Jesus as the pre-existent logos even though we know this identification was a commonplace in most second-century Christianities and suspect that such a connection was made in the bishop's ecclesiastical theology.[79] Therefore, in the same way that I have characterized his doctrine regarding man, I am also defining his doctrine regarding the agents of God. Theophilus is engaged in protreptic theology.

Notes

1. The bishop's detail in his teaching on the logos far exceeds what he has to say about the sophia and the pneuma and, therefore, one could include his discussions of all three under the rubric of logology rather than the more classical term pneumology or the more exotic sophology.

2. Theophilus does not address the origin of the pneuma.

3. R. M. Grant, *Greek Apologists of the Second Century* (Philadelphia: The Westminster Press, 1988), 173. While Grant makes this claim, he does not spend much energy in formulating Theophilus' distinction between the three. He does speak at some length of the importance of Theophilus' contribution regarding the generation of the logos, but does not detail the unique functions of the sophia, the pneuma and the logos.

4. W. O. E. Oesterly and G. H. Box, *The Religion and Worship of the Synagogue* (London: Oxford University Press, 1911), 169. R. A. Norris, "Hypostasis," *EEC*, 443-45, says "hypostasis" is the "Greek word variously rendered in English as 'person,' 'substance,' 'subject,' or 'subsistence.' " Norris' article demonstrates the historical development of the term. He says: "A noun formed from the verb *hyphistemi* (stand under, support, stand off or down from), *hypostasis* first achieved wide currency as a medical term meaning a deposit, sediment, or precipitate. It joined the language of philosophy, under Stoic auspices, as signifying real, concretely existent being, that is, the actual 'deposit' or 'precipitate' in reality of unactualized possibility. In this sense, hypostasis was also contrasted with insubstantial appearance or merely notional existence. Thus, it came to mean the actuality or reality of something (whether in the sense of its nature, its existence, or its source), or simply as an actuality, a real thing (*pragma*): connotations that, it is important to note, could also attach to the term 'substance' (*ousia*). 'Hypostasis' often bore the sense of that which lies behind and beneath an appearance (its reality) or an activity (its plan or purpose); but just as frequently, it was used to emphasize the fact of concrete existence. 'Hypostasis' figured in the theological language of the patristic era in two primary ways: in the development of the doctrine of the trinity and in the formulation of the doctrine of the incarnation." According the Cappadocian fathers (fl. at the end of the 4th century), Norris points out, "the hypostases of the trinity, then, were objective realities that completely shared the same nature or substance, but were differentiated from one another, and so individualized, by the relations of origination and derivation in which they stood to one another." According to Theodore of Mopsuestia (d. 428), the terms "hypostasis" and "nature" were equivalent. In Norris' continuing description, "both denote a real, concrete individual considered both as an independent subject of action and attribution and as having a distinctive constitution or character." According to Cyril, at the council of Chalcedon (451), Norris concludes, "there is in Christ one sole hyposta-

sis—that of the divine son, considered as a real individual who is the ontological subject of an incarnate life."

5. So as not to violate his language or the possible intention behind his ambiguity by suggesting their status as personal intermediaries or objective realities, no citation of the sophia, the pneuma (spirit) or the logos in this book, in contrast to R. M. Grant's varied translations, begins with a capital letter or is left unqualified (usually by the definite article). Furthermore, given that the sophia, the pneuma and the logos are his Greek terms, they will be used consistently in my analysis rather than wisdom, spirit and word (reason), respectively. One further point should be made at the outset. Theophilus' language of personification is widely distributed in his many discussions of God's activity in the cosmos and thus one could say that he speaks of numerous agents of God's work. Nevertheless, his three major personified agents are unquestionably the sophia, the pneuma and the logos.

6. Irenaeus (d. ca. 200), who was a contemporary of Theophilus, uses a similar motif. Irenaeus, *AH* 3.21.10, 4 preface 4, 4.20.1, 5.1.3, 5.5.1, 5.6.1, 5.28.4 and *Demonstration* 11 are the key passages. According to R. M. Grant, *Jesus,* 99: "Like Theophilus (1.5, 2.18), Irenaeus speaks of God's hands at work in creation, especially the creation of Adam. But while Theophilus defined the 'hands' as God's logos and sophia (2.18), Irenaeus is careful to identify them as son and spirit (4 preface 4, 5.6.1, 5.28.4) or logos and spirit (5.1.3) or to explain that logos and sophia are the same as son and spirit (4.74, 4.20.1). He knows that the combination son-spirit is biblical, while logos-sophia is not." See also J. Mambrino, "Les Deux Mains de Dieu' dans l'oeuvre de saint Irénée," *Nouvelle Revue Théologique* 79 (1957), 355-70. A case has been made for Irenaeus' intentional use of Theophilus by F. Loofs, *Theophilus von Antiochien Adversus Marcionem und die anderen theologischen Quellen bei Irenaeus* (Texte und Untersuchungen zur Geschichte der altchristlichen Literatur 46.2, 1930). His theory of a literary and conceptual connection between Theophilus and Irenaeus has been criticized by F. R. M. Hitchcock, "Loofs' Theory of Theophilus of Antioch as a Source of Irenaeus," *Journal of Theological Studies* 38 (1937), 130-39. However, Grant (in his above book, 99-100) has gone even further, suggesting that Irenaeus consciously corrected the Antiochene bishop.

7. J. Quasten, *Patrology. Volume One: The Beginnings of Patristic Literature* (Utrecht and Brussels: Spectrum, 1950), 239.

8. J. N. D. Kelly, *Early Christian Doctrines* (San Francisco: Harper and Row, 1978), 102.

9. D. F. Wright, "Trinity," *EEC,* 912-13.

10. The lacuna will be explained shortly.

11. How ironic and ignoble it would be if the embryo of the doctrine of the Trinity, a doctrine which D. F. Wright, "Trinity," *EEC,* 911, calls "one of the most distinctive and fundamental tenets of the Christian faith," and in which Athanasius (ca. 300-373), the Cappadocians (ca. 329-395) and Augustine (354-430) played such formative roles, should have actually been conceived in the mind of someone reading Theophilus.

12. Genesis 1:26. The two Greek terms εἰκών and ὁμοίωσις are often treated as interchangeable, but Theophilus may have assumed that they possess special or technical distinction given their juxtaposition in this famous biblical text.

13. R. M. Grant added a definite article in his translation (which I underlined) when the Greek text does not provide it. I think Grant may have been thinking that Theophilus identified the sophia and the logos with the image and the likeness. But I see nothing in the Theophilian argument to warrant this connection.

14. Namely, γενηθήτω φῶς, γενηθήτω στερέωμα, συναχθήτω τὸ ὕδωρ, γενηθήτωσαν φωστῆρες, ἐξαγαγέτω τὰ ὕδατα ανδ ἐξαγαγέτω ἡ γῆ ("let there be light," "let there be a

firmament," "let there be water collected," "let there be lights," "let the waters bring forth," and "let the earth bring forth").

15. That is, ποιήσωμεν ἄνθρωπον ("let us make man").

16. See his pomegranate analogy in 1.5, which will be discussed shortly.

17. The only other mention of divine hands in Theophilus' books are in the biblical quotations, Psalm 94:4 (1.4) and Isaiah 45:12 (2.35).

18. I would translate the word σοφία in each of these instance, all occurring in the *Syngramma*, as "sophia" and thus include them in the statistics of agency (bringing the number to 21).

19. More often than not, when the pneuma is qualified in these ways it is accompanied by anthropomorphic language and thus treated as an agent comparable to the sophia and the logos. R. M. Grant claims in "Theophilus of Antioch to Autolycus," *Harvard Theological Review* 40 (1947), 251, that for Theophilus the spirit is a "medium of revelation" but "not quite a personal agent like logos or sophia." Further, he claims the "spirit is not primarily a person or hypostasis," but "lifegiving breath of God." However, since I am not so sure that Theophilus considered the logos and the sophia as actual persons or hypostases, but merely tools for personifying God's work in the world, I am not as inclined to separate them from the pneuma in the bishop's underlying theological system. Having said this, as will shortly become clear, I would fully agree with Grant that the pneuma is for Theophilus both lifegiving breath and the medium of revelation.

20. In both of these instances R. M. Grant capitalized the initial letter of "Word," and so I have added them to my statistics on the logos of agency (bringing the number to 29).

21. Theophilus does not seem inclined toward interpreting the term logos as "reason." His preference for the logos in the *Syngramma* might also reflect a growth in his audience's capacity to move beyond the LXX sophia and pneuma, and deal with the Johannine concept of the logos. But as we shall see, while he draws explicitly on the Johannine logos, he chooses not to develop it in the christological fashion of the New Testament.

22. In fact, Theophilus quotes Proverbs some five times in *Ad Autolycum* (1.11; 2.10, 35; 3.13).

23. As examples of such readings see J. L. Crenshaw, *Old Testament Wisdom* (Atlanta: Knox, 1981), R. B. Y. Scott, *The Way of Wisdom* (New York: Collier Books, 1971) and G. Von Rad, *Wisdom in Israel* (Nashville: Abingdon, 1972).

24. R. M. Grant suggests in his edition that Theophilus is reading Job 38:31, 9:9 and Psalm 146:4 as he composes this passage.

25. Ephesians 3:10—"That through the church the manifold wisdom of God might now be made known to the principalities and powers in the heavenly places."

26. The usage of the term sophia in this passage parallels its usage in the Ephesians 3:10.

27. R. M. Grant, "Theophilus of Antioch to Autolycus," 250.

28. R. M. Grant translates sophia as Wisdom, with the initial capital letter, perhaps sensing a certain ambiguity in the bishop's usage.

29. Consider the serious warnings of the Sibyl which Theophilus reveals to Autolycus in 2.36.

30. Theophilus uses two different but related Greek words in referencing God's breath, namely, ἀναπνοή (which could mean the drawing or recovery of breath, that is, inhalation) in the earlier text and πνοή (which can refer to exhalation or the blowing of wind) here. While he may not have intended any semantic difference between the two, a reader so inclined could assume the bishop's earlier text was referring to the human act

of accepting or taking in the pneuma and the latter text to the divine act of sending the pneuma into the world.

31. The word λεπτόν may be used in all of these ways, and can also be used as a substantive, meaning a "light breeze."

32. Is Theophilus an evolutionist? No! In 2.15 he says, taking the Genesis creation story to be actual history, that the "luminaries" were created on the fourth day even though the earth was "adorned" with vegetation on the third day. According to Theophilus, God ordered the creation in this manner so as to provide a refutation of "foolish philosophers," i.e., the evolutionists of his day who were of the opinion that life and growth are connected with the activity of sun. Theophilus' argument is, in R. M. Grant's words, "Theophilus of Antioch to Autolycus," 236, "what is posterior cannot produce what is prior." On the premise of the Genesis creation story, this same argument is found even today among certain "young-earth" Fundamentalists, who claim that God created some prehistoric fossils to confuse "old-earth" Evolutionists.

33. While Theophilus does not explicitly formulate a polemic against the Jewish community or their ideas anywhere in *Ad Autolycum,* his language could be read as pejorative, implying a lesser status to the Jewish (Hebrew) prophets.

34. G. Kittel, *Theological Dictionary of the New Testament* (Grand Rapids: Eerdmans, 1965), volume 3, 132, documents the Hellenistic history of this term, especially in connection with Moses. Cf. Numbers 12:7.

35. D. Winston, *The Wisdom of Solomon,* The Anchor Bible (Garden City, NY: Doubleday), 99.

36. See the phrase "lover of learning" in 2.29, 30, 32, 38; 3.15 and 17, which is used by the bishop almost like a code phrase for ecclesiastical candidacy. Theophilus genuinely anticipates Autolycus' conversion and encourages him to become a real φιλομαθής, thus preparing him for Christian citizenship. Cf. the similar protreptic usage of the Greek term φιλομαθής in Plato's Phaedo 67b and 82c, and Lysis 218a.

37. D. F. Winslow, "Logos," *EEC,* 544-48, offers a fine article on the logos in which he says "the Greek term *logos* is patient of many meanings and, depending on the context, can be translated in a seemingly infinite variety of ways: 'speech,' 'discourse,' 'proclamation,' 'story,' 'reason,' 'rational principle,' 'logic,' 'commandment.' For the theology of the early church, however, its most significant, and at the same time most problematic, rendering is as 'word' or 'Word,' and it is as a pivotal term in the Prologue (Fore-'word') to the Fourth Gospel that *logos* was to become highly determinative for the development of Christian doctrine." Both Theophilus and Autolycus were surely aware of the nuanced nature of the logos and especially its usage in the Gospel of John in reference to the historical Jesus.

38. Cf. Mark 2:17 and parallels, where Jesus is portrayed as an ἰατρός. See the discussion of this New Testament text and the conception of God the healer in Hellenistic tradition in G. Kittel, *Theological Dictionary,* volume 3, 204f.

39. Arndt and Gingrich, 342b.

40. Liddell and Scott, 1312b.

41. The Greek word τύφλωσις is generally understood as the act of making someone blind, as opposed to τυφλότης, the state of being blind (Liddell and Scott, 1838a.).

42. A common expression for the actual state of blindness is πήρωσις τῶν ὀφθαλμῶν (Liddell and Scott, 1401b-1402a). The reader of R. M. Grant's translation would not know that two different Greek word, τύφλωσις and πήρωσις, are used because he consolidates them.

43. Cf. James 2:17, 24 and 26.

44. While Theophilus' citation of the LXX version of Proverbs 3:19-20 is a faithful quotation, he paraphrases Psalm 32:6, which reads: "By the word of the Lord the heavens were established; and all the host of them (πᾶσα ἡ δύναμις αὐτῶν) by the breath of his mouth (τῷ πνεύματι τοῦ στόματος αὐτοῦ)."

45. Cf. I Cor.15:53-54—"For this perishable nature must put on the imperishable, and this mortal nature must put on immortality. When the perishable puts on the imperishable, and the mortal puts on immortality, then shall come to pass the saying that is written: 'Death is swallowed up in victory.' "

46. No doubt in contrast to οἱ ἀθάνατοι of Autolycus' pagan world.

47. *EEC,* 546.

48. Cf. the figurative usage of this term, σπλάγχνα, in NT passages like Luke 1:78, II Corinthians 7:15, Philippians 1:18 and 2:1, Colossians 3:12 and I John 3:17, where it is the seat and source of love and usually translated as heart or affections.

49. M. Dods translated ἐξερευξάμενος as "emitting" in *ANF,* volume 2, 98a. He was praised for doings so by A. C. Coxe in his notes to the volume, but then reprimanded by Coxe for mentioning the literal translation of "belching or vomiting," in fn. 2. Notwithstanding Coxe's delicate sensibilities, Dods was as linguistically justified for his note as R. M. Grant is in his translation. Liddell and Scott, 591a, give "vomiting forth" or "pouring forth" as important translations of the verb ἐξερεύγομαι, citing its use in the highly visual contexts of honey when boiled, tumors breaking out, rivers emptying themselves and veins discharging. Further, the noun ἡ ἐξέρευξις is used in a number of instances for the exercise of belching. The question for the reader is what is Theophilus' dominant metaphor? Are we dealing with an image of illness, of ecstatic utterance, or of pregnancy and birth. Given his language, ἐνδιάθετος, ἐγέννησεν and ἐξερευξάμενος, any one of these three metaphors could be used. Grant chooses the image of illness and Dods chooses ecstatic utterance. I am inclined toward the third choice given a later text, to be discussed shortly, from the *Syngramma.*

50. See LXX Psalms 109:3c–ἐκ γαστρὸς πρὸ Ἑωσφόρου ἐγέννησά σε ("I have begotten you from the womb before the morning") and 44:1a–ἐξηρεύξατο ἡ καρδία μου λόγον ἀγαθόν ("My heart has uttered a good matter"). The γαστήρ can be the belly or paunch, and even stand for appetite or gluttony, but is just as often used in late antiquity for the womb in the context of pregnancy.

51. Cf. John 1:3–πάντα δι αὐτοῦ ἐγένετο.

52. Theophilus concludes this passage paraphrasing the LXX Proverbs 8:22-30.

53. Ἐν ἀρχῇ ἦν ὁ λόγος, καὶ ὁ λόγος ἦν πρὸς τὸν θεόν. Cf. John 10:38–ἐν ἐμοὶ ὁ πατὴρ κἀγὼ ἐν τῷ πατρί.

54. My alteration and emphasis. Notice the prepositions.

55. Theophilus emphasizes the actual syntactical order of the Greek words. The LXX text has the adverbial phrase and verb preceding the subject: 1) Ἐν ἀρχῇ 2) ἐποίησεν 3) ὁ θεός. Thus, consistent with my alteration, Theophilus was imagining a translation that would read something like the following: "By the beginning created, i.e., God, the heaven and the earth."

56. Cf. Theophilus' ἐπὶ κενῷ ωιτη τηε ἐπὶ ματαίῳ of the LXX. By κενός the bishop could mean "void of content."

57. The Greek preposition ἐν is very common, and it is used with a great variety of meanings, typically of place, state, condition, position, instrument, means, manner, time and number.

58. Cf. Tatian's *Oratio ad Graecos:* "For matter is not without beginning (οὔτε ἄναρχος ἡ ὕλη) like God, nor because of having beginning is it also of equal power with

God; it was originated and brought into being by none other, projected by the sole creator of all that is."

59. Namely, the so-called "Triad" and "Hands" passages (2.15 and 18, respectively).

60. It is curious that only God's omnipresence is of concern in Theophilus' arguments with Autolycus and never divine omnipotence or omniscience.

61. I Corinthians 1:24—"But to those who are called, both Jews and Greeks, Christ [is] the power of God and the wisdom of God." Theophilus is intentionally substituting the logos for the Christ of the Pauline tradition.

62. See J. H. Charlesworth, "The Jewish Roots of Christology: The Discovery of the Hypostatic Voice," *Scottish Journal of Theology* 39 (1985), 19-41; O. Betz, "φωνή" in G. Kittel, *Theological Dictionary of the New Testament* (Grand Rapids: Eerdmans, 1974), volume 9, 278-301; and J. Neusner, *From Politics to Piety: The Emergence of Pharisaic Judaism* (New York: Prentice-Hall, 1979), 129-32. Charlesworth's article is particularly helpful in framing the discussion. He says (23): "It is clear that one cannot see a sound or a voice . . . [but] one can see a hypostatic creature." Furthermore, "it is well known that both many Jews and many early Christians knew about a heavenly voice; what is not clear is whether by circa A.D. 100 there had developed a concept of a heavenly being, the Voice." Neusner speaks of the Bath Qol ("daughter of a voice"), the divine voice who reveals God's will, as "the heavenly echo." He is of the opinion that the Jewish concept was used as early as A.D. 150, basing it upon a couple of stories preserved in Tosephta Sotah 13.3 and the Babylonian Talmud, Yoma 9b. Charlesworth (29-30) traces the notion of a hypostatic Voice to a couple of fragment Targumim, which render Genesis 3:8 and 10: "And they heard the voice of the word of the Lord pacing about in the garden . . . And [Adam] said, 'the Voice of your word I heard pacing about in the garden.' " But he concludes (36-37), after finding evidence for the hypostatic voice primarily within apocalyptic documents, that "the apocalyptists forced metaphors until they became conceived as hypostatic creatures," thus "the fantastic is realistic." And, moreover (38), "that the voice had developed in early Jewish theology from the voice of God to the Voice from God . . . a member of God's celestial court." While Theophilus was probably aware of this apocalyptic usage, he does not force the metaphor beyond his need to convince Autolycus of the reliableness of the Christian scriptures.

63. This Genesis 2:15 text is quoted in 2.20.

64. Neither Autolycus or Theophilus seem to be interested in the equally thorny problem of coordinating omnipresence with absolute transcendence.

65. Theophilus' rendition of this Genesis 3:8-10 text is quoted in 2.21.

66. From time to time he speaks of the physically conceived sons of Zeus or Dionysus (1.9, 2.5, 3.6).

67. The term counsellor is used in only one other place, namely, in the conclusion to his collected works (3.30)—"If you will, read these books carefully so that you may have a counsellor and pledge of the truth (σύμβουλον καὶ ἀρραβῶνα τῆς ἀληθείας)."

68. Notice βουλή (Isaiah 9:6a) instead of σύμβουλος (2.22).

69. b) καὶ τὶς αὐτοῦ *σύμβουλος* ἐγένετο...

70. a) Τὶς ἔστη ἐν ὑποστήματι κυρίου, b) καὶ εἶδε τὸν *λόγον* αὐτοῦ...

71. This appears to have been done in the doxological quotation of it in Romans 11:34.

72. 1.3. See C. Brown's *Dictionary of New Testament Theology* (Grand Rapids: Zondervan, 1986), volume 1 667-69, for a complete discussion of this phrase "first born of all creation," especially its usage in Colossians 1:15.

73. Never far from the bishop's mind is his concern over the "nonsense" of polytheism.

74. Thus, Theophilus' use of the Greek participle ἐξερευξάμενος in 2.10 might better be understood in terms of reproduction rather than regurgitation or even articulation.

75. Cf. Romans 13:1-3, 7-8 and I Timothy 2:1-2. Theophilus seems to be referencing Pauline traditions, while crediting the logos with the insights. To translate θεῖος λόγος as "divine word," as R. M. Grant does, could indicate that Theophilus was legitimizing Paul's work as scripture.

76. The content of the first lacuna in the above text.

77. The content of the second lacuna.

78. It should be pointed out as well that even in 2.10 the sophia is not the dominant subject of generation. Consider this slightly revised translation of that Greek text: "God, having his own logos innate in his own bowels, generated him (together with his own sophia)." Whose sophia? Given other passages, particularly 2.18, it is obviously God's sophia. But even the syntax of this earlier sentence tends to reduce the prominence of the sophia.

79. Both Theophilus and Autolycus were surely aware of the usage of the logos in the Gospel of John in reference to the historical Jesus as the pre-existent Christ figure. It is likely that Theophilus has replaced christology with logology in *Ad Autolycum* in order to provide his readers with a philosophically acceptable and politically correct statement of his religion. However, to what extent christology, with its potential for apocalyptic references to Jewish messianism, would have been politically dangerous in late second-century Antioch is unclear. In this regard, consider the two highly respected books by G. Downey, *A History of Antioch in Syria from Seleucus to Arab Conquest* (Princeton: Princeton University, 1961) and *Ancient Antioch* (Princeton: Princeton University Press, 1963); and the three fine studies by R. Brown and J. Meier, *Antioch and Rome: New Testament Cradles of Catholic Christianity* (New York: Paulist Press, 1983); W. A. Meeks and R. L. Wilken, *Jews and Christians in Antioch in the First Four Centuries of the Common Era,* Society of Biblical Literature Sources for Biblical Study 13 (Missoula, MT: Scholars Press, 1978); and especially D. S. Wallace-Hadrill, *Christian Antioch: A Study of Early Christian Thought in the East* (Cambridge: Cambridge University Press, 1982). Also, see the two articles by R. R. Hann "Judaism and Jewish Christianity in Antioch: Chrisma and Conflict in the First Century," *Journal of Religious History* 14 (1987), 341-60; and C. Kraeling, "The Jewish Community at Antioch," *The Journal of Biblical Literature* 51 (1932); as well as the three encyclopedia articles on Antioch by F. W. Norris, listed in the bibliography, particularly, "Antioch of Syria," in D. N. Freedman, *The Anchor Bible Dictionary* (New York: Doubleday, 1992), volume 1, 265-69.

Chapter 5

The Nature of Salvation

In this fifth chapter Theophilus' doctrine of salvation, or soteriology, is analyzed.[1] In light of the observations made in the previous three chapters, Theophilus' soteriological focus may be considerably clearer. That focus is now examined in detail. The bishop's teaching on salvation is here presented in terms of the question: How is salvation achieved?

Within my presentation of his doctrine on man, I indirectly addressed his responses to the questions: What is salvation? Why is salvation necessary? and Who can achieve salvation? While progression to divine status was the goal of primal man, the goal of fallen man is salvation to immortal status. These goals are essentially the same in Theophilus' formulation of them, but the method for achieving them has changed. Now man must be saved from the human condition within a designated period of time; in individual terms he is speaking about that period between birth and physical death, and in a larger communal sense he is speaking about the post-paradise period which reaches an end with the divine resurrection. But in its teleological essence the "what" of salvation is the same as that of progression, namely, the achieving of the goal of human immortality and deification. The "why" of salvation is taken for granted by the bishop. He believes man's nature is inclined toward assuming immortal and divine status. In other words, divine immortality is the natural destiny of humanity. To achieve such immortality in paradise meant overcoming impatience. To do so in the post-paradise (or the fallen world) means overcoming sin. The human realization of this goal, in both of these dispensations, entails obedience to God. As for "who" can achieve salvation, it is the fallen man who becomes repentant and morally righteous.[2]

And so, with this last point in his doctrine on man, we come to the question of "how" one becomes morally righteous and achieves his goal of divine immortality. This question leads Theophilus and his readers into discussions regarding the significance and the content of the law (nomos), and the roles of the prophets and the holy churches. This chapter, in the manner of chapters three and four, concludes with my formulation of the Theophilian theory of salvation.

The Philosophy of Religious Law

Theophilus addresses the subject of "positive law"[3] in terms of the Greek word νόμος (nomos) twenty-six times throughout his three books. The nomos is mentioned only once in his *Homilia,* thirteen times in his *Syngramma* and twelve times in his *Hypomnema.*[4] Moreover, it is perhaps on this topic that the bishop shows his greatest intensity of thought.

His single use of the term nomos in his first book occurs in a polemic against emperor worship. Before introducing the nomos, the bishop says of such worship:

> Accordingly, I will pay honour to the emperor not by worshipping him but by praying for him. I worship the God who is the real and true God, since I know that the emperor was made by him. You will say to me, "Why do you not worship the emperor?" Because he was made not to be worshipped but to be honoured with legitimate honour. He is not God but a man appointed by God. . . . Similarly worship must be given to God alone. . . . Honour the emperor by wishing him well, by observing him, by praying for him, for by so doing you will perform the will of God. (1.11)

In this passage Theophilus has incorporated a number of notions which are also promoted in the New Testament.[5] The bishop is telling Autolycus that he should not treat the emperor as a god. He should honor, show good will to, observe and pray for the emperor. Why? Because this is the will of God. Before Autolycus could ask Theophilus how he knew God's will, the bishop introduces him to the source of his information regarding the divine mind, that is, the nomos. While the modern reader, given that this is Theophilus' first mention of the nomos of God, might expect the bishop to draw upon the centerpiece of biblical legislation—namely, Exodus 20:3 ("You shall have no other gods but me"), which he eventually does in the *Hypomnema* (3.9) in a passage discussing the Ten Commandments—he does not even quote from the Torah (or law section) of the Bible. Rather, he paraphrases a passage from Proverbs (24:21-22a). In the bishop's words:

> The law of God says, "Honour, my son, God and the king, and be disobedient to neither one; for they will suddenly destroy their enemies." (1.11)[6]

What is interesting here is not that he introduces his paraphrase with New Testament ideas, but the fact that he chooses to formulate his polemic against emperor worship using Proverbs as a source of nomos. As we shall see, Theophilus never limits nomos by a strict definition. In some fashion, nomos is always larger than a mere body of legislation (like, for instance, the Mosaic law). His nomos is found wherever he hears the voice of God, be it in the garden of paradise or in the preaching of the gospel. For Theophilus one thing about the nomos remains constant, as I will argue—what one hears the "nomos" commanding, one must do to achieve salvation.[7]

In his *Syngramma* Theophilus develops a broadly based philosophy of nomos, while in his *Hypomnema* he establishes the general corpus of nomos. Or, to put it another way, the bishop uses his exegesis of the creation story to explain the significance of the law, and he uses his presentation of the Christian life to lay out what I will call his curriculum of the law. In the *Syngramma* Theophilus appears to imply a philosophical distinction between what modern readers would call natural and positive law, although his language blurs the categories from time to time. This distinction is of no importance in the practical concerns of the *Hypomnema*. Let us now look at his extensive comments in both of these documents in turn.

He begins what one might call his philosophy of law with an exegetical comment regarding the third day of creation. It was then that God separated the earth from the seas. Now for the bishop, who sees "a pattern and type of a great mystery" (2.15) in the formation of the cosmos, there is much to learn from the sea. So he explains to Autolycus the meaning of this analogy. He says:

> And we say that for us the world is in the likeness of the sea. For just as the sea, if it did not have the flow of rivers and springs as a supply of nourishment, would long ago have been parched because of its saltiness, so also the world, if it had not had the law of God and the prophets flowing and gushing forth with sweetness and compassion and righteousness and the teaching of God's holy commandments, would already have failed because of the evil and sin abounding in it. (2.14)[8]

Juxtaposing natural law and positive law the bishop constructs an analogy. The sea is compared to the world, and the latter is apparently inclusive of all sentient beings and not just human society. The bishop maintains that the ecology of the sea could not survive if it were not for the fresh water supplied by the land rivers.[9] Likewise, as the rivers nourish the sea, so the nomos nourishes humanity, and therefore also animal life.

In his view there is a moral connection between the two types of creatures. Consider again this passage quoted earlier:

> Wild animals are so called from their being hunted. They were not originally created evil or poisonous, for nothing was originally created evil by God; everything was good and very good. The sin of man made them evil, for when man transgressed they transgressed with him. If the master of the house does well, his servants necessarily live properly; if the master sins, his slaves sin with him. Just so, it turned out that man, the master, sinned and the slaves sinned with him. (2.17)

The nomos of God flows like rivers wherever prophets teach specific commandments. The bishop does not reduce nomos to commandments, but a collection of commands are included in nomos. And why is nomos necessary? Because evil and sin abound in the world and would have "dried" it up if it were not for this nomos. Such language treats the nomos as though it were natural law withstanding the force of sin as coeternal chaos. However, with the information provided in the last passage above, it may be inferred that the need for nomos, as he prefers to use the term, presupposes the existence of human sin. It is the sin of man that created an evil earthly environment and necessitated this divine nomos Thus, it would seem the bishop believes that divine nomos is simply God's reaction to the human condition of sin. In other words, the nomos Theophilus is speaking about, in this context, is positive law.

Theophilus finds the creation story a gold mine for his philosophy of nomos. He says, again juxtaposing natural and positive law, in the context of the fourth day of creation:

> The disposition of the stars corresponds to the arrangement and rank of the righteous and godly men who keep the law and the commandments of God. For the stars which are clearly visible and radiant exist in imitation of the prophets; for this reason they remain unswerving, not passing over to one position from another. Those which possess a secondary degree of radiance are types of the people of the righteous. On the other hand, those which pass over and flee from one position to another and are called "planets" are a type of the men who depart from God, abandoning his law and ordinances. (2.15)

Here, those who are law-abiding are compared to stars that shine and the lawless to planets. First, what is the central idea in this comparison? How do those who keep the law imitate the stars and how do those who abandon the law resemble the planets? We can imagine that Theophilus looked into the sky and saw the steadiness of the stars and the movement of the planets, and abstracted the notion of reliability and consistency which the stars suggested to him as characteristic of nomos keepers. The movements of the planets probably seemed erratic to him and thus an example of the unreliable and inconsistent nomos breakers. A second aspect regarding nomos which is suggested by this text is derived from the fact that some stars shine brighter or are more radiant than others. The brighter ones are like the prophets who presumably give greater testimony to the nomos, while the lesser lights, who are no less righteous or godly, probably do not share the same responsibility.

Along similar lines, the nature of nomos is revealed in the events of the fifth day of creation. The bishop adds:

> But also the great fish and the carnivorous birds are in the likeness of greedy men and transgressors. For as marine animals and birds are of one nature, and some remain in their natural state, not harming those weaker than themselves but keeping the law of God and eating seeds from the earth, but some of them transgress the law of God, eating flesh and harming those weaker than themselves, so also the righteous who keep the law of God do not bite or harm anyone but live in

> holiness and justice, but robbers and murderers and the godless are
> like great fish and wild animals and carnivorous birds. They virtually
> consume those weaker than themselves. (2.16)

This is an important passage, for not only do we have a direct comparison drawn between humans and other sentient beings, but here the bishop actually speaks of a "natural" state or condition as the law of God, a law that is understood as pre-existent to the human context. In this text the law-abiding men are like law-abiding fish and birds that do not harm others, and lawless men are like lawless flesh-eating fish, carnivorous birds and wild animals. According to Theophilus, as was pointed out earlier (2.17), some creatures actually become lawless in the context of human sin. Thus their state of lawlessness, or transgression, is not their "natural state." They were created as law keepers and not as neutral entities with no intrinsic inclination. Obviously they had the physical capacity to change their orientation, but in the bishop's mind that original orientation was indigenous to their "first-formed" existence and, therefore, they were distinct from man in some sense which he has not made altogether clear as of yet. This law informed creatures not to harm "those weaker than themselves" and not to "consume flesh." This kind of law, which is pre-existent to (though apparently not unaffected by) the circumstances of sin and evil, would be called natural law. At least one can say that the kind of nomos he has in mind here deals with the natural conditions of non-human creatures.[10]

When discussing the tree of knowledge and God's charge not to eat of it, the bishop does not want anyone to suppose it was God's original command, or the tree itself, that is responsible for man's eventual sin and death. So he says:

> Again, when a law commands abstinence from something and some-
> one does not obey, it is not the law which results in punishment but
> the disobedience and the transgression. For a father sometimes orders
> his own child to abstain from certain things, and when the child does
> not obey the paternal command he is beaten and receives chastise-
> ment because of his disobedience. The commands themselves are not
> the blows; the disobedience results in beatings for the disobedient
> one. So also for the first-formed man, his disobedience resulted in his
> expulsion from paradise. It was not that the tree of knowledge con-
> tained anything evil, but that through disobedience man acquired
> pain, suffering and sorrow, and finally fell victim to death. (2.25)

Theophilus makes it abundantly clear in this passage that man is to be held responsible for his own sin and death. If Autolycus failed to understand this fact upon his first reading of the paradise story, Theophilus does not want him to miss this essential truth now. Why is this fact essential? Perhaps Autolycus would not go so far as to blame God for evil or even for pain, suffering, sorrow and death. But God may have created a situation which is to blame for evil and its consequences. After all, God made the tree of knowledge. It is unlikely that Autolycus, philosophically speaking, would have considered this tree as a source of evil, even with his untutored reading of the paradise story. But the bishop is taking nothing for granted. He tells his readers that God attached a single positive law or command (ἐντολή) to the existence of this tree (2.24). Theophilus is aware of his readers' philosophical problem with this story. It is an easy problem to formulate: the presence of this original nomos is what leads to evil and its consequences, which includes God's wrath and punishment. No nomos, no problem. Autolycus may well have argued that without this particular law humanity, like the animal kingdom, would have remained in a natural state. But the bishop is prepared to defend God's original nomos. Notice how he formulates his defense. A child is punished by his father when a paternal command is disobeyed. Of course this punishment only makes sense given that such a child is conditioned by the knowledge of right and wrong.[11] Theophilus apparently believes in the idea of original morality. The force of his argument is that the child conditioned by moral knowledge is no different than first-formed man. It is interesting to note that at one point Theophilus implies that Adam and Eve were infants (2.25). But of course, the assumption is that they were morally innocent but not morally ignorant. However, this analogy may have created a problem for his readers. Autolycus may still have understood Theophilus' explanation of the origin of sin as an example of blaming the innocent victim. By the second century this problem had been well defined in terms of theodicy. The oppressive presence of God, in the form of divine testing, was carefully considered and for many resolved in the wisdom traditions.[12]

After a short pause the bishop re-engages his argument, even though satisfied that he has explained his most significant point, that is, why man is held responsible for his own sin and death. Theophilus says:

> For God made man free and with power over himself. What man acquired for himself through his neglect and disobedience, [this thing] God now freely bestows upon him through love and mercy, when man obeys him. For as by disobedience man gained death for himself, so by obedience to the will of God whoever will can obtain eternal life for himself. For God gave us a law and holy commandments; everyone who performs them can be saved (δύναται σωθῆναι) and, attaining to the resurrection, can inherit imperishability. (2.27)

This is a key passage for understanding Theophilus' notion of salvation. I know of no other statement in early Christian literature that is quite like this one. If Autolycus was not convinced by Theophilus' argument, and still held God responsible for the human condition, then Autolycus has failed to appreciate fully the freedom of the human will. It is the inborn attribute of freedom to make moral choices that somehow characterizes man and ultimately, though not inexorably, leads to his condemnation. While this observation of human nature is not unique to the bishop, what comes after sounds somewhat strange in his Christian context.

The bishop goes on to say it is man's doing of nomos, conformity of his will to God's will, which saves him. It is true for Theophilus that grace is not precluded from his understanding of salvation.[13] But divine grace, or mercy or favor, is the counterpart to divine wrath. Just as the consequence of God's wrath for man's disobedience was punishment which resulted in pain, suffering, sorrow and finally death, so the result of God's grace for man's obedience is the blessing of eternal life. And so, for Theophilus, both grace and eternal life are contingent upon man's obedience to nomos.[14] Apparently, grace is not actually "unmerited" favor in the bishop's understanding. The bishop says in the above passage that divine "love and mercy" are shown toward man only "when man obeys him." And what are the specifics of this obedience? While he does not itemize here, as he will in the *Hypomnema,* he is definite and unambiguous. God provided, he says, a law and commandments, and "everyone who performs them can be saved and, attaining to the resurrection, can inherit imperishability." The fact that man should get a second chance to achieve his original goal, is the proof of God's mercy and grace. But, that second chance is a conditional one. The point being made here is that, while primal man progressed through patient observance of a single commandment, salvation and resurrected imperishability are the products of an extensive quid pro quo system that also rewards performance.

The bishop briefly addresses the content of this nomos, which is essentially the teachings of the prophets, in terms of a list of vices. He says:

> The God and Father and maker of the universe did not abandon mankind but gave a law and sent holy prophets to proclaim and to teach the human race so that each one of us might become sober and recognize that God is one. They also taught us to abstain from unlawful idolatry and adultery and murder, fornication, theft, love of money, perjury, anger, and all licentiousness and uncleanness; they taught that whatever a man does not want done to himself he should not do to another; and that thus a person who acts righteously may escape the eternal punishments and be judged worthy of receiving eternal life from God. (2.34)

God's work was not over after the creation was concluded. Nor did God abandon the human race after man stumbled in paradise. But God did penalize man for that mistake by charging him to keep an extensive set of commandments. The bishop tells us that it was the holy prophets who accurately conveyed this additional legislation. This nomos is designed, in the first instance, to sober people up to the truth of monotheism. Idolatry is perceived by the bishop as a particularly insidious problem. But injunctions against several moral failings are also included in the teachings of the prophets, ranging from murder to anger. Theophilus is even of the opinion that the Golden Rule, expressed in its negative form here, is the product of prophetic teaching.[15] He now proclaims that the human goal is two-fold; first, to escape eternal punishments, and second, to receive eternal life—both of which are the consequences of righteous activity. His understanding of righteous activity is yet to receive a systematic presentation. In the above passage he is prepared to do no more than offer a causal look at a random selection of moral concerns.

However, he seems to think that central to the "divine nomos" is the rejection of the worship of images.[16] He says:

> The divine law ('Ο θεῖος νόμος) forbids not only the worship of idols
> but also the worship of the heavenly bodies such as the sun, the
> moon, or the other stars, or of heaven or earth or sea or springs or
> rivers. Only the real God who made the universe is to be worshipped,
> with holiness of heart and a sincere mind. For this reason the holy
> law (ὁ ἅγιος νόμος) said, "You shall not commit adultery, you shall
> not kill, you shall not steal, you shall not bear false witness, you shall
> not covet your neighbor's wife." So also the prophets. Solomon
> teaches us not to sin even by a glance, saying, "Let your eyes look
> straight and let your eyelids incline justly." (2.35)

In this passage Theophilus distinguishes "the divine law (ὁ θεῖος νόμος)" from "the holy law (ὁ ἅγιος νόμος)." While his use of these terms in a couple of other passages do not seem to highlight any distinction, here they are used substantively to focus on a major division in what he is going to call the *Deka Kephalaia* of God's legislation.[17] This divine law consists of the credal charge to reject idolatry and pantheism, and to practice monotheism exclusively. And how is one to practice this religion? It is the holy law that lays out the specifics in what could be called an ethical pentalogue. The bishop clearly understands righteous activity as beginning with emotional and intellectual commitment to monotheism, but then extending to morality. While the origin of his so-called divine law is probably Exodus 20:3-5, the source of his holy law is found in Exodus 20:13-17.[18] However, the teaching of the nomos moves beyond mere external good works to the internal state of the heart and mind. Again, this notion is attributed not to the Torah, but to Solomon, with an exact quotation from the Septuagint version of Proverbs 4:25.[19]

In the last of these texts from the *Syngramma*, the bishop tells his readers that the Greek poets, among whom are Aeschylus and Euripides, predicted the just punishment of men who commit evil acts. Of them he says:

> Whether, then, they spoke of an unjust oath or any other fault they
> virtually predicted that God would inquire into it; and willing or un-
> willing they made declarations about the conflagration of the world
> in harmony with the prophets, though they were much more recent
> and stole these things from the law and the prophets. (2.37)

Occasionally the pagan poets were in virtual harmony with his prophets. But the bishop would not concede to the poets' originality in articulating the truth. When the poets proclaimed truth it was always derivative—stolen goods. The law and the prophets are absolute sources of reliable information about everything from chronology to morality. The phrase, "the law and the prophets," used only in the first nomos passage of the *Syngramma* and here in the last (2.14 and 37), is most surely a reference to the common Matthean phrase which parallels the rabbinic division of the Hebrew scripture into the Torah and the Nevi'im (the Law and the Prophets).[20] Nowhere does Theophilus appear to be speaking of the Ketuvim (Writings) as a third collection of biblical texts, even though it technically supplies him with a considerable amount of nomos. The point to be made here regarding this final *Syngramma* text, however, is that, while Theophilus is aware of a Mosaic collection of sacred books that are called the Law, he does not equate the salvific nomos he wishes to teach with this collection. As we have briefly seen, for him nomos extends beyond the law of Moses or the so-called biblical law books.[21] Theophilus also seems to count the original command (ἡ ἐντολή) of God to the primal parents and a variety of moral teachings (αἱ ἐντολαί) from other prophets in his miscellany of nomos.

These are all of the references to nomos in the *Syngramma* and they supply a kind of philosophy of law. In the *Syngramma* the bishop uses his exegesis of the creation story to explain the significance and nature of God's law. God's law is important because it nourishes humanity and all creation, a creation which would dry up and die without it (like the ocean would without rivers). The law keeps men from harming others (as the natural state of the beast prevented carnivorous activity). While this divine law is predicated on man's free-will and thus is not itself the origin of evil, it is an efficacious mandate leading to salvation. But the law is a matter of intellectual and emotional commitment, as well as, morality. For Theophilus the significance of the law of God demands more than mere honor; in human terms nomos is a necessity for the acquisition of eternal life. In contrast to the bishop's treatment in the first and second books, the third book is much more specific about the content of this nomos.

The Curriculum of Religious Law

Early on in his *Hypomnema*, Theophilus contrasts his Christian position with pagan thought by first analyzing a selection of biblical law and then providing a somewhat systematized Christian ethic. He opens his discussion of Christian nomos with monotheistic language. He says:

> We acknowledge a god, but only one, the founder and maker and demiurge of this whole universe. We know that everything is governed by providential care, but by him alone. We have learned a holy law, but we have as legislator the real God (νομοθέτην ἔχομεν τὸν ὄντως θεόν), who teaches us to practice justice and piety and beneficence (δικαιοπραγεῖν καὶ εὐσεβεῖν καὶ καλοποιεῖν). (3.9)

In this passage from the ninth chapter of the *Hypomnema* Theophilus is contrasting his Christian position to the paganism he had outlined in the previous eight chapters. Actually, his presentation of Greek religious thought consisted of little more than a polemic against selected philosophical inconsistencies and crude and vulgar myths. Contrary to the confusing polytheism of paganism, Christianity speaks of "the real God," that is, the God of monotheism.

For Theophilus the difference between paganism and his Christianity is crystal clear. The distinction is based on the identity of the legislator and the content of his legislation. In fact the only other place Theophilus speaks of a legislatoris in reference to the son of Zeus whom he claims taught debauchery (3.6). The legislator whom he is referring to is "the real god" who may be known by a number of names but is the one creator and governor of the universe. But what does this legislator legislate? Theophilus proceeds to divide what he will shortly call the "Ten Chapters" (δέκα κεφάλαια), or more precisely an octalogue plus a selection of other appropriate materials, into three parts, namely, piety (εὐσέβεια), beneficence (καλοποιεῖν) and justice (δικαιοσύνη).[22] He says of each in this first systematic collection of nomos:

> Concerning piety [God] says, "You shall have no other gods but me. You shall not make for yourself an idol or the likeness of anything in the heaven above or in the earth below or in the waters under the earth. You shall not worship them or serve them, for I am the Lord your God." Concerning beneficence he said, "Honour your father and your mother, so that it may be well for you and that you may live long upon the land which I, the Lord God, give you." And concerning justice: "You shall not commit adultery; you shall not kill; you shall not steal; you shall not bear false witness against your neighbor; you shall not covet your neighbor's wife, you shall not covet his house or his field or his servant or his servant girl or his ox or his ass or any of his animals or anything that belongs to your neighbor. You shall not pervert the judgment of the poor man in judging him: from every unjust word you shall stand aloof. You shall not kill the innocent and righteous man. You shall not vindicate the ungodly man and you shall not take bribes, for bribes blind the eyes of those who see and they do harm to just words." (3.9)

The following chart, based on the preceding passage, is designed to show how Theophilus' understood the nomos in the context of his reading of Exodus.

A THREE-FOLD DIVISION OF PRIMARY NOMOS

Types of Nomos	Divisions of Nomos	Commandments of Nomos[23]
The Divine Law	Piety	You shall have no other gods but me (Exodus 20:3)
The Holy Law	Beneficence	Honor your father and your mother (Exodus 20:12)
	Justice	You shall not commit adultery, kill, steal, bear false witness or covet (Exodus 20:13-17); plus, you are to show good judgment and live honestly (Exodus 23:6-8)

According to Theophilus, the "Ten Chapters (δέκα κεφάλαια, *Deka Kephalaia)* of this great and marvelous law, which suffices for all righteousness" (3.9)[24] serves as a primary ritual and moral code that is superior to anything in Greek literature. It is interesting that his *Deka Kephalaia* is two commandments short of the famous Mosaic version. He does not include the third commandment on taking God's name in vain or the fourth commandment on keeping the Sabbath. Rather, he adds several miscellaneous social laws from a later section of Exodus.[25] Curiously, Theophilus' omissions are the violations of which Jesus was accused, namely, blasphemy and Sabbath-breaking.[26]

Theophilus closes this initial discussion of divine legislation with a few brief comments on an injunction from Exodus 23:9 regarding the beneficial treatment of "sojourners (προσήλυτοι)" (3.10). Why does he choose this piece of legislation to include in his selective collection of nomos? The Greek word προσήλυτος can be translated "sojourner," "proselyte" and "convert," or simply as "one who has come over." I do not believe that Theophilus was citing this obscure passage simply to embellish his already finely tuned discussion of nomos. Rather, it seems plausible that he was making a veiled invitation to his protégé Autolycus that he ought to convert from his paganism and become a Christian. In case Autolycus thought that God's nomos is impersonal or an inhuman burden, Theophilus brings closure to this discussion by demonstrating the empathetic nature of divine nomos. Theophilus, speaking of the ancient Israelites, says "God taught them through the law, saying . . . " (3.10). Saying what? I believe Autolycus is being invited by Theophilus, albeit indirectly, to understand nomos in very personal terms and to read himself into this ancient injunction:

> "You shall not oppress the sojourner (προσήλυτον), for you know the life of the sojourner; you yourselves were sojourners in the land of Egypt."

The bishop is subtly saying that he understands the weighty burden of the law for he too was once a sojourner, and so Autolycus need not fear "oppression" within the church as a sojourner who might convert to Christianity.

The bishop maintains that while Moses was the minister (διάκονος) of this divine law, it is God himself who is the legislator (νομοθέτης) and is thus teaching the human race his expectations of them. In Theophilus' words:

> Of this divine law the minister (διάκονος) was Moses, the servant of God, not only to all the world but especially to the Hebrews (also called Jews). . . . God taught them through the law. (3.9 and 3.10)

Concerning the nomos and its relationship to repentance he says:

> Now when the people transgressed the law which God had given them, because God is good and merciful and did not want to destroy them he not only gave the law but later sent prophets from among

> their brothers to teach and remind them of the content of the law and
> to convert them to repentance so that they would no longer sin. But
> the prophets predicted that if they continued in their evil deeds they
> would be delivered under the hand of all the kingdoms of the earth;
> and it is obvious that these things have already happened to them.
> (3.11)

These statements are packed with historical references that are blended into a
general philosophical notion about divine providence. The particular people
Theophilus is speaking about in the above text are the Hebrews and the Jews of
the previous text. The nomos they are said to have transgressed is the law ad-
ministered by Moses, presumably of both the divine and holy varieties. Neither
here nor anywhere else in the bishop's *Ad Autolycum* does he have anything
negative to say about Hebrews or Jews, a fact which sets him apart from almost
every other second-century Christian author. While he does not describe the content of nomos here in the latter text, it is likely that he still has his earlier mentioned *Deka Kephalaia* in mind.[27] His greater concern at this point in his
argument is not the specific content of nomos but Autolycus' recognition of the
fact of human transgression and the remedy for it. Theophilus wants his readers
to know that as a historian he can document this human transgression and its
consequences. However, what is overwhelmingly important is how God reacts
when humanity breaks the nomos divinely set forth. Because God is good and
merciful,[28] he sent prophets to teach and to remind people of the content of the
nomos.[29] Therefore, with the moral teaching of the Mosaic law, humanity is
given a second chance. They can convert to repentance, or rebuff the opportunity.

This nomos-based opportunity is the bishop's preeminent point and he
quotes a number of scriptural texts to support it, the foremost passage being
from Ezekiel 18:21-23:

> If the lawless man is converted from all the lawless deeds he has
> done and keeps my commandments and performs my ordinances, he
> will truly live and will not die; all his iniquities which he has done
> will not be remembered, but by the righteousness which he has done
> he will live; for I do not desire the death of the lawless man, says the
> Lord, so much as that he may be converted from the evil way and
> live. (3.11)

Ezekiel's soteriological notion—that turning away from evil and lawless deeds
to observing righteousness ultimately leads to life without death—is for Theophilus the essence of God's merciful treatment of humanity, as well as an example of a prophetic reminder. For Theophilus, as for Ezekiel, conversion is a
matter of law keeping; law keeping translates into righteousness and righteousness leads to eternal life.

Over the course of several chapters in the *Hypomnema* (3.11-14), Theophilus
appears to turn from the *Deka Kephalaia* to a second collection of nomos. As we
shall see, he believes that the teachings of the prophets and also the gospels are

consistent with the first collection. Notice the phrase "the prophets and the gospels." The bishop teaches that the prophets and the gospels are compatible collections of sacred literature possessing a conceptual solidarity with "the law and the prophets" when it comes to nomos. The consistency of the prophets and the gospels in providing nomos is insured by the fact that the authors of these equivalent repositories of truth were actually human agents inspired by the same divine agent, namely, the pneuma. The nomos cannot be misrepresented by either of these sources, prophets or gospels, given this fact. And it is the integrity of this nomos that must be preserved if human conversion and restoration are to become a reality. In order to demonstrate this consistency, Theophilus quotes a number of biblical passages from both the Septuagint and the New Testament. In contrast to his earlier three-fold division of primary nomos, which he discovered in what he called the law of Moses or the *Deka Kephalaia,* he now establishes additional nomos, which he discovered in the prophets and the gospels. The bishop presents this material as a fourfold division of secondary nomos and it can be organized in the following manner:

A FOUR-FOLD DIVISION OF SECONDARY NOMOS[30]

Divisions of Nomos	Biblical Sources
Repentance (μετάνοια)	Isaiah 55:6-7 Ezekiel 18:21-23 Isaiah 31:6 & 45:22 Jeremiah 6:9
Justice (δικαιοσύνη)	Isaiah 1:116-17 Isaiah 58:6-8 Jeremiah 6:16 Hosea 12:7 & 13:4 Joel 2:16 & 1:14 Zechariah 7:9-10
Chastity (σεμνότης)	Proverbs 4:225-26 Matthew 5:28 & 32 Proverbs 6:27-29
Good Will (εὔνοια)	Isaiah 66:5 Matthew 5:44-46 & 6:3 Titus 3:1 I Timothy 2:1-2 Romans 13:7-8

Theophilus says "repentance" is an example of God's mercy which extends beyond the earlier law, "for God always wants the human race to turn away from all its sins" (3.11). And "justice" is described in the law, but:

> The teaching of the prophets and the gospels is consistent with it be-
> cause all the inspired men made utterances by means of the one spirit
> of God. (3.12)

While Theophilus mentions the gospels in regard to justice he saves his New Testament quotations for his presentation of "chastity" and "good will." Chastity is required not only in deed but also in thought, a point that can be illustrated from the observations of Solomon, but also "the gospel voice provides a stricter teaching about purity" (3.13). Good will is to be practiced towards all people thus weakening the temptation to become "sycophants" (3.14). Such teachings are a protection against pagan promiscuity, cannibalism and adultery, lessons which are being taught in Theophilus' parish.[31]

The reader should notice four particulars in Theophilus' presentation of the sources of this secondary collection of nomos. First, it is treated not so much as additional law, but as a natural extension of the earlier *Deka Kephalaia*. It even retains one of the terms (the Greek word δικαιοσύνη) of that earlier collection of nomos. Second, the work of Solomon, that is, Proverbs, plays a significant role as prophetic nomos. Third, it is Matthew's Gospel which Theophilus relies upon as his primary gospel source of nomos. And last of all, Theophilus appears to include Pauline teachings under his rubric of gospel nomos. All four of these points are considered in the next chapter of this book, but for now the reader should be aware that the bishop is engaged in a systematic presentation of mo-rality (rather than ritual or credal law), designed to bridge the ancient Hebrew world with his contemporary Hellenistic context. In doing so he uses the phrase "the prophets and the gospels" to mobilize a variety of biblical materials in his protreptic cause.

As he concludes his presentation the bishop says that "law is the guiding principle (πολιτεύεται)" (3.15) and, therefore, "one must . . . become a student of the legislation (μαθητὴν τῆς νομοθεσίας) of God" (3.17). This key sote-riological imperative does not contain a call for faith or hope based on a passive acceptance of grace. It is not associated with a special person or a unique place or an unusual event. Rather, it has a pragmatic character. Theophilus is implor-ing Autolycus to convert by becoming a student. And so the bishop has carefully laid out a curriculum on nomos and provided the textbooks Autolycus needs to study. Why must one become such a committed student of the legislation of God? Because, as was said, nomos is at a minimum a guiding principle. But there is a less abstract and more concrete way of answering this question, which is provided by someone whom Theophilus believes Autolycus admires. The bishop implies that Plato was actually promoting a Christian parochial educa-tion: "As Plato himself admitted when he said that accurate learning cannot be obtained unless God teaches it through the law" (3.17).[32] This is how Theophilus leaves it in his *Hypomnema*.

Is Theophilus promoting Mosaic law? If by Mosaic law one means the entire Torah, as it was understood in a both a Hellenistic and Rabbinic context, with its variety of ritual laws and purity rites (such as circumcision), this is clearly not what the Christian bishop is talking about.[33] Theophilus is interested primarily in credal (θεῖος) and moral (ἅγιος) nomos, the nomos of piety (εὐσέβεια), beneficence (καλοποιεῖν) and righteousness (δικαιοσύνη). It should also be mentioned in this regard that Theophilus would probably not have agreed with the following general statement of Paul, which suggested that there was no nomos at all from Adam to Moses: "Sin indeed was in the world before the law was given, but sin is not counted where there is no law. Yet death reigned from Adam to Moses" (Romans 5:13-14). There was for the bishop (and Paul as well, despite the above statement) an original commandment to Adam and Eve which represents positive law based on moral appropriation.[34] Even if the primal parents did not fully comprehend the moral implications of the nomos given in paradise, its existence implies their capacity to understand and keep it. They were morally bound to keep this law, a law which Theophilus presents as an archetype for all subsequent nomos. After humanity sinned and thus defeated the idea of progression, the idea of salvation dependent upon human enlightened and conversion to a life of obedient nomos keeping replaced it. As humanity needed to be taught and reminded about the specifics of this obedient lifestyle, God (as νομοθέτης) could be said to have reformulated that original imperative of the garden into the *Deka Kephalaia* of the Mosaic law and even more fully into the four-fold division of repentance (μετάνοια), justice (δικαιοσύνη), chastity (σεμνότης) and good will (εὔνοια) of the prophets and the gospels. However, before drawing any conclusions about Theophilus' understanding of the contributions of the prophets and the gospels to his curriculum of nomos, we should consider what he has to say about the human agents of nomos.

The Roles of Prophets and Churches

What are the roles of the prophets[35] and of the so-called holy churches in Theophilus' soteriological scheme? As this section demonstrates the prophets are the agents of, and the churches are the sanctuaries for, "the teachings of the truth" (2.14). Let us begin with a discussion of these agents of truth. When Theophilus compared the world to the sea, he claimed that this world would have already "failed," by which he seems to have meant that it would have ceased to exist, if it had not been for "the law of God" (2.14).[36] While it is nomos as natural law which supports the world's existence, Theophilus blends this concept with that of nomos as positive law. According to him nomos (whether that be natural or positive law) is revealed in "the prophets flowing and gushing forth with sweetness and compassion and righteousness and the teachings of God's holy commandments" (2.14). The role of the prophets is second in importance only to the significance of the nomos itself in Theophilus' soteriological landscape. The "prophet" is not merely Theophilus' "basic classification for Old Testament writers" as R. M. Grant has rightly said,[37] but is his preeminent figure for promoting the source of salvation, namely, the nomos. Let us consider the role of the prophet in two parts: First, the general character of prophethood, and second, the work of specific prophets.

In the *Homilia* Theophilus confesses his personal debt to the holy prophets. He says:

> At that time I encountered the sacred writings of the holy prophets, who through the spirit of God foretold past events in the way that they happened, present events in the way they are happening, and future events in the order in which they will be accomplished. (1.14)

It was their historical accuracy, and apparently their predictive power, that convinced him of the prophets' reliability in all things, even with respect to reports about "eternal tortures." Of these he claims:

> These tortures were predicted by the prophets, but later poets and philosophers stole them from the holy scriptures in order to make their own teaching seem trustworthy. In any case, however, they too foretold the punishments to come upon the ungodly and the incredulous, so that these punishments might be attested to all and no one might say, "We did not hear nor did we know." (1.14)

While it is fun to notice how Theophilus insistently claims that pagan thinkers are often, what I would call, "ideological kleptomaniacs," it is especially important to see that the eternal punishment of which he speaks is directed at both the impious and the unbeliever. The concern he is trying to invoke in the majority of his audience, who may sense they fall into one or both of these two categories, is how they might escape this disaster. The bishop tells Autolycus:

> If you will, you too must reverently read the prophetic writings. They will be your best guides for escaping the eternal punishments and for obtaining the eternal benefits of God. (1.14)

The three passages above represent Theophilus' only discussion of the prophets in the *Homilia*. But from them we learn of his deep commitment to the prophetic scriptures as the "best guides," but little about the actual role of the prophets themselves. The *Syngramma* formulates this notion.

The key passages regarding the prophets occur early in the *Syngramma*. The bishop tells us:

> All the historians and poets and so-called philosophers are deceived in every respect, and so are those who pay attention to them . . . . So unwillingly they admit that they do not know the truth. (2.8)

This is bold rhetoric. Theophilus is addressing an audience that is apparently well versed in pagan intellectual culture. In debate some of his readers may have conceded to an agnostic position, though not without resistance. Furthermore, the bishop believes he can explain the ignorance and pride of the pagan intellectuals. He says of the great authors, and perhaps implying the same of some of his readers:

> Inspired by demons and puffed up by them, they said what they said through them. (2.8)

However, of the poets specifically, and this appears to be a rare event in the bishop's mind:

> Sometimes some poets, becoming sober in soul and departing from the demons, made statements in agreement with those of the prophets in order to bear witness to themselves and to all men concerning the sole rule of God and the judgment and the other matters they discussed. (2.8)

With perhaps a touch of sarcasm he tells his readers that even pagans, in moments of sobriety, occasionally get it right and acknowledge divine monotheistic providence—not to mention human responsibility. This observation, however, is merely an introduction leading up to his claim for the inspiration of and truth in the writings of the Hebrew prophets.

In the following protracted passage, Theophilus explains who these prophets are and how their careers developed. In this important text he says:

> The men of God, who were possessed by a holy spirit and became prophets and were inspired and instructed by God himself, were taught by God and became holy and righteous. For this reason they were judged worthy to receive the reward of becoming instruments of God and containing wisdom from him. Through wisdom they spoke about the creation of the world and about everything else; for they also prophesied about pestilences and famines and wars. There were not just one or two of them but more at various times and seasons among the Hebrews, as well as the Sibyl among the Greeks. All of them were consistent with one another and with themselves, and they described events which had previously occurred, events in their own time, and events which are now being fulfilled in our times. For this reason we are persuaded that their predictions of coming events will prove correct, just as the former events took place exactly. (2.9)

Who are the prophets? They are certain individuals first possessed by the pneuma and then deemed worthy to be inspired and instructed by God himself. Thus, they became instruments of God. As instruments they were filled with the sophia of God, which allowed them insights on a wide range of concerns. They spoke on subjects as diverse as the events of creation to specific future catastrophes. Their reliability is certain, Theophilus maintains, given their internal consistency and unimpeachable record. It is important to notice that the bishop promotes not just the continuity of the truth from one generation to another, but he suggests the universality of this truth. Not only were the Hebrews privy to information about historically vital events, but so were the Greeks as is evinced in the prophecies of the Sibyl. While the inclusion of the Sibyl among the authentic prophets has become apologetic convention in the second century,[38] Theophilus' endorsement is more vigorous than most.

It is the teachings of this lengthy but important statement which Theophilus continually expands upon in the rest of the *Syngramma*. To once again address a previously mentioned passage, he says of the source of the prophets' inspiration:

> It was [the logos], spirit of God and beginning and sophia and power of the most high, who came down into the prophets and spoke through them about the creation of the world and all the rest. (2.10)

Theophilus sees the prophets as special individuals because they have been used in a special way by a powerful and unique force in the cosmos. This divine force, although characterized by several names, here appears to be a singular agent of God. While this is the sole example of the phrase "power of the most high" in Theophilus' books,[39] "power" is an important term for God in the bishop's thought (1.3, 2.4). It has already been suggested in chapter four that certain figures like these—the pneuma, the beginning, the sophia and the power—are occasionally blended, by the bishop, with the logos. In this instance, his language promotes this idea, so much so that it can be said the many-named logos is the personified source of powerful prophetic speech. However, the bishop is continually shifting these terms around.[40] At any rate, it is this cosmic force or divine presence that has made certain individuals appear remarkable, and thus the bishop says of these people and their writings:

> For the stars which are clearly visible and radiant exist in imitation of the prophets. (2.15) . . . The books which belong to us, the worshippers of God, are proved to be writings not only more ancient but also more true than all historians and poets. (2.30)

And how can this be proven? The bishop continues:

> Those who love learning and antiquities can judge whether what has been said by us through the holy prophets is merely recent or not. (2.32)

He proposes the comparative study of historical texts, confident critical thinking will support his claim that he possesses the best and most ancient of books—the textbooks for Autolycus' education.

In the last section of the *Syngramma*, the bishop tells the story of how the world was settled after the deluge. Answering his own provocative question, he says:

> Which of the so-called wise men or poets or historiographers was able to say what was true in regard to these matters? They lived long after them and introduced a multitude of gods . . . . For this reason it

is plain that all the rest were in error and that only the Christians have
held the truth—we who are instructed by the holy spirit who spoke in
the holy prophets and foretold everything. (2.33)[41]

Here for the first time Theophilus connects the work of the pneuma and the
words of the prophets with Christianity, and with himself in particular. Christians possess the truth, he says. And where did they get it? Did it come directly
from God? In a very real sense, though the bishop does not explore the phenomenon, Christians are instructed by the pneuma when they read the prophets.
Continuing in his task to cultivate the critical mind of his readers, Theophilus
enjoins Autolycus:

Furthermore, you must devotedly search the things of God, I mean
those spoken through the prophets, so that by comparing what is said
by us with what is said by the others you will be able to discover the
truth. (2.34)

To put it in other words, Christians are the only people who possess the truth in
total, which is the *paideia* of the pneuma via the holy prophets. The only way to
ascertain the truth is through a careful and spiritual study of the prophets.[42]
    And what exactly is this "truth" that the prophets will proclaim and teach to
the Christians? They taught history and they made predictions which ought to be
carefully considered. But their most important responsibilities are the preservation and presentation of salvific nomos. The bishop said:

God . . . gave a law and sent holy prophets to proclaim and to teach
the human race so that each one of us might become sober and recognize that God is one. They also taught . . . that a person who acts
righteously may escape the eternal punishments and be judged worthy of receiving eternal life from God. (2.34)[43]

First and foremost is the prophetic teaching of monotheism, followed by specific
legal and moral obligations that lead to salvation from eternal punishment to
eternal life. How can one be certain that their teachings are accurate? The bishop
adds:

It is obvious how agreeably and harmoniously all the prophets spoke,
making their proclamation by one and the same spirit concerning the
sole rule of God and the origin of the world and the making of
man. . . . And why should I list the multitude of the prophets, since
they are many and made countless statements in agreement and harmony? For those who desire to do so can read what was said through
them and acquire accurate knowledge of what is true, and not be led
astray by speculation and pointless labour. These persons whom we
have mentioned were prophets among the Hebrews; they were illiterate men and shepherds and uneducated. (2.35)

Over against sophisticated pagan philosophy the bishop is recommending to Autolycus writings composed by illiterate and uneducated men. Theophilus actually seems to value their illiteracy as proof of their worth. While he does not expound upon this notion, he does claim that they were reliable instruments of divine truth rather than producers of human speculation. The bishop resists listing the actual individuals about whom he is talking because he has made access to their writings easy and he seems to suggest that all he can do in his arguments, in the present work, is introduce Autolycus to the masters. The conversion of Autolycus is, in his mind, an event which will occur if he too encounters the truth of the prophets first hand. This was his experience and he is recommending it to all skeptics.

The subject of the prophets is addressed in the *Hypomnema* as well. In fact, it is here that we learn of the prophets' teaching regarding repentance and of their relationship to the gospels. The prophets are sent to teach and remind people of "the content of the law and to convert them to repentance so that they would no longer sin" (3.11). Furthermore, "the teaching of the prophets and gospels is consistent . . . because all inspired men made utterances by means of the one spirit of God" (3.12). The essential difference between the prophets' teaching of nomos and that of the gospels' is that "the gospel voice (ἡ εὐαγγέλιος φωνὴ) provides a stricter teaching about purity" (3.13). The bishop does not take this opportunity to brag about the superiority of the gospel voice over the voice of the Hebrew prophets. Why? Because the voice of the gospel is presented by the bishop as providing an extension, or perhaps a refinement, of only certain aspects of the teachings of the prophetic voice. After all, the bishop's ultimate point is one of comparison and not contrast, of solidarity and not contravention. His comparison of the prophets and the gospels leads him to claim their solidarity, in other words, they are essentially the product of the same voice speaking in a different context.

The bishop once again asserts the harmony of the prophets with ever increasing enthusiasm when he says:

> How much more, then, shall we know the truth, since we learn it from the holy prophets, who were filled with the holy spirit of God? For this reason all the prophets spoke harmoniously and in agreement with one another when they predicted what was going to happen to the whole world. The very outcome of the previously predicted and fulfilled events can teach those who love learning—or rather, love truth—that their proclamations are really true. (3.17)

He concludes his general statement on the prophets in the context of establishing a reliable chronology. He says:

> From the compilation of the periods of time and from all that has been said, the antiquity of the prophetic writings and the divine nature of our message are obvious. This message is not recent in origin,

nor are our writings, as some suppose, mythical and false. They are actually more ancient and more trustworthy. (3.29)

Our writings? The bishop has made his argument for the consistency, the antiquity and the divine character of the message of the prophets and the gospels. Both of these collections are for Theophilus Christian documents which must be studied as essential to conversion and ultimately serve as the foundation of a Christian education that leads to salvation.

Now what does Theophilus say about the work of specific prophets, and whom does he consider a prophet? The bishop mentions by name Isaiah (2.13), Jeremiah (2.35.), Ezekiel (3.11), Hosea (2.35), Joel (3.12), Habakkuk (2.35), Malachi (2.38, 3.12), Zechariah (3.12, 23) and even Daniel (3.29), and assembles a massive amount of quotations from most of them.[44] Their value for him is found in what they have to say about the conflagration, the end times and especially repentance. What they provide as chronological evidence is equally important for his needs. Included in his list of prophets is Adam (2.28). According to Theophilus, Adam not only introduced Eve to the "world" but also predicted the nature of human wedlock. In his words:

> Adam said to Eve, "This is now bone from my bones and flesh from my flesh," and in addition he prophesied, saying "For this reason a man will leave his father and mother and will cleave to his wife, and the two shall be one flesh." *This is actually fulfilled among us.* For what man who marries lawfully does not disregard his mother and father and his whole family and all his relatives, while he cleaves to his own wife and unites with her, loving her more than them? For this reason husbands have often suffered death for the sake of their wives. (2.28)[45]

Adam, who was the first human being, was also the first prophet.[46] Even the Sibyl, as was suggested earlier, is considered a prophet deserving respect (2.36). Theophilus uses the term prophet some forty-six times; and the most prominent of these personalities is, without a doubt, Moses.

Moses is mentioned twenty times by name in the *Syngramma* and *Hypomnema*. He is seen as an instrument used by the logos of God (2.10). How so? Consider the following information supplied by the bishop. Both the logos and Moses are called "servants" of God. Of the logos, Theophilus says God "used this logos as his servant in the things created by him" (2.10). Regarding Moses, the bishop says:

> Of this divine law the minister was Moses, the servant of God, not only to all the world but especially to the Hebrews. (3.9)[47]

These are the only two instances of Theophilus speaking about servants or helpers of God in his three books. Moses administers the positive law of God reflecting perhaps the bishop's understanding of the logos' administration of natural law in the creation process. In this sense both the logos and Moses are dispensers of a divine nomos, and as such they are servants of God. Moses, however, is said to be an instrument used by the logos, while it is the pneuma who actually speaks through him (2.30). Perhaps the bishop, as was suggested earlier, sees the logos as the actual source of prophetic legal speech. The pneuma would then be the breath that carries that speech into and through the prophet. After all, the logos is said to be the "command of God" (2.13),[48] who can "give orders" (3.14) and thus "lead" the human race (3.15). Moses is called "our prophet" (3.18), "minister of God" (3.18, 23) and "leader of the Jews" (3.20), and Theophilus believes that he has proven that Moses is "more ancient than all writers" (3.29). In fact it is not just Moses' relationship with God but his chronological seniority that makes his presumed writings superior to those of the pagans (3.21, 23, 24).

Theophilus shows nearly as much interest in King Solomon as a prophet as he does Moses. Solomon is mentioned thirteen times by the bishop. Solomon's prophetic role is essentially derived from the value the bishop places on the words of Proverbs and the sophia tradition in general.[49] However, as we have seen in several quotations above, Solomon is a teacher of nomos as well, albeit a stricter sort of morality (2.35),[50] and even a commentator on future events (2.38). The bishop does not overlook the fact that Solomon was known as a wise man who built the great Jewish temple (3.21, 22, 25), nor does he exclude the value of his seniority over the Greeks when pressing the point of his superior moral nomos (3.28).

Therefore, Adam, Moses, Solomon and the authors of the Hebrew Nevi'im were all prophetic voices proclaiming the truth about many things but most of all about man's salvation by nomos. However, their united voices from the past were not the only voices that must be heard. The bishop says of the prophetic witness:

> All these matters will be understood by everyone who seeks for the wisdom of God and is pleasing to him through faith and righteousness and good deeds . . . . He who loves learning must really love it. Endeavor to meet with us more often, so that by hearing a living voice you may accurately learn what is true. (2.38)

Both faith and good deeds, as well as the desire for the sophia of God, are necessary to the Christian life Theophilus proclaims. And where does one encounter the sophia of God? God's wisdom can be found in the living voice; that is, it can be heard in the words of Theophilus and those of his community. There is also the gospel voice, mentioned earlier, which "provides a stricter teaching about purity" (3.13). For example, this gospel voice says "love your enemies and pray for those who insult you" (3.14).[51] The bishop stresses that the voice of the prophets is consistent with the voice of the gospel. But in the passage above, Theophilus is introducing Autolycus to another voice apart from what he considers to be the scriptural voice. It is the voice which is "our teaching" (2.1), "the proof of our truth and our teaching" (3.4) "our message" (3.4),[52] which possesses "a divine nature" and "is not recent" (3.29). The bishop is introducing Autolycus and his readers to the voice of his church.

What is the gospel voice according to Theophilus' teaching? On the one hand, a case could be made for this voice being simply that of the historical Jesus. After all, the bishop quotes Jesus' Sermon on the Mount five times (3.13, 14). On the other hand, a case can be made for this voice being the personified logos expressing itself in the context of an explanation of divine providence. Is it then possible, plausible and maybe even probable that Theophilus thought of the historical Jesus as uniquely possessing the logos? The bishop does formulate his doctrine on the logos of God in the context of the initial verses of the prologue to the Gospel of John (2.22). Could it be that the bishop has substituted the term logos for Jesus? In other words, did Theophilus prefer, for whatever reason, to present a logology rather than an explicit christology? As was pointed out earlier, while it was the Hebrew prophets who taught repentance (3.11) and justice (3.12),[53] it was the logos who is said to have taught the central lessons of the Sermon on the Mount, namely, chastity (3.13) and good will (3.14). Nevertheless, on closer inspection, it can be seen that the logos in question "taught" and "gave orders" not only through the voice of Jesus, but also through the voices of Solomon and Paul.[54] While neither Jesus or Paul are mentioned by name, as is Solomon, it is plausible to assume that Theophilus understood them both to be recipients of the prophetic gift provided by the divine logos. Therefore, while I am suggesting that Theophilus took the "gospel voice" to be primarily the voice speaking through the Gospel texts, that is, the voice of the historical Jesus, it is difficult to assess whether or not he thought of Jesus himself, anymore than Solomon or Paul, as uniquely possessing the logos.[55] I think it is more probable that just as he took Solomon to be one of the Hebrew prophets, he took some Pauline teachings to be included under the rubric of the gospel voice. As was made clear in chapter four, Theophilus' doctrine on the logos (which includes some Johannine quotations[56]) is a tool for interpreting the creation story and to a lesser degree for explaining the prophetic teaching of nomos. What should be understood by the reader at this point is that the logos is not his tool for developing a christology.[57] Theophilus does not even suggest a person-centered christology, let alone a passion-centered soteriology, in his three extant books. Furthermore, if the person of Jesus the Christ had been introduced to Autolycus, given the context of the protreptic theology of *Ad Autolycum,* it seems to me he would have been presented as a prophet and not the subject of atonement. In *Ad Autolycum,* Theophilus is committed to teaching the idea that atonement for sin is achieved through a life lived in accordance with nomos.

Before laying out the Theophilian theory of soteriological *paideia* in schematic form and before drawing conclusions regarding the relationship of the logos and the nomos consider this final question: Where does salvation take place? Or, where is salvation to be found? Apart from his usage in the context of the Noah story (3.18-19) and in relationship to the nomos (2.27), the bishop only employs the Greek verb σώζω (to save) in one other passage. In his analysis of the third day of creation, he compares the sea to his contemporary world, which "if it had not had the law of God . . . would already have failed because of the evil and sin abounding in it" (2.14). Thus, he says:

> God gave the world, which is agitated and tossed by sins, certain as-
> semblies (συναγωγάς) called holy churches, in which as in havens
> with good mooring-places are the teachings of truth. In these will
> take refuge those who wish to be saved (οἱ θέλοντες σῴζεσθαι),
> when they are lovers of truth and want to escape the wrath and judg-
> ment of God. (2.14)

Theophilus is consistent. Those who abide by the nomos of God are invited to
takeup residence in "synagogues" called holy churches. For Theophilus the
Christian synagogues are the repositories of the teachings of truth, which I take
to be an alternative way of speaking about the teaching of God's nomos. In these
places people who are lovers of truth show their receptivity as those wishing to
be saved. Therefore, for Theophilus, the "whoever will" of his primary soteriological text (2.27) is a potential member of this Christian institution. It is here
in the Christian synagogue (or church) that salvation is to be found and nurtured.
While the abstract process of conversion takes place in the individual life of a
nomos keeper, Theophilus is convinced that realization of this enlightenment is
best tutored and safeguarded within the asylum provided by the Christian
church.[58] It is within such an institution that sanctuary is found, not so much
from the influence of other religious perspectives or even persecution of the
world, but from the wrath of God. It is within the Christian community that the
nomos doer is saved in the most concrete sense—a synagogue where the prophetic word is continued in the gospel voice as it becomes a living voice, or
more simply, where the bishop teaches God's nomos.

Theophilus' Theory of Salvation

Having now address the significance and the content of the nomos and the roles
of the prophets and the holy churches in the preservation and the teaching of the
nomos, how might the Theophilian theory of salvation finally be organized? For
Theophilus, there are four divine dispensations, creation, paradise, a fixed period
of time (τακτὸς χρόνος) and resurrection. It is in the first three dispensations
that the reader must reckon with a shift in the notion of nomos. Most importantly
for the bishop's work in *Ad Autolycum,* it is on the third dispensation that he
focuses his attention. He believes that fallen humans can be recalled to paradise
and addresses the procedure for such transformation in terms of education
(παιδευθείς). Though he does not explain any of the details of this recall
(ἀνάκλησις) to a paradise (perhaps he has something like purgatory in mind), he
appears to think of it as the natural result of hearing and doing God's nomos.
With these words as an introduction, consider the following schematic:

THE THEOPHILIAN DISPENSATIONS OF NOMOS[59]

Creation	Paradise	A Fixed Period of Time for Education		Resurrection
		Primary Nomos (Moses' *Deka Kephalaia*):		For
		The Divine Law	Piety	Recall
The Command ἡ διάταξις	The Command ἡ ἐντολή	The Holy Law	Beneficence Justice	To
		Secondary Nomos:		Paradise
		Nevi'im	Repentance Justice	And
		Solomon	Chastity	Then
		Jesus	Chastity Good Will	Eternal
		Paul	Good Will	Life

Originally the nomos of paradise consisted of only a single commandment (ἐν-τολή). But man failed himself as well as God when he broke that single command. Man was then removed from the garden; and access to the tree of life, which had prolonged his mortal body as he sought maturation through progression, appeared to be permanently interrupted. Now his salvific education—that is, his opportunity to acquire divine *paideia*—began. What he called the Mosaic "Ten Chapters (*Deka Kephalaia*) of the great and marvelous law" (3.9) was primary to this education. It was originally divided into two categories of divine law (θεῖος νόμος) and holy law (ἅγιος νόμος) and then later subdivided into the three categories of piety, beneficence and justice. But when Theophilus wanted to demonstrate how scripture expanded upon that *Deka Kephalaia,* he organized the teachings of other prophets—that is, the Nevi'im, Solomon, Jesus and Paul—as a fourfold nomos containing commandments dealing with repentance, justice, chastity and good will. Thus, this secondary nomos, as a "guiding principle," was also essential to his educational way of life (πολιτεία) that led toward the goal of salvation. This primary and secondary *paideia* which Theophilus teaches, promotes a salvation achieved through a life lived in accordance with God's nomos.

Now, with this summary complete, let us briefly consider the specific relationship of the nomos to the logos, such as it is, in *Ad Autolycum*. God's logos (as well as his sophia and pneuma) does seem, in my opinion, to be linked to nomos in the bishop's thought. The bishop introduced divine agency in order to explain the transcendent God's activity in the world without disturbing his idea of monotheism. While the personification of the logos is one of Theophilus' ways of addressing God's work in the creation, it is also his instrument for speaking about God's participation in the prophetic witness to salvific nomos. For Theophilus, the logos informed individuals and communities of the content and meaning of salvific nomos. From the primal voice (φωνή), which was called the command (διάταξις) of creation—and the garden voice, which was "the" command (ἐντολή) to Adam and Eve, then later the prophetic words of Moses, Solomon and the authors of the Nevi'im, which included the gospel voice (Jesus and Paul) and, in all probability, even the living hermeneutic voice of Theophilus and his community—God's logos has been busy articulating nomos. The logos first spoke with the voice of natural law, that is, the nomos of the physical universe. Then the logos spoke with the voice of positive law, that is, the nomos for human behavior. Initially, in the garden, the logos imparted nomos designed to give humanity an opportunity for progress. But after the Fall the logos publicized nomos designed to give humanity an opportunity for repentance.

However, it is the post-paradise salvific nomos that is of practical importance for Theophilus' readers. This salvific nomos, I would suggest, is presented by the bishop as having the vivifying effect of the fruit of the tree of life in the post-paradise dispensation. And, furthermore, God has made it widely accessible to humanity. The logos' salvific activity was especially prolific in the teachings of Moses and Solomon, the authors of the Nevi'im and the Sermon on the Mount. But such activity is also present in the epistles of the New Testament and even in the living voice of the contemporary church as it expounds throughout the world the significance of nomos for eternal life. Apparently, when it comes to nomos there is a chain of prophets who are all informed by the logos of God. But while the logos is the prophetic voice which proclaims nomos and the hermeneutic voice which teaches nomos, it is perhaps also the protreptic voice which fashions nomos into an appropriate invitation to Christian faith.

Notes

1. For two fine representative articles on the definitions of religious salvation see M. Slusser, "Salvation," in *EEC,* 823-26 and D. G. Dawe, "Salvation," in Keith Crim's *The Perennial Dictionary of World Religions* (San Francisco: Harper Collins, 1989), 643-46.

2. With this first mention here of Theophilus' teaching on morality it is important to define the concept and distinguish it from ethics. In a most recent discussion of early Christian morality, W. A. Meeks, *The Origins of Christian Morality* (New Haven: Yale University Press, 1993), 3-4, says: "In modern English, the word *ethics* has come to have a more stately resonance than the word *morality* . . . . 'Ethics' and 'morality' are often used synonymously—the one word comes from the Greek, the other from the Latin word that Cicero coined to translate the Greek . . . . I take 'ethics' in the sense of a reflective, second-order activity: it is morality rendered self-conscious; it asks about the logic of moral discourse and action, about the grounds for judgment, about the anatomy of duty or the roots and structure of virtue. It is thus, as the *Oxford English Dictionary* has it, 'the science of morality.' 'Morality,' on the other hand, names a dimension of life, a pervasive and, often, only partly conscious set of value-laden dispositions, inclinations, attitudes, and habits." As we shall see, *Ad Autolycum* comprises little more than a rudimentary code of behavior. Its teachings do not add up to a comprehensive ethical

system of commandments, but only provides exemplary law sufficient to make the bishop's case regarding its significance in his soteriology. Therefore, while Theophilus is dealing with and reflecting upon morality in a protreptic context, one could refer to his accomplishment as a micro-system of ethics.

3. H. L Hart, "Legal Positivism," *The Encyclopedia of Philosophy* (New York: Collier-Macmillan, 1972), vols. 3 and 4, 418f., says: "Since at least the fourteenth century, the expression 'positive law' has been used to refer to laws laid down or made by human beings in contrast to natural or divine law, which is regarded as something discovered and not made by man. But the expression 'positive law' has also long been used to refer to any law brought into being by a command or act of will and so includes the law of God as well as human legislation." While clearly distinguishing divine and human law, I do not think Theophilus has made a conscious distinction between natural law and positive law. But he does indirectly speak of the law of creation, of the law of paradise and of the law of the post-paradise world. Therefore, I am using the term nomos in both the ontological sense (creational law) and the normative sense (mandated law) as reflective of his intent.

4. See 1.11; 2.14, 15, 16, 25, 27, 34, 35, 37; 3.9, 10, 11, 12, 15, 17, 23. In every discussion from 1.11 to 2.16, Theophilus qualifies nomos as "the law of God." After 2.16 he never again uses this phrase. When he does qualify the term nomos, it is a "divine law" (2.35; 3.9, 23) or a "holy law" (2.35, 3.9). In one instance he refers to the nomos as "a great and marvelous law" (3.9). Theophilus speaks of the commandments (ἐντολαί) of God five times (2.14, 15, 27;' 3.11, 24), and of the singular commandment (ἡ ἐντολή) to the primal parents three times (2.19, 24, 27). However, the term laws (νόμοι, the plural of νόμος) is used only four times in Theophilus' books and never in the context of divine nomos. In 1.5 human laws and commandments are spoken of in contrast to the nomos of God. In 3.6 he twice speaks of human laws against inappropriate sexual intercourse, and in 3.16 the plural appears in a quotation from Plato. The bishop clearly prefers to speak of God's legislation in the collective singular. He also addresses the subject in terms of God's "ordinances" three times (2.15—προστάγματα; 3.11, 15—δικαιώματα).

5. Cf. the ideas and language of Romans 13:1; I Timothy 2:1-2 and I Peter 2:13-17 (particularly verses 15 and 17).

6. Theophilus appears to have substituted the imperative τίμα (honor) in his paraphrase for the Septuagint's φοβοῦ (fear), which seems an odd shift given the price of disobedience. He also concludes his piece of law by substituting τοὺς ἐχθρούς (the enemies) for τοὺς ἀσεβεῖς (the ungodly).

7. See similar language of hearing and doing in Psalm 94:8 as quoted in Hebrews 3:7-8, 15 and 4:7. Cf. I Timothy 4:16.

8. The phrase, "the compassion and sweetness" (τὴν εὐσπλαγχνίαν καὶ γλυκύτητα), is also used in *I Clement* 14:3 (with the terms reversed).

9. The bishop demonstrates scientific acumen by suggesting that the rivers actually nourish the sea by controlling the level of saline.

10. His language of "transgression," "remaining," "harming" and "keeping," is suggestive of a bestial will and morality. But it is obvious that the bishop is using anthropomorphic language for purposes of drawing a connection between man and the animal kingdom.

11. A child may not understand exactly why something is right or wrong, but obedience is expected when the child has been conditioned to know right from wrong. Until such knowledge is acquired, however, all parental disciplining is little more than conditioning and not really punishment in the strictest sense of the word. Thus, an infant who does not possess a moral capacity cannot understand the concept of punishment.

12. See J. L. Crenshaw's *Theodicy In The Old Testament* (Philadelphia: Fortress, 1983) and *A Whirlpool of Torment: Israelite Traditions of God as an Oppressive Presence* (Philadelphia: Fortress, 1984). Also consider J. D. Levenson's *Creation and the Persistence of Evil: The Jewish Drama of Divine Omnipotence* (San Francisco: Harper and Row, 1988), especially 47-50.

13. The term χάρις (grace) is mentioned only twice by the bishop in 3.15 and 23 with no discussion.

14. As we shall see shortly, R. M. Grant believes that Theophilus' language in this passage is an actual polemic against Paul's theology. Whether this is so or not, it certainly is a polemic against so-called "cheap grace."

15. See the fine analysis provided by A. Dihle, *Die goldene Regel: Eine Einführung in die Geschichte der antiken und frühchristlichen Vulgärethik,* Studienheft zur Altertumswissenschaft 7 (Göttingen: Vandenhoeck und Ruprecht, 1962), 109-14. Cf. the positive forms in Leviticus 19:18; Matthew 7:12 and Luke 6:31 with the more typical negative forms in Tobit 4:15; *Letter of Aristeas* 207; Ms. D of Acts 15:29; *Didache* 1:2 (perhaps the closest in wording to Theophilus) and R. Hillel, b. Shabbat 31a.

16. Cf. I Peter 4:3.

17. The term ἅγιος νόμος (holy law) is used in only one other place, 3.9, where it is associated with moral injunctions. In that same passage the term θεῖος νόμος (divine law) is used without any specific reference, though it is said that Moses was the minister of this nomos. Both divine and holy nomos could be merely alternative terms for the δέκα κεφάλαια (the *Deka Kephalaia,* the Ten Chapters, mentioned only in 3.9). The only other instance of θεῖος νόμος is in 3.23, where it says only that this nomos was "given us through Moses." Therefore, I would suggest that while it is possible that the usage of these terms could be little more than a matter of style on the bishop's part, it is plausible given this initial usage that they represent a substantive distinction in his mind.

18. He does not follow the biblical arrangement of this legislation. Cf. 3.9, discussed shortly, which is his more complete version of Christian nomos. There the pentalogue has given way to an octalogue. As we shall see, Theophilus does not provide the expected decalogue.

19. Cf. 3.13, where the text is revisited in a slightly more systematic setting.

20. See Matthew 5:17; 7:12; 11:13 and 22:40. Cf. Luke 16:16 and Acts 24:14. Regarding this Rabbinic pentateuchal division, see G. Wigoder, *The Encyclopedia of Judaism,* "Bible" (New York: Macmillian, 1989), 114-24, and J. Neusner, *Between Time and Eternity: The Essentials of Judaism* (Belmount, CA: Wadsworth, 1975), 7-8.

21. It will also become clear in the next section that the Theophilian nomos is exclusive of much that is in the law of Moses.

22. Notice Theophilus' use of the infinitive καλοποιεῖν, although a substantive like καλοποιός (paralleling καλλοποιός)would have made a more balanced comparison.

23. For purposes of conciseness, his quotations have been abbreviated.

24. Given that the bishop managed to distinguish ten elements in this collection of commandments, suggests that the title, "Ten Commandments" (or "Chapters") is an unassailable tradition for him, even if its content is not.

25. R. M. Grant, *Greek Apologists of the Second Century* (Philadelphia: The Westminster Press, 1988), 161, points out that the covenant code (Exodus 20:22-23:33) is included in the *Didascalia Apostolorum* as basic law, but not in the *Apostolic Constitutions.* See, however, Theophilus' comments on honoring the Sabbath in 2.12. Cf. Grant's most recent comments on the subject in *Heresy and Criticism: The Search for Authenticity in Early Christian Literature* (Louisville, KY: Knox, 1993), 90-91, where he says of Theophilus' position: "The essential law of God, transmitted through Moses, dealt with

piety, well-doing, and justice. It had ten chapters or headings—but not the ten listed in Exodus or Deuteronomy. Instead, Theophilus retained only commandments 1-2 and 5-10, adding to these several 'judgments' from Exodus 23:6-9." With this understanding of nomos in the context of his ultimate synthesis of the law, the prophets and the gospels, Grant does not see him completely outside the trajectory of orthodoxy. He continues: "By 181, then, relatively orthodox Christian leaders were using the critical weapons of their opponents. About a century later the Syriac *Didascalia Apostolorum* insists that the true Old Testament law consists only of the decalogue and the 'judgments' expressed in Exodus 21-23." Thus Grant concludes of Theophilus' work: "This is defensive exegesis of the Bible, directed against Marcion." Given the likelihood that he wrote an anti-Marcionite document it seems probable that *Ad Autolycum* would reflect similar concerns.

26. Both Matthew 19:18-19 and Mark 10:19 have Jesus cite six commandments, though they do not indicate the same six. The charge of blasphemy and its context is found in John 10:30-39 and in the tradition of the inquisition before Caiaphas and the Sanhedrin in Mark 14:64 and parallels. The charge of Sabbath-breaking is found in John 5:18; 9:16 and is justified in Matthew 12:1-8 and parallels. Theophilus surely knew the third commandment and he alluded to the fourth commandment in 2.10 and 12.

27. It is not clear in *Ad Autolycum* that the bishop's amendments are to be understood as emendations and improvements, that is, his changes in the *Deka Kephalaia* from Exodus 20 are not discussed or presented as corrections in the "old covenant law."

28. Compare the usage of οἰκτιρμός (mercy) in Romans 12:1; II Corinthians 1:3; Colossians 3:12; Philippians 2:1 and Hebrews 10:28 (a text where violation of the law of Moses is said to lead to death without οἰκτιρμός).

29. This couplet of teaching and reminding is a common Jewish idea that is embellished in the New Testament. See John 14:26, where it is the paraclete who is sent, and of whom Jesus says: "He will *teach* you all things, and bring to your *remembrance* all that I have said to you." Theophilus, however, never speaks of a paraclete.

30. This chart, which is here offered in place of the bishop's entire set of quotations, is a modification (see the next footnote) of R. M. Grant's schematic on, and analysis of, the same material, "Theophilus of Antioch to Autolycus," *Harvard Theological Review* 40 (1947), 243. What follows this chart is a discussion of the nature of the commandments involved in this collection of nomos.

31. Theophilus employs descriptively accurate terms which may fit the well known paradigm of "cardinal virtues," but, he does not use this paradigm per se, at least not consistently. R. M. Grant tries to negotiate a tighter fit between Theophilus and the paradigm by inserting a notion which the bishop addressed earlier in a different context, namely, φιλανθρωπία (see 2.27) replacing Theophilus' own term, εὔνοια (here in 3.14). The fourfold division of Stoic virtues, φρόνησις, σωφροσύνη, ἀνδρεία and δικαιοσύνη (prudence, temperance, courage, and justice) is partially represented in Hellenistic Judaism, in 4 Maccabees 2:2-4 and Wisdom 7:7. Also, Philo, in *Allegorical Interpretation* 1.63, spoke of the four Stoic virtues in conjunction with the four rivers of Eden; and he revised this list in *The Special Laws* 2.63, where he spoke of "the regulating of one's conduct towards God by the rules of piety (εὐσέβεια) and holiness (ὁσιότης), and of one's conduct towards men by the rules of humanity (φιλανθρωπία) and justice (δικαιοσύνη)." According to E. R. Goodenough, *An Introduction to Philo Judaeus* (New Haven: Yale University Press, 1940), 44, Philo's treatise *On Virtues*, "which may have originally included a section on piety (περὶ εὐσεβείας), is now divided under the heads of bravery (περὶ ἀνδρείας), love of mankind (περὶ φιλανθρωπίας), repentance (περὶ μετανοίας), and nobility (περὶ εὐγενείας)."

32. Theophilus' Platonic reference is probably to the *Meno* 99e. Notice that the bishop's context for this text is simply an argument pointing out the antiquity of the law, however. As he says in 3.23, "the scriptures of the divine law given us through Moses actually antedate not only the reign of Zeus in Crete but also the Trojan war."

33. As S. Sandmel, *The Genius of Paul* (New York: Schocken Books, 1970), 46-47, makes clear even the terms of "law" and "revelation" were not precisely distinguished: "For modern Judaism, the Hebrew word torah is a broad term. For Hellenistic Judaism, the casualness with which the Hebrew word torah was translated by the Greek word *nomos*, 'law,' is apparent on every page of the surviving literature. Greek Jews nowhere raised the question of whether torah really means *nomos*, law! And whenever they defended their Jewish convictions, it was always on the premise, startling to modern Jewish students, that *nomos* did adequately translate *torah*. To Palestinian Jews, and their spiritual descendants, the word torah never had so restricted a connotation; they equated *torah* with our word 'revelation.' While they would have conceded that torah was a revelation which *included* 'law,' they would properly have denied that revelation and 'law' were interchangeable." Oddly enough, when Theophilus uses the Greek term νόμος he is typically referring to God's revelation regarding the moral way a life should be lived.

34. Paul seems to promote the idea of such primal law in Romans 1, making it quite clear that he was not suggesting by his later statement that man was not morally responsible before Mosaic law was enforced. Rather, his statement must be read as a polemic against Mosaic law as the sole arbiter of morality and salvation. Unlike Paul, Theophilus is not given to making polemics against Mosaic law. He embraces what he wants of it and then expands the concept of nomos to include the law of creation, of the garden, of the prophets and of the gospels, but he finds nothing in the term nomos itself to take sharp issue with. He has no perceptible bias against any particular notion of biblical nomos. For discussions of Paul and his understanding of the the law, see A. F. Segal, *Paul the Convert* (New Haven: Yale University Press, 1990), 255-67; E. Sanders, *Paul, the Law, and the Jewish People* (Minneapolis: Fortress, 1983), 123-35; F. Watson, *Paul, Judaism and the Gentiles* (Cambridge: Cambridge University Press, 1986), 102-9; and again S. Sandmel, *The Genius of Paul* (New York: Schocken Books, 1970), particularly 36-60. Sandmel offers an intriguing comparison of Philo and Paul. He says, in general terms: "Philo's acceptance of torah as *nomos* is paralleled, though not precisely, by Paul" (47).

35. While Theophilus speaks of those Hebrew Bible authors who are commonly included in the collection of books called the Nevi'im as prophets, as we will see, he also seems to include Adam, Moses, Solomon (and perhaps even Jesus and Paul) in this same category. Theophilus may not have thought of Jesus and Paul as Hebrew prophets, as he clearly does Adam, Moses and Solomon, but he offers nothing which would suggest a good reason for excluding them from his category of true prophets.

36. Cf. *Mishnah Avot* 1:2, which says, "By three things is the world sustained: by the law, by the [temple-]service, and by deeds of loving-kindness."

37. R. M. Grant, *Greek Apologists*, 162.

38. See Justin's *I Apology* 20.1, 44.12; Athenagoras' *Legatio* 30.1; Tatian's *Oratio Ad Graecos* 41.1; Hermas 2.4.1; and the discussions by R. M. Grant, *Greek Apologists*, 15, 103-4 and 134. Theophilus quotes the Sibyl only in his second book (2.3, 31 and 36), but always approvingly.

39. Given the Gospel allusion (Luke 1:35), "power of the most high," this passage could be seen as a veiled reference to the pre-existent Christ.

40. For example, the logos is the ἀρχη; in 1.3, and the δύναμις and the σοφία in 2.22.

41. See 2.37, where Theophilus contrasts the reliability of the Hebrew prophets with the Greek poets, who may not have always been forthcoming.

42. Presumably this included selected passages of the Sibyl. As was suggested earlier, this text could be read as depreciating the Hebrew prophets capacity to fully understand what they reported and recorded, given that Christians "hold" the truth for which the prophets are the "instruments" of transmission. However, I do not think this is Theophilus' intent.

43. Cf. I Peter 4:3; and the "apostolic decree" in Acts 15:20 & 29, of which R. M. Grant (*AA*, 85, note 1) points out that Theophilus' list of abstentions and his quotation of the "negative golden rule," is the text of Codex Bezae.

44. He quotes Isaiah ten times in all (2.35, 38; 3.11, 12, 14). He quotes Jeremiah six times (3.11, 12). He quotes Hosea four times (2.38, 3.12). Using the divisions of the Hebrew Bible, while the bishop quotes the Torah eleven times (Genesis seven times and Exodus four times) and the Ketuvim seven times (the Psalms twice and Proverbs five times), he quotes from the Nevi'im or Prophets twenty-six times.

45. This is his reading of Genesis 2:23-24. It is on the basis of this passage alone that R. M. Grant, *AA*, ix, claims that Theophilus was probably married.

46. Compare the similar claim for Adam in Qur'anic teachings (Surah 3.33-34).

47. Cf. 3.23. The fact that the bishop uses different Greek words (2.10— ὑπουργός and 3.9—θεράπων), which are both translated by R. M. Grant as "servant," is probably not a highly important point. But it does suggest a possible reservation on Theophilus' part with identifying the logos too closely with an actual person.

48. An interesting choice of words. Why did the bishop use διάταξις in this instance rather than the more common ἐντολή? He could also have used synonyms like διάταγμα or διαταγή. Rather, he chose an obscure term that is more often used for describing how things are ordered, like troops on a battle field or topics in a book. Perhaps the key is in the LXX Psalm 118:91, which says: "By your command (διάταξις) the day continues; for all things are your servants (δοῦλα)." This Greek word διάταξις may have occurred in what was for Theophilus an important context. Could it be that the linkage in the Psalm of these two ideas, command and servant, led the bishop to his description of the logos as both command and servant?

49. See especially 2.10 in this regard.

50. Cf. his comment on the Gospels in 3.13.

51. Quoting Matthew 5:44f.

52. The Greek text reads ὁ ἡμῶν λόγος.

53. Although Theophilus includes the "gospels" in the teaching of δικαιοσύνη he does not quote any Gospel text to support his several texts from the Nevi'im.

54. See the chart on "A Fourfold Division of Secondary Nomos." In 3.13 he quotes Proverbs 4:25-26 and 6:27-29 to support Matthew 5:28 and 32 on the matter of chastity (σεμνότης), and in 3.14 he quotes Titus 3:1; I Timothy 2:1-2; Romans 13:7-8 to support Matthew 5:44-46 and 6:3 on the subject of good will (εὔνοια).

55. Once again, one must keep in mind the protreptic nature of the bishop's project in *Ad Autolycum*.

56. His Johannine quotations (2.22) even seem to have about them a perfunctory character: "Hence the holy scriptures and all those inspired by the spirit teach us, *and one of them*, John, says . . ." That is not to say the Gospel of John is any less precious to him than the scriptures of the Hebrews. But rather to point out that John's information regarding the logos is not only consistent with them, but a part of the larger recognized authority of "holy scripture." Theophilus does not seem willing in *Ad Autolycum* to suggest that a New Testament document should take priority over the Hebrew scriptures.

57. Again, this is not to say that the bishop did not use the logos to develop a christological perspective, like that of Ignatius or some of the apologists, elsewhere in the context of an ecclesiastical theology.

58. While Theophilus' *Ad Autolycum* clearly does not teach the christology of Acts 4:12 ("And there is salvation in no one else, for there is no other name under heaven given among men by which we must be saved."), nor does he teach an ecclesiology equivalent to that of Cyprian's *Epistles* (*"Extra ecclesiam nulla salus."* See *ANF*, volume 5, 378, as well as, 318 and 333.).

59. Whereas the earlier schematic on the Theophilian dispensations of man was presented so as to demonstrate the bishop's theory of human nature and development, the following schematic on the Theophilian dispensations of nomos is presented so as to demonstrate his theory on the evolution of the divine law.

PART THREE:
AN ANALYSIS

Chapter 6

A Protreptic Theology

In this chapter I am addressing the nature of what I have called Theophilus' protreptic theology. The first section below observes how the bishop defines a Christian. The second section, which is closely connected to the first, is an analysis of a key, though somewhat surprising, feature of his theology. As I have mentioned throughout this study Theophilus' extant writings do not make any reference to the historical Jesus or the person of Christ. While this literary disinterest in Jesus is not dissimilar from other second-century writings on Christian apologetics, it is highly peculiar given the bishop's attempt to offer his readers a refined definition of what it means to be a Christian. My analysis of this feature of the bishop's work will of necessity include a critique of a highly intriguing and carefully argued thesis by R. M. Grant, one of the most well known early church historians of our day.

Defining a Christian

Theophilus calls himself a Christian. What does he think a Christian is? While the bishop does not mention the name of Jesus or his title "the Christ" anywhere in his three extant books, this fact alone does not mean he failed to write about the historical Jesus or the Christ of faith elsewhere. After all, many of his reported writings have not survived. Nevertheless, as we have already seen, J. Bentivegna has called Theophilus' doctrine, "a Christianity without a Christ."[1] His central comment in this regard is worth repeating:

> After having read the work of Theophilus . . . nobody would have the slightest idea that Christian doctrine might have anything to do with the person of Christ.[2]

Therefore, Bentivegna has concluded that Theophilus' work contains no "real" christology. But, he adds, given Theophilus' "explanation of the faith of Christians," his teachings could be called a "christianology."[3] That is to say, Theophilus proposes a study of what it means to be a Christian.

In the light of Bentivegna's observation, consider the bishop's precise language regarding the term "Christian" (Χριστιανός). In the opening chapter of the *Homilia,* Theophilus says to Autolycus:

> You call me a Christian (χριστιανὸν) as if I were bearing an evil name, I acknowledge that I am a Christian (χριστιανός). I bear this name beloved by God (θεοφιλὲς) in the hope of being useful (εὔχρηστος) to God. (1.1)

Obviously there is a significantly negative history surrounding the term Christian to which Theophilus forcefully objects. In no uncertain terms he makes it clear from the outset of his trilogy that he is a Christian and proud to be one. In the closing chapter of the *Homilia,* Theophilus defines, in provocative language, what it means to be a Christian. He says:

> As for your ridiculing me when you call me a Christian (χριστιανόν), you do not know what you are saying. In the first place, what is anointed (χριστὸν) is sweet and useful (εὔχρηστον), not ridiculous. What boat can be useful (εὔχρηστον) and seaworthy (σώζεσθαι) unless it is first caulked (χρισθῇ)? What tower or house is attractive and useful (εὔχρηστός) unless it is whitewashed (κέχρισται)? What man on entering this life or being an athlete is not anointed with oil (χρίεται ἐλαίῳ)? What work of art or ornament can possess attractiveness unless it is greased (χρισθῇ) and polished? Furthermore, the air and everything under heaven is anointed (χρίεται), so to speak, by light and spirit (φωτὶ καὶ πνεύματι). Do you not want to be anointed with the oil of God (χρισθῆναι ἔλαιον θεοῦ)? We are actually called Christians just because we are anointed with the oil of God (χριστιανοί ὅτι χριόμεθα ἔλαιον θεοῦ). (1.12)

In these two texts Theophilus does not expose the nature of the ridicule he believed was directed at him when the Greek term Χριστιανός was used, except to say that those using it seem to have thought it denoted something "evil."[4] Furthermore, the bishop admits to being exceedingly proud of his own Greek name, "Theophilus" (θεόφιλος), which he points out is linguistically related to the term "beloved of God" (θεοφιλές). Nevertheless, his primary concern is that his readers understand the precise meaning and significance of the honorable title "Christian."

In the first passage above (1.1), Theophilus suggests a connection between the terms "Christian" and "usefulness," although he does not explain in so many words how he as a Christian (Χριστιανός) intends to be useful (εὔχρηστος). Clearly he has more to say about the matter in the second passage (1.12). Here he employs the term "useful" three times in an obvious play on the sounds of several Greek words, especially the substantive τὸ χριστὸν (the anointed).[5] But, of course, this phonetic similarity is not the most significant relationship between these terms. Theophilus appears to be saying that "what is τὸ χριστόν is εὔχρηστον."[6] In other words, the thing that is anointed in some fashion—as a boat is "caulked," a tower or house is "whitewashed," a baby or athlete is "oiled," an art work or ornament is "greased or polished"—is thus made useful. Or maybe "rightly serviceable" is an even better definition of the Greek word εὔχρηστον in this context. In fact, Theophilus explicitly says that anointing is in a sense a universal event in that God's entire creation was anointed by light (φῶς) and pneuma (πνεῦμα). Though he qualified this claim ("so to speak"), it seems the bishop is pointing out that what God has made is not arbitrary. Everything serves a purpose. In this regard he may well have considered the Septuagint Psalm 118:91, which says: "The day continues by your arrangement (διατάξει); for all things are your servants (δοῦλα)." As was pointed out before, this biblical passage may have specifically suggested the notion of the logos as servant, but it also supports the bishop's general teaching that all of creation has a role to play in the divine plan.

Therefore, using his several analogies, the reader is being taught an appropriate definition for this highly significant title, Χριστιανός. Theophilus has gone to some trouble to make sure his definition is understood, that is: "We are actually called Christians just because we are anointed with the oil of God" (1.12).[7] It would appear the bishop, at least in *Ad Autolycum,* is of the opinion that it is not the personal noun "Christ" (Χριστός) but the verbs "anoint" (χρίω) and "to be anointed" (χρίσθηναι) which provide the primary etymological meaning for the term Christian. Thus, Theophilus seems to be inviting Autolycus not to follow a particular person who is a "christ" (an anointed one), but simply to "be anointed with the oil of God" himself. Given the candid and assertive nature of the bishop's explanation, I think it is unlikely that Theophilus' readers would have misunderstood his point.

Having appropriately defined the title Christian as one who has been anointed, consider Theophilus' brief comment on the nature of this anointing. There is something called "the oil of God" (τὸ ἔλαιον θεοῦ), mentioned here but nowhere else in the bishop's three books. What is this oil of God? It seems to be a physical substance with which to anoint a person, even Autolycus if he desires it. To my mind it is plausible to suggest that Theophilus is a baptist. When he later addresses the "repentance and remission of sins through water and a bath of regeneration" (2.16), in his *Syngramma,* he appears to be speaking of the ritual anointing called baptism. Thus, the waters of that "bath of regeneration" are surely his symbolic oil of God. He does not specifically allude to the olive oil of the chrismatory used in the prebaptismal and postbaptismal anointings of the early western or Syrian traditions.[8] At any rate, whether he is speaking of water or oil, it is the function of this anointing that he seeks to emphasize. The purpose of this oil of God is not so much to identify people as Christians as it is to initiate believers in Christian service. That is to say, this ritual symbolically appoints people to a titled office making them serviceable to do their divinely ordained and soteriologically effective duty.

There are two matters regarding Theophilus' definition of the term Christian which concern me, a minor one and a major one. Let me address the minor one now and the more serious one at the conclusion of this chapter. It seems to me that some of the bishop's fastidious Greek readers might have objected to his eccentric usage of the term Χριστιανός for the anointed one, when technically the term χριστός (christ) would have been the more obvious choice. In other words, etymologically, being anointed should identify one as a "Christ" more than as a "Christian." If this is so, an educated Greek reader could have asked, then why doesn't Theophilus simply call himself a Christ and abandon the term Christian altogether? Unfortunately his extant books yield nothing with which to formulate a certain answer to this question. However, given his wide reading of the New Testament and its specific usage of the title Christ and given the entrenchment of the term Christian in the second-century ecclesiastical tradition, especially at Antioch,[9] I doubt that the bishop would ever have thought of himself or any of the members of his community as Christs.[10]

Disinterest in Jesus

R. M. Grant claims that the most surprising feature of Theophilus' theology is its "complete silence in regard to Jesus and his acts."[11] Theophilus of Antioch, the author of *Ad Autolycum,* identifies himself as a Christian even though he appears to ignore the historical Jesus.[12] In fact, Theophilus is silent regarding not only Jesus, the Christ, but also the incarnation and the passion, both of which were important in the development of second-century Christian theories of sacrificial atonement.[13] It should also be pointed out, in what many scholars consider to be comparable literature of this period, that neither of the works of Athenagoras of Athens nor of Tatian the Syrian mentions the name of Jesus or the title of Christ. H. Y. Gamble explains this phenomenon of apparent disinterest in the historical Jesus as a matter of apologetic convention and scope. He says:

> The Christianity of the apologists, however, cannot be read off the apologies alone. Their projects were so focused on specific criticisms that they appear to support hardly more than monotheism, moral responsibility, and the expectation of resurrection and judgment and to be uninterested in Jesus as a human figure, in the corporate life of the Christian community, or in the deeper resources and expression of early Christian piety. The apologists were not disingenuous, but their task was of limited scope.[14]

Observe that Gamble is speaking of the lack of certain apologetic interest in Jesus as a "human figure" and not necessarily as a divine one. However, Gamble's point is well taken when one considers the scope of apologists like Justin, Athenagoras and Tatian. These authors, given their perceptions of hostile audiences and of a need for immediate and reciprocal responses, do not draw specific attention to the story of the historical Jesus, discuss ecclesiastical matters or explore the foundations of Christian piety. They were preoccupied with self-defense and community preservation. Be that as it may, one should keep in mind that the scope of Justin's apologies did not deter him from mentioning Jesus and the Christ.[15] If, however, the question of appropriate scope did deter Athenagoras and Tatian, as it might have Theophilus, one should also observe that the socio-political context of their apologies was much more limiting than was that of the bishop's *Ad Autolycum*. This collection of books appears to be written in a context free enough to not only address "the deeper resources and expression of early Christian piety," but to take on as we have seen the additional task of carefully defining what the term "Christian" actually means (1.12).[16]

Having acknowledged that Theophilus does not provide his readers with a christological discussion, let us see what Athenagoras and Tatian offered the formation of an early christology. It is fascinating to observe that, unlike Theophilus, neither Athenagoras or Tatian sought to define a Christian. Nevertheless, Athenagoras—though not directly dealing with the incarnation or passion, and as we have said, without mentioning the name of Jesus—does discuss at some considerable length trinitarian ideas in his book *Legatio*. He acknowledges "men . . . who [speak of] God the Father, God the son, and the holy spirit; and who proclaim both their power in their unity and their diversity in rank" (*Legatio* 10.5). Furthermore, he contends:

> We say that there is God, and the son his word, and the holy spirit, united in power yet distinguished in rank as the Father, the son, and the spirit, since the son is mind, reason, and wisdom of the Father, and the spirit an effluence like light from fire. (*Legatio* 24.2)[17]

As a longtime student and translator of Athenagoras' work, W. R. Schoedel has said of this apologist:

> Athenagoras' doctrine of God culminates in trinitarian theology. For apologetic reasons, however, he avoids its most controversial feature—the doctrine of the incarnation.[18]

However, in one instance, Athenagoras does ask an incarnationally interesting question: "Yet if a god assumes flesh by divine dispensation (οἰκονομίαν), is he forthwith a slave of lust?" (*Legatio* 21.4). In posing this rhetorical question, Schoedel says:

> Athenagoras anticipates objections which could be directed on the same grounds against the Christian "dispensation" [οἰκονομία]—a term by now virtually technical for "incarnation."[19]

Whether or not Schoedel is correct, it seems to me that in the light of Athenagoras' trinitarian and sonship language, one might reasonably infer from this question his capacity to defend a Christian belief in divine incarnation. Nevertheless, with respect to the quality of Athenagoras' theological language, Schoedel believes he can claim:

> Athenagoras anticipates later "orthodox" teaching in his emphasis on
> the distinctions within the godhead and the eternity of the word,
> [even though] the "generation" of the son is still bound up with his
> emission for the purpose of creation.[20]

Tatian, in contrast to Athenagoras, is inclined to offer nuggets suggestive of
his explicit understanding of the theological role of the historical Jesus.[21] In his
book, *Oratio Ad Graecos,* this Syrian claims to be a disciple of the "barbarian
philosophy" that is Christianity (*Oratio* 35, 42). He says, at one point:

> We are not fools, men of Greece, nor are we talking nonsense when
> we declare that *God has been born in the form of man.* You who
> abuse us should compare your own stories with our narratives. (*Oratio* 21)

In the context of a withering attack on pagan mythology Tatian clearly defends
the idea of the incarnation.[22] In an earlier passage located in a discussion of the
doctrine of the two spirits, the material spirit and the divine spirit, Tatian seems
to be making a reference to the passion as well. He says:

> God's spirit is not given to all, but dwelling among some who be-
> haved justly and being intimately connected with the soul it revealed
> by predictions to the other souls what had been hidden. The souls
> which were obedient to wisdom attracted to themselves the *kindred
> spirit,* but those which were disobedient and rejected *the servant of
> the suffering God* were clearly shown to be enemies of God rather
> than his worshippers. (*Oratio* 13)

Tatian maintains that his philosophy teaches "that God has been born in the form
of man" and that the disobedient rejected "the servant of the suffering God." The
"suffering God" may refer to the crucified Jesus,[23] and thus the phrase appears to
support the idea that Tatian promoted a divine Christ figure. Furthermore, the
"servant" of this God is probably the "kindred spirit," which no doubt inspires
Tatian himself, as a soul "obedient to wisdom." Thus, this servant/kindred spirit
may very well be the third element of Tatian's trinity. With regard to this Syrian
apologist, Eusebius informs us that in Tatian's writings, "Christ is spoken of as
God" (*EH* 5.28.5). In summary, even though they do not mention Jesus or Christ
by name, the extant works of Athenagoras and Tatian can be examined more
easily for some sort of explicit christology.

What is so peculiar in Theophilus' extant books is his lack of any hint about
the incarnation, the passion, and the resurrection of Christ, or for that matter the
trinity.[24] Theophilus simply has nothing to say about Jesus or the Christ within
the scope of *Ad Autolycum.*[25] The most obvious explanation for this phenomenon, discounting any charge of being disingenuous, is that Theophilus' theological needs in *Ad Autolycum* do not require any christological discussion.
Although peculiar, given the theological content of his writings, this christological lacuna in *Ad Autolycum* alone does not mean he failed to write about the his-

torical Jesus or the Christ of faith elsewhere. After all, many of his reported writings have not survived. However, the expectation on the part of modern readers that Theophilus' *Ad Autolycum* would offer some christological content, at least comparable to what Athenagoras and Tatian have put forth, should not surprise anyone. It seems extraordinary to me that Theophilus would have been more successful than they were at suppressing unneeded material of this nature.

Now with regard to Theophilus' greater scope and opportunity for christological discourse, consider the following argument. On the one hand, the bishop wrote what I believe are three independent works over a period of perhaps several years. While these three books are linked together as conversations with a particular individual, Autolycus, they yet retain their own unique qualities, so much so, that it can be said they possess a variety of topical concerns reflecting distinguishable purposes. In other words, on the basis of the length and depth of his acknowledged relationship with Autolycus and the range of interests revealed by the books themselves, it is reasonable to anticipate some suggestion of a christology. On the other hand, Athenagoras and Tatian have left only one academically oriented treatise apiece and, in both instances, they seem more strictly defined in scope than the books of *Ad Autolycum*. Actually, Theophilus' three books, taken together, account for nearly twice as much written material as is preserved for either Athenagoras or Tatian. And, moreover, the type of material preserved by the bishop allowed for a considerably wider expression of Christian concerns.

The point behind all of this comparative information can be stated as follows: Theophilus may have chosen not to mention Jesus or the Christ as did both Athenagoras and Tatian, but it does not appear in his case for lack of opportunity. Where these two apologists had limited their scope, offering no theological explanation for how they chose to identify themselves, the bishop actually expanded his scope, even to the degree of explaining the derivation of the name "Christian." The bishop's variety of preserved materials and its sheer amount distinguish him from the other two men and thus it seems to me would have allowed him the latitude to discuss Jesus or the Christ in a less hostile and perhaps more receptive context than they may have had.[26] Nevertheless, whether Theophilus would have disagreed with Athenagoras and Tatian (not to mention Ignatius and Justin) regarding the role of Jesus, or simply thought that any such christological suggestions might interfere with his project, the extraordinary fact remains that such material is clearly absent from *Ad Autolycum*. While I do not wish to put too fine a point on it here, I will be suggesting in the conclusion of this book that Theophilian Christianity, as it is framed in *Ad Autolycum,* may not anticipate later Nicene standards in the same way that many other second-century Christian theologies seem to do. By this I do not mean to suggest in any way that he would have promoted heresy.

However, one modern scholar has suggested just that. R. M. Grant has made a case for defining Theophilus' reconstructed christology as a good example of a Jewish-Christian theology that would describe the role of Jesus only in human-prophetic terms, that is, as an example of "low christology." Grant begins this reconstruction on the basis of what I have already acknowledged to be a significant feature of Theophilus' theology, namely, the "complete" silence regarding Jesus and any of his salvific acts. In what follows I will attempt to present Grant's case and then offer an evaluation of it.

Grant's presentation of what he takes to be Theophilus' christology is found in two of his most recent books.[27] These discussions are the culmination of a lifetime of work in patristics and the summary of a massive number of his own articles on this particular bishop. After discussing several examples of second-century christological teachings, Grant contrasts Theophilus' thought primarily with that of Justin and Irenaeus, claiming:

> A very different kind of christology appears in the writings of Theophilus of Antioch . . . . His views will seem strange, but we recall that in his time there was wide diversity over this doctrine even at Rome. There Theodotus of Byzantium identified Jesus as a man who was born of a virgin and worked miracles after the Christ, the spirit "in the form of a dove," entered him. He became God either when the spirit descended or after he rose from the dead. Theodotus' followers went on to claim that this had been the apostolic doctrine at Rome to the end of the second century but was then falsified.[28]

Theodotus is often cited as an example of adoptionist christology, and Grant believes that Theophilus' "christological" language, such as it is, is closer to Theodotus than to Justin or Irenaeus. Actually, I would prefer to say it is Theophilus' theological language (which lacks the particular type of christological content found in Justin and Irenaeus) that leaves the bishop open to an adoptionist charge, and a possible ideological connection with this Theodotus. Nevertheless, Theophilus' connection to an adoptionist position is the point of Grant's argument.

This observation, Grant admits, is not exactly original. He cites A. Robinson, who made the rather confessionally oriented claim that in Theophilus' writings:

> There is no Christian theology, properly so called, propounded: the Incarnation, Passion, Resurrection of our Lord are not mentioned; the very names Christ and Jesus are absent: the Gospels are referred to only in passing for moral precepts.[29]

In a similar vein Grant discusses a highly provocative article, mentioned and briefly quoted above, by J. Bentivegna. As we have seen, Bentivegna maintained that Theophilus' *Ad Autolycum* was "a Christianity without Christ." Grant noticed that this line of thought resonated the concerns of S. Laeuchli, who criticized Theophilus' teachings as "the first grave problem of Christian apologetic language."[30] Laeuchli believed that the Hellenistic reader of *Ad Autolycum* could have been "converted to diaspora Judaism" as easily as to Christianity.[31] According to Grant, "clearly Theophilus is a Christian" but "he is also a Hellenistic Jewish theologian."[32] It is not my intent here to evaluate that particular statement, but simply to discuss Grant's sense that with Theophilus' *Ad Autolycum*, we have a theology, and perhaps a christology, that corresponds with a position that would later be declared heretical.

Having highlighted Theophilus' teachings on God's transcendence and what he calls Theophilus' doctrine of "reticent monotheism,"[33] as well as the bishop's unique reading of the logos' function as divine thought and word, Grant hones in on what he believes Theophilus would have said about the role of Jesus. He claims Theophilus' silence about Jesus is based on his "peculiar doctrine about Christ"[34] or his "unique christology."[35] This "peculiar doctrine" does however include, according to Grant, a singular allusion to Jesus. In his words:

> All Theophilus could really say about Jesus is that he was born after the "power of the most high" came down upon Mary (Luke 1:35, alluded to in 2.10). Theophilus seems to believe in the virginal conception but not the incarnation. He thus resembles the adoptionist Theodotus of Byzantium, who taught that "Christ was a man like others but born of a virgin by the will of God when the holy spirit overshadowed her."[36]

However, the passage in *Ad Autolycum,* from which Grant is quoting, is a discussion of how the creation is accomplished through the work of the logos and, it seems to me, not a covert description of Jesus. The text explicitly says that a further function of the logos is to reveal the story of creation. Consider Theophilus' words:

> It was [logos], spirit of God and beginning and sophia and power of the most high, who came down into the prophets and spoke through them about the creation of the world and all the rest. (2.10)

However one might argue an implicit reference to Jesus in this passage, it is on the foundation of the bishop's use of this unique phrase, "power of the most high," that Grant argues Theophilus is primarily working with the Gospel of Luke.[37]

Grant expands upon his claim that Theophilus is using the Gospel of Luke in an analysis of an important anthropological discussion in *Ad Autolycum.* He says of Theophilus:

> He used Luke's verse about the infant Jesus for his portrait of the infant Adam (2.24-25), and claimed that God gave Adam an "aptitude for progress (Luke 2:52) so that he might grow" in stature (Luke 1:80, 2:40) and thinking (equivalent to the "wisdom" of Luke 2:40, 52). In this context he used the expression "with God and men" (Luke 2:52) and spoke of human beings as "subject to parents" (Luke 2:51, 43)—though obviously neither statement could properly be made of Adam. There were no other humans in Adam's infancy, and he had no parents. Theophilus also notes that children must be obedient to God (cf. Luke 2:49), a point irrelevant to the early life of Adam, except insofar as Adam could be called "son of God" (Luke 3:38).[38]

Convinced that Theophilus is using Luke's language to correlate the life of Jesus with that of Adam and perhaps with other Jewish heroes,[39] Grant sees the makings of Theophilus' unique christology in Lucan terms.[40] He says of Theophilus' position:

> Adam was created neither mortal nor immortal but with two potentialities. If he had really progressed, he would have become "mature" or "perfect" (Eph. 4:13; cf. Matt. 5:48), would have been "declared a god," as Jesus was declared (John 20:28), and would have ascended into heaven, as Jesus did (Luke 24:52). This picture implies that neither Adam nor Jesus was originally perfect. Theophilus relies on the Jewish Christian doctrine of Christ as the second Adam, partly in agreement with I Corinthians 15:45-49 and Philippians 2:5:11 (he knows both letters) and partly in an even more Jewish manner. Nemesius of Emesa tells us that "the Jews say that man was created neither mortal nor immortal but in a state poised between the two." This is Theophilus' doctrine.[41]

The Syrian, Nemesius, who was bishop of Emesa around 390, is a fascinating parallel. Nemesius employed the philosophical, medical and ethical discussions of his day in the composition of his sole surviving work, *On the Nature of Man*.[42] Grant's quotation from this work not only demonstrates the prevalence of a particular doctrinal notion, but, given Nemesius' favorable leanings toward this so-called Jewish conception, it suggests a possible Syrian theological connection extending back to at least the work of Theophilus. However, all that Grant has said so far regarding Theophilus' christological position is brought to a climax in a Pauline context.

Grant suspects that Theophilus is substituting Adam for Christ in selected New Testament passages so as to set the stage for his "revision" of and likely polemic against Pauline christology (and, of course, Pauline soteriology too). His demonstration of this matter is presented by paralleling a passage from Theophilus (*Ad Autolycum* 2.27) with similar texts from Paul (Romans 5:15-21; 7:12; I Cor. 15:50) that "contrast Adam in the past with humanity in the present."[43] The Theophilian passage in question formulates this contrast, he says, "without any explicit reference to Christ."[44] Consider the following passages as they are laid out by Grant:

Ad Autolycum 2:27	**Romans 5:15-21**
What Man acquired for himself through his neglect and disobedience, God now freely gives him through love and mercy.	Many died through one man's trespass. The grace of God and the free gift abound for many.
For as by disobedience *man* gained death for himself, so by obedience to the will of God . . .	As by *one man's* disobedience many were made sinners, so by *one man's* obedience . . .

Now Theophilus, says Grant, "begins to diverge rather sharply from Paul's christological statement."[45] Continuing the above quotations:

whoever will can obtain eternal life for himself. For God gave us a law and holy commandments; *everyone* who does them can be saved and attaining to the resurrection can inherit imperishability.	many will be made righteous to eternal life. 7:12 – The law is holy and the commandment is holy and just and good (cf. Gal. 3:12). I Cor. 15:50 – inherit imperishability.

Setting aside the question as to whether these ought to be categorized as christological or soteriological discussions, what does Grant conclude from this purported Theophilian revision of Pauline doctrine? He says:

> Theophilus insists that God will reward those who seek imperishability through good works and strongly emphasizes justice as a virtue proclaimed by the prophets and the holy law of God . . . . His Jewish Christian emphasis on obedience to the law of justice makes him view the work of Christ as exemplary, not efficacious.[46]

Grant also mentions one other passage in which he contends that Theophilus "rephrased Paul" thus "intentionally or not, minimized the saving work of Christ."[47] In the heat of debate Theophilus reminds Autolycus that he once supposed the bishop's "message (logos) to be foolishness" (2.1). In contrast, Paul had said of nonbelievers: "For the [message] (logos) of the cross is [foolishness] to those who are perishing, but to us who are being saved it is the power of God" (I Corinthians 1:18).

In the light of what he takes to be Theophilus' genuine understanding of the role of Jesus and implicit christology, Grant goes on to compare the bishop's thought with the heretical doctrines of the Ebionites and the "certain unorthodoxy" of the *Clementine Homilies*. Maintaining the accuracy of his portrait of the Theophilian Jesus, Grant does concede a difficulty in coordinating the

bishop's "picture of Jesus" with "his doctrine of logos and sophia."[48] Nevertheless, Grant adds:

> If Jesus differed from others, it was in the obedience for which God
> finally gave him the name above every name and made him Lord and
> Christ (Phil. 2:8-9) or, indeed, God (2.27). Theophilus does refer to
> the logos of God as "also his son," but the logos is preexistent, not
> incarnate (2.22). And while he does allude to a verse in Luke about
> the conception of Jesus (2.10), this goes no further than Theodotus of
> Byzantium, who used the same verse.[49]

Thus, Grant believes that Theophilus' teachings "did justice" to certain aspects
of New Testament thought, like Luke's, and not to others, like Paul's. Furthermore, Grant says, Theophilus' so-called "reticent monotheism" represents a
"sharp break" at Antioch with the incarnational christology of Ignatius, and so
demonstrates in this quarter a "startling diversity" in second-century theology.[50]

While I hope this discussion has done justice to Grant's presentation of
Theophilus' understanding of the role of Jesus in Christian theology, I think that
a fair critique of his deeply informed analysis would not have been possible
without our consideration of the genre of the documents collectively known as
Ad Autolycum and our thorough study of the theology within those documents.
For this reason, I did not want to address Grant's controversial thesis until after
the primary work of this book. I would like to credit him with the persistent observation of what I believe is truly a peculiar "missing-Jesus" feature in Theophilian theology. In fact it is because of the comprehensive nature of this feature
that I do not believe Theophilus' theology in *Ad Autolycum* supplies us with
enough data to suggest, let alone reconstruct, his christology per se. Thus, I cannot join Grant in proposing a description of Theophilus' christology, at least not
in terms of the person of Jesus. However, the theological discourse of *Ad
Autolycum* does supply us with a soteriology that I believe is not muted by this
"missing Jesus" feature. And so, while appreciating Grant's observations and
without minimizing his suspicions, I am reluctant to embrace all of his conclusions.[51]

So let me offer a modest critique of the thesis and speculations of R. M.
Grant. Grant has presented an interesting thesis, namely, that Theophilus' silence about Jesus is based on his "peculiar doctrine about Christ" or his "unique
christology." While Grant parallels Theophilus' theology with the adoptionist
christology of Theodotus, it seems to me that the implied adoptionist charge is
built on an argument from "silence." I am not at all sure that Theophilus' silence
regarding Jesus should necessarily lead us to assume with Grant that the sixth
bishop of Antioch was a promoter of a low christology. It may be true that
Theophilian Christianity, as framed in *Ad Autolycum,* may not anticipate later
Nicene standards in the same way that many other second-century Christian theologies seem to do. However, that is not to say that Theophilus of Antioch,
bishop of a Syrian Christian church, did not have a great deal to say about Jesus,
his divinity and perhaps even the salvific nature of his acts elsewhere. Moreover,

given that Theophilus is a bishop in the Christian church, given that he is in good standing with Eusebius and Jerome (two preeminent representatives of the later orthodox community), and given that he makes use of a number of New Testament texts (especially the Gospel of John, with its high christology), it seems likely that he would have believed in both the incarnation and the passion of Jesus the Christ.[52]

While I found Grant's thesis seductive, my own analyses of the bishop's doctrines in *Ad Autolycum* and my identification of these doctrines as protreptic theology leave me much less inclined to argue on his behalf. This is not to say that I have not benefited from his observations and speculations, but only that his thesis, and the wealth of insight behind it, lies beyond the evidence that I have been able to gather. Therefore, on the basis of my research, I have come to the following conclusions regarding Grant's thesis. While the protreptic theology of *Ad Autolycum* presents us with a nomos-based soteriology, it is entirely possible that the ecclesiastical theology of the sixth bishop of the Christian church at Antioch would have contained a passion-based soteriology. Further, while the protreptic theology of *Ad Autolycum* may recommend a low christology in which the preexistent logos inspired Jesus in his adult life as a prophet, it is entirely possible the ecclesiastical theology of the sixth bishop of the Christian church at Antioch would have involved a high christology in which the pre-existent logos became incarnate in Jesus at his conception. While *Ad Autolycum* does not speak of, or even hint at, the incarnation or passion of Jesus, there is no evidence in these documents to suggest that the sixth bishop of Antioch did not teach such ideas in his Christian church and there celebrate the Holy Eucharist.

Grant has also made another bold claim regarding Theophilus, contending that he was "a radical Judaizer who upheld the liberal Judaism of the Diaspora."[53] He adds:

> The existence of Theophilus as bishop of Antioch proves conclusively the indistinctness of the line between orthodoxy and heresy in the late second century, as well as of the line between Judaism and Christianity.[54]

Before commenting let me address one element of the bishop's thought that might have led Grant to make this claim. In *Ad Autolycum* Theophilus did not explicitly seek to develop a polemic against Judaism. When it came to Antiochene Jewish influence, even though we know very little about its distinguishing marks, Theophilus clearly was not on the same page with his famous predecessor, Ignatius, for example.

There are several polemical passages in Ignatius' letters that even though they were occasioned by particular controversies in the Asian churches nevertheless must reflect his experience of the religious environment of Antioch. To paraphrase what I take to be Ignatius' concern, the religion of Judaism was obsolete and Jewish teachings within the church were at least heterodox if not heretical.[55] He said:

> Do not be deceived by strange doctrines or antiquated myths, since they are worthless. For if we continue to live in accordance with Judaism, we admit that we have not received grace . . . . It is utterly absurd to profess Jesus Christ and to practice Judaism. For Christianity (Χριστιανισμός) did not believe in Judaism, but Judaism ('Ιουδαϊσμός) in Christianity, in which "every tongue" believed and "was brought together" to God. (*Magnesians* 8.1, 10.3)

In another place he warns his readers to beware false teaching, but also seems to make an interesting distinction and judgment regarding the source of that teaching.

> But if anyone expounds Judaism to you, do not listen to him. For it is better to hear about Christianity from a man who is circumcised than about Judaism from one who is not. But if either of them fail to speak about Jesus Christ, I look on them as tombstones and graves of the dead, upon which only the names of men are inscribed. (*Philadelphians* 6:1)

Trying to clarify Ignatius' understanding of Christianity as a separate religion and his understanding of its ethnic origins, W. A. Meeks argues that the second bishop of Antioch is more concerned with certain Gentiles, who most probably were Christians but adopted Jewish practices (i.e., Jewish Christians), than he is with Christians of Jewish origins (i.e., Judaeo-Christians).[56] However, the sixth bishop of Antioch nowhere in *Ad Autolycum* suggests that Hebrew thought was "antiquated myth," as did the second bishop.[57] Clearly Theophilus embraced what he believed to be the morality of the Hebrew scriptures. For him, selected teachings from Jesus' Sermon on the Mount and from Paul's Epistles appear to be reformulations or extensions of the earlier Hebrew morality.

Now returning to Grant's identification of Theophilus with the "liberal Judaism of the Diaspora," I am certain the bishop would not have been attracted to the Rabbinic idea of an eternal pre-existent Torah.[58] Moreover, I do not think he would have promoted the ritual Mosaic law of Hellenistic Judaism. If I am correct then one might ask what sort of liberal Diaspora Judaism Grant has in mind. Perhaps he is thinking of gnostic Judaisms. Nevertheless, it might be better, given the bishop's unmistakable acknowledgement that he is a Christian, to say he held a moralistic form of Christianity that understood nomos as salvific. Furthermore, regarding Grant's conclusion that Theophilus blurs "the line between Judaism and Christianity," it might be better to say that Theophilus' *Ad Autolycum* (not the bishop) represents the "indistinctness of the line between orthodoxy and heresy" within the early church alone.

In conclusion, getting back to Theophilus' definition of the term Christian, it seems to me that some of Theophilus' more educated readers would have been aware of the linguistic connection between the historical Jesus as the "Christ" and the term "Christian." If this is so, then why doesn't the bishop acknowledge this connection as a necessary part of his definition of the term Christian?[59] Again, his extant books yield nothing with which to formulate a certain answer to this question. However, the term Christian is a name or title which he clearly believes is associated with ritual anointing. He says nothing which would suggest that he is ambivalent on this point. Nor does he equivocate on what it means to be a Christian. To be a Christian is to be anointed, to be anointed is to be useful, to be useful is to be law abiding. To be law abiding is a choice to live a righteous life that ultimately leads to immortality.

If one believes the bishop had more to say about Jesus in this regard, then it is possible to conclude that Theophilus' profile of this first-century figure was situated in an appropriate ecclesiastical context and thus a part of an ecclesiastical theology. In any case, one can suggest that the protreptic nature of *Ad Autolycum* would have had much to do with such a self-imposed silence. The protreptic nature of *Ad Autolycum* and its theology—its doctrines on the human condition, the agents of God and the nature of salvation—would have limited the bishop's attention. Theophilus sought Autolycus' conversion. He wanted Autolycus to join his community. So the bishop was careful not to exceed his theoretical needs in formulating an attractive invitation to the Christian faith. He would not have wanted to complicate or do anything that might have distracted his readers. So, what theological material could he dispense with as unessential for his invitation? On the one hand, he certainly could not leave out any information necessary to effect Autolycus' salvation. On the other hand, he could postpone discussions about the person of Christ, whose works may only have been exemplary for human salvation. Without necessarily minimizing the work of Jesus, he must emphasize the moral teachings of Moses, Solomon and the Prophets, along with the reformulations of those teachings by the Gospel voice (what I take to be his selected materials from the New Testament). It is the word of the law in those teachings that the protreptic theology of *Ad Autolycum* must promote. As it stands I think it is fair to say that Theophilus' books present his readers with a protreptic theology that invites them to become Christians by being anointed to a life of law-abiding service to God. With this in mind, let us consider the nature of the religion promoted in *Ad Autolycum*.

Notes

1. J. Bentivegna, "A Christianity Without Christ by Theophilus of Antioch," *Studia patristica* 13 (1975), 107.
2. J. Bentivegna, "A Christianity Without Christ," 128.
3. J. Bentivegna, "A Christianity Without Christ," 128.
4. For an excellent review on how the name was use in the early Christian context see E. Bickerman, "The Name of Christians," *Harvard Theological Review* 42 (1949), 109-24.
5. Notice the compact usage of the bishop's thirteen similar sounding Greek words: χριστιανόν, χριστόν, εὔχρηστον, εὔχρηστον, χρισθῇ, εὔχρηστος, κέχρισται, χρίεται, χρισθῇ, χρίεται, χρισθῆναι, χριστιανοὶ and χριόμεθα.
6. He could have made his point even more obvious by using the slightly less emphatic Greek word χρηστόν (useful), but chose a degree of subtlety.

7. See J. Bentivegna, "A Christianity Without Christ," 108f, who stresses this Theophilian definition. R. M. Grant, *Greek Apologists of the Second Century* (Philadelphia: The Westminster Press, 1988), 146, contends that "Autolycus attacks the name but does not recognize either the utility of oil or the fact that 'Christian' comes from being chrismated with the oil of God."

8. The sacred olive oil blended with myrrh, cinnamon, aromatic cane and cassia, spoken of in Exodus 30:22-25, became the prototype tool for sacred events such as the installations of sanctuaries and cult objects (Exodus 40:9-12), as well as kings, priests and prophets (Isaiah 11:2-9; Psalms 45; 89; 110; Isaiah 42:1; 48:16; 61:1). Olive oil became the choice of many Christians in the prebaptismal anointing, symbolizing healing, exorcism and the enabling of the candidate for battle with Satan. Scented oil was often used after the baptism and it symbolized the gift of the Holy Spirit. See *EEC*, 43-45 and 131-34 for a discussion of recent scholarship on anointing in conjunction with baptism in the early church.

9. See Acts 11:26c—"And in Antioch the disciples were for the first time called Christians."

10. A Latin contemporary of Theophilus, Tertullian, *On Baptism* 7, said: "Aaron is called 'christ,' from the 'chrism,' which is 'the unction'; which, when made spiritual, furnished an appropriate name for the Lord, because he was 'anointed' with the spirit by God the Father . . . . In our case, the unction runs carnally, (i.e. on the body,) but profits spiritually; in the same way as the act of baptism itself too is carnal, in that we are plunged in water, but the effect spiritual, in that we are freed from sins." Tertullian's use of this sort of language may reflect a tradition in which Christians might be referred to as Christs at some point after baptismal anointing. It has been widely argued that Tertullian's theology presents us with a form of adoptionism or a low christology. See *EEC*, 12-13 and 89, for definitions of adoptionism, and R. M. Grant, *Heresy and Criticism: The Search for Authenticity in Early Christian Literature* (Louisville, KY: Knox, 1993), 67-73, for a discussion of adoptionists as biblical scholars. According to this doctrine, the divinity-imparting pneuma is not innate to the historical Jesus. Rather, it is acquired by him at his baptism, when the Father makes Jesus his divine Son.

11. R. M. Grant, *Jesus After the Gospels: The Christ of the Second Century* (Louisville, KY: Knox, 1990), 77. He makes a similar claim in the earlier *Greek Apologists*, 165.

12. The possibility that the bishop understood the logos to be the pre-existent Christ figure uniquely indwelling the person of Jesus from birth, seems plausible and probable given his uncritical use of the Prologue to the Gospel of John, but it is not demonstrable on the evidence of *Ad Autolycum*. Therein lies the problem.

13. F. M. Young, "Atonement," in *EEC*, 115-21. See also the older works be H. E. W. Turner, *The Patristic Doctrine of Redemption* (London: Mowbray, 1952) and F. W. Dillistone, *The Christian Understanding of Atonement* (London: Nisbet, 1968).

14. H. Y. Gamble, "Apologetics," in *EEC*, 70.

15. See Justin's *I Apology* 12.9; 23.2; 34.2; 35.6; 42.4; 63.3, 10; 66.2; 67.7; *II Apology* 6.4, 6; 8.4, 5; and 22.1. He avoided discussing Jesus' history but hardly his status.

16. With regard to differing socio-political contexts, see both W. R. Schoedel's *Athenagoras: Legatio and De Resurrectione* (Oxford: Clarendon, 1972), xi-xxxvi and M. Whittaker's *Tatian: Oratio Ad Graecos* (Oxford: Clarendon, 1982), xv-xx, as well as, *EEC*, pp.112-13 and 882. The treatise *On the Resurrection* does not appear to belong to Athenagoras as both Schoedel and R. M. Grant, "Athenagoras or Pseudo-Athenagoras," *Harvard Theological Review* 47 (1954), 121-29, have convincingly shown. Both Athenagoras and Tatian are primarily defenders of an unpopular religion and so they formulate

careful strategies that will avoid unnecessary offense. Given that the report of a divine man who was born, executed and resurrected in a specific historical context might cause such offense, they generally found a more appropriate defensive stance in philosophical speculation. Theophilus did not share the same constraints in his more comfortable environment. I would contend that he did not intend to conceal any essentials in his explanation of the Christian faith. Further, I believe he thought himself to have explained his Christian faith as fully as he could while at the same time addressing a certain set of topics which were important to him and his particular audience. After all, he was seeking the conversion of an old and well informed acquaintance. I certainly do not think he was in any way "disingenuous." Nor do I consider the teachings of *Ad Autolycum* reductionist theology.

17. See Justin's ranking in *I Apology* 13: "[Jesus Christ] is the son of the true God himself, and holding him in the second place, and the prophetic spirit in the third, we will prove."

18. W. R. Schoedel, *Athenagoras*, xviii. Athenagoras' extensive trinitarian and sonship discussions are found in *Legatio* 10.2-5; 4.2; 6.2; 12.3; 18.2 and 24.2.

19. W. R. Schoedel, *Athenagoras*, 47, fn. 2. Schoedel adds: "Probably this concern explains Athenagoras' willingness to grant the corporeal nature of the gods and to go on from there in criticism of them."

20. W. R. Schoedel, *Athenagoras*, xviii. L. W. Barnard supports Schoedel's conclusions in his study, *Athenagoras: A Study in Second Century Christian Apologetic* (Paris: Beauchesne, 1972), 96-111.

21. M. Whittaker, *Tatian*, xv, says of Tatian's theology that it is difficult to comprehend given his "hortatory rather than didactic" style, a style in which "systematic exposition is continually interrupted by outbursts of polemic." Nevertheless, his extant apology does appear to leak out incarnation and passion ideas.

22. I would not qualify Tatian's claim by saying that he is simply defending the "feasibility" of the incarnation in comparison with pagan myths as does M. Whittaker, xv. In the heat of an involved debate Tatian seems to be acknowledging a firm position, although he has no need for developing it.

23. R. M. Grant, *Greek Apologists*, 129-30, believes this to be so.

24. I believe that the τριάς reference in 2.15 (evaluated in chapter four), usually taken to be an allusion to the theological idea of the trinity, has become the subject of unwarranted scholarly conjecture.

25. Again, Theophilus (2.10) does "appear" to quote Luke 1:35, naming the logos "power of the most high," and thus may support the idea that the beginning of the logos' incarnate life is in the womb of Mary. However, the beginning of the logos' "incarnation" is explicitly located if at all in the garden of paradise, where the logos is said to be the φωνή (voice) that both talks and walks. The logos is uniquely present in a "voice" and not in a person per se. Theophilus also quotes the Johannine Prologue (2.22), but ostensibly in support of this sort of "incarnational" divine activity. Perhaps it would even be better to speak of the φωνή in terms of the logos' "immanency," rather than a possible non sequitur like "incarnation."

26. Their rhetoric suggests they were engaging hostile audiences. On this point see the introductions to both W. R. Schoedel's *Athenagoras* and M. Whittaker's *Tatian*.

27. See R. M. Grant's *Jesus*, 68-82 and *Greek Apologists*, 165-74.

28. R. M. Grant is drawing his information on this Theodotus, also called "The Leatherworker," from Eusebius' *EH* 5.28; Hippolytus' *Refutation* 7.35 and 10.23; and Epiphanius' *Panarion* 54. See the brief entry on Theodotus in *EEC*, 894. Grant believes Theodotus' use of the phrase "in the form of a dove" is taken directly from Luke 3:22.

29. J. A. Robinson, *St. Irenaeus: The Apostolic Preaching* (London: SPCK, 1920), 54.

30. S. Laeuchli's *The Language of Faith: An Introduction to the Semantic Dilemma of the Early Church* (New York: Abingdon, 1962), 165.

31. S. Laeuchli, *The Language of Faith,* 165.

32. R. M. Grant, *Greek Apologists,* 165.

33. R. M. Grant, *Greek Apologists,* 173 and *Jesus,* 81. What does Grant mean by this term, "reticent"? He does not offer an explanation. If he is suggesting that Theophilus is disinclined or is too reserved or too restrained or simply too cautious to speak about God's oneness, he would be mistaken. In point of fact, Theophilus is effusive on the subject of God's singularity, as I point out in chapter four. If, on the other hand, Grant is simply claiming that the bishop modulates his monotheism by employing the tool of divine personification, his point is well taken given that this is the general character of Hellenistic monotheism, Jewish as well as Christian.

34. R. M. Grant, *Jesus,* 77.

35. R. M. Grant, *Greek Apologists,* 165.

36. R. M. Grant, *Jesus,* 77. Grant is citing Hippolytus' quotation of Theodotus in *Refutation* 10.23.1. Cf. Epiphanius' quotation of a claim by Theodotus, in *Panarion* 54.3.5: "The gospel itself says to Mary, 'The spirit of the Lord will come upon you'; it does not say, 'The spirit of the Lord will be born in you.' "

37. R. M. Grant believes that the Gospel of Luke contains a low christology. I think it is plausible that when Theophilus used the phrase in question he could have had the Christmas story in mind. But isn't it more likely, given the context of its usage here, that the phrase was simply part of his stock of significant terms, terms employed when he needed to emphasize a particular point—perhaps as sermonic rhetoric? This question, of course, cannot be fully answered. But it does hint at the degree of ambiguity we face when reading Theophilus.

38. R. M. Grant, *Jesus,* 77.

39. Here R. M. Grant mentions the language used of Moses, Samson, Samuel, David, Solomon and even Josephus, as can be found in Judges 13:24; I Samuel 2:21, 26, 30:6; Josephus' *Antiquities* 2.230-31, 8.49; and *Life* 8. Grant also includes Paul's claims regarding his own "youthful progress as a Jew" in Galatians 1:14.

40. R. M. Grant focuses primarily on 2.27.

41. R. M. Grant, *Jesus,* 78.

42. R. M. Grant's quotation is taken from Nemesius' *On the Nature of Man* 5. See *EEC,* 640 for sources on this little known bishop and author.

43. See R. M. Grant's *Jesus,* 78 and *Greek Apologists,* 172. One should also notice that Theophilus and his contemporary Irenaeus (*AH* 3.21.10), who supports the Pauline formulation with almost the exact same words, would seem to hold sharply different opinions on this matter. See F. R. M. Hitchcock, "Loofs' Theory of Theophilus of Antioch as a Source of Irenaeus," *Journal of Theological Studies* 38 (1937), 130-39, as supporting Grant's argument that Theophilus is engaged with polemics against Paul's theology, while advancing his own case for Irenaeus intentionally correcting this Theophilian polemic.

44. R. M. Grant, *Jesus,* 78.

45. R. M. Grant, *Jesus,* 78.

46. R. M. Grant, *Jesus,* 79. He points to 1.3, 11, 14 (cf. Rom. 2:7); and 2.34 to support his claim that Theophilus believes in the efficacious nature of "good works." The passages that Grant cites emphasizing the prophetic notion of "justice as a virtue" are 2.8, 37; 3.9, 12 and those which suggest that the biblical figures Adam, Moses and Solo-

mon were prophets, "and probably Jesus himself," are 2.10, 28, 30, 38; 3.13. Grant believes Theophilus' view of Jesus is in certain respects not unlike the Gospel of Luke, where "Christ's saving work disappears." This reading of Luke is supported by his citation of W. Schmeichel, *Soteriology in the Theology of Luke* (Ph.D diss. University of Chicago, 1975), 236-80. A somewhat different reading of Luke's soteriology in found in "The Anchor Bible" commentary by J. A. Fitzmyer, *The Gospel According to Luke I-IX,* (New York: Doubleday, 1981), 219-27, where he points out that Luke "alone among the Synoptists calls Jesus 'Savior' (2:11; cf. Acts 5:31; 13:23)." We might also consider the Lucan citation of the Petrine statement in Acts 4:12—"And there is salvation in no one else, for there is no other name under heaven given among men by which we must be saved." However, in the pages cited above, Fitzmyer seems to concede that the scholarly consensus would support a position more like the one we find in Grant. Also, Grant points to an apparent agreement between Origen (*Commentary on Matthew* 13.26) and Nemesius (*Nature of Man* 5), "that Adam could have become perfect by moral progress," as sharing in Theophilus' opinion.

47. R. M. Grant, *Jesus,* 79.

48. R. M. Grant, *Jesus,* 81.

49. R. M. Grant, *Jesus,* 81.

50. R. M. Grant, *Jesus,* 81-82.

51. I am unwilling to speak of the christology of *Ad Autolycum* or of the reconstructed christology of Theophilus. By refusing to address his understanding of the role of Jesus in the protreptic context of these documents, Theophilus unwittingly left us bereft of any solid evidence for reconstructing his christology. But given his thoughtful definition of the term Christian and his explicit teachings regarding the logos and the prophets, in these extant books, R. M. Grant has with some effort speculated on what Theophilus might have believed regarding the role of Jesus as a "Christ" figure. For Grant, *Ad Autolycum* offers information regarding the relationship between the logos and the prophets that can be correlated with what it means to be a Christian in a way that is sufficient for understanding how the bishop may have presented the role of Jesus in his heresiological writings or his ecclesiastical theology. All of this may sound a bit too hazardous for some readers, and I am inclined to agree. I think *Ad Autolycum* offers a great deal of interesting theology despite a lack of data upon which to reconstruct a clear christology.

52. Here I am in agreement with W. R. Schoedel, where he claims, in his fine article "Theophilus of Antioch: Jewish Christian?," *Illinois Classical Studies* 18 (1993), 294, that Grant puts "insufficient weight" on Theophilus' quotation from John 1:1-3.

53. R. M. Grant, "The Problem of Theophilus," *Harvard Theological Review* 43 (1950), 194.

54. R. M. Grant, "The Problem," 196. My emphasis. Grant concludes the above statement with the following claims: "In the third century the line became considerably sharper, as Paul of Samosata discovered, and the works of Theophilus became lost in obscurity. Were it not for one eleventh century manuscript we could never have imagined his Christian Judaism." This last statement is noteworthy. Grant is saying that Theophilus' theology in *Ad Autolycum* represents a point of view that is truly non-normative, a view with which I am in agreement. But I do not think, as Grant seem to, that Theophilus was a closet heretic, left undetected by his Nicene readers.

55. R. R. Hann, "Judaism and Jewish Christianity in Antioch: Chrisma and Conflict in the First Century," *The Journal of Religious History* 14 (1987), 356.

56. W. A. Meeks and R. L. Wilken, *Jews and Christians in Antioch in the First Four Centuries of the Common Era,* Society of Biblical Literature Sources for Biblical Study

13 (Missoula, MT: Scholars Press, 1978), 20. Both V. Corwin, *St. Ignatius and Christi-anity in Antioch* (New Haven: Yale University Press, 1960), 61-64, and R. M. Grant, "Jewish Christianity at Antioch in the Second Century," *Recherches de Science Re-ligieuse* 60 (1972): 97-108, maintain that these Antiochene Jewish Christians show af-finities with the Qumran Essene sect. Meeks, 45, disagrees.

57. It seems unlikely to me that Ignatius and Theophilus would have felt theologi-cally at home with each other. However, it is unclear to what extent Theophilus would have disagreed with Irenaeus' polemical language, when he described Judaism as "the first synagogue" whose "husband was the law" but Jesus Christ was "Lord of the law," and his followers who are called Christians had "no need of the law as tutor," given that they "kept the Sabbath perpetually" through serving God (Irenaeus, *Demonstration* 96). See W. H. C. Frend, *The Rise of Christianity* (Philadelphia: Fortress, 1984), 247-48, where he says of Irenaeus' thought: "The Old Testament recorded how humans moved from infancy towards maturity, each stage being marked by a covenant with God, that of Noah, of Abraham, and of Moses, leading through the prophets to the supreme manifes-tation of God through the word, his son, at the incarnation . . . . Each covenant had been valid for its time but had been superseded when it had served its purpose." Theophilus would have appreciated Irenaeus' extensive contribution to historical analysis and salva-tion history, and perhaps would not have objected too much to Irenaeus' polemic against Jewish nomos as ritual law.

58. For the a recent discussion and up-to-date bibliographical information on the idea of the preexistence-of-the-Torah, consider G. Boccaccini's "The Preexistence of the To-rah: A Commonplace in Second Temple Judaism, or a Later Rabbinic Development?" *Henoch* 17 (1995), 329-49. Also, see E. E. Urbach's standard discussion of the notion in *The Sages: The World and Wisdom of the Rabbis of The Talmud* (Cambridge, MA: Har-vard University Press, 1979), 684-85.

59. Given his historical context, his community, his audience and, what I we have ob-serve in the this chapter, as the limited permission of apologetic convention to address the person of Christ (Justin) and the work of Christ (Athenagoras and Tatian), it does indeed seem odd that he does not take this appropriate opportunity to mention the person and work of Christ. Nevertheless, I offer the following explanation as sufficient, if not satisfying, for our understanding of Theophilus' intent.

Chapter 7

A Nomistic Christianity

Having characterized the nature of his theology, we can now probe deeper into the kind of Christianity Theophilus promotes. In order to situate his thought in the complex of early church history, I will compare the soteriological teachings of *Ad Autolycum* with those of the New Testament epistles of Paul and, especially, James, and then compare what I take to be Theophilus' soteriology with that of his contemporary, Irenaeus of Lyons. This approach should be sufficient to give us a clear view of Theophilus' unique place in the history of Christian thought. The upshot of this probe is my identification of Theophilus as a proponent of a "nomistic" Christianity, one that emphasizes the necessity of law or nomos. In conclusion, I will venture a brief assessment of my book's subject— Theophilus the bishop and theologian of Antioch.

Where does Theophilus' concept of nomos keeping fit in the larger picture of second-century Christian pluralism? As we have seen, Theophilus promotes a type of moralistic Christianity that some scholars, like R. M. Grant, have been inclined to call Jewish-Christian in orientation. Given my comments in the previous chapter of this book, I would be opposed to speaking about Theophilus' thought in this manner. Yet, it is clearly a type of non-normative Christianity. What kind of Christian is Theophilus?

In order to understand someone's theological position it is often helpful to see what it is they oppose. On the one hand, there is in Theophilus no hint of an anti-Pharasaic polemic as is found in many of the New Testament documents, or an anti-Rabbinic polemic as in many patristic documents. On the other hand, Theophilus offers only a conventional polemic against Greek pagan philosophies and mythologies in general. Unhappily, therefore, Theophilus' protreptic language in *Ad Autolycum* gives no direct help in identifying his brand of Christianity. However, his extraordinary emphasis on nomos and good works does suggest that his Christianity is dissimilar to that of Paul while being similar to that of the Epistle of James. Let us consider this possibility.

What is James' conceptual position on nomos, particularly moral law, in comparison with the position of Paul? The teachings of James, contrary to some suspicions, are closer to those of Paul than to those of Pharisaic Judaism.[1] James and Paul speak about the Mosaic law, presumably with primary emphasis on the moral mandates, in nearly the same terms. James says: "Whoever keeps the whole law *but fails in one point* has become guilty of all of it" (2:10). Paul is arguably making the same point when he comments on a text from Deuteronomy 27:26, saying: "All who rely on works of the law are under a curse; for it is written, 'cursed be everyone who *does not abide by all things* written in the book of the law, and do them'" (Galatians 3:10). Paul then reinforces his point of view, while suggesting his negative opinion of the contemporary Pharisaic community, with the words: "I testify again to every man who receives circumcision that he is bound to keep *the whole law*" (Galatians 5:3).[2]

Given that Paul and James are promoting the teachings of Jesus as they understood them, what did their master teach on this subject? The weight of Jesus' personal teachings, as reported in the Gospels, is evidence that he believed obedience to Hebrew law is not in and of itself a merit-making enterprise. Furthermore, as both James and Paul have contended, he seems to have believed that humanity would be condemned even for the smallest of transgressions. In fact, Jesus radicalizes the law, interpreting it more rigidly than even the scribes and Pharisees. Consider the following well-known story from the Synoptics:

> And as [Jesus] was setting out on his journey, a man ran up and knelt before him, and asked him, "Good Teacher, what must I do to inherit eternal life?". . . And Jesus looking upon him loved him, and said to him, "You lack one thing; go, sell what you have, and give to the poor, and you will have treasure in heaven; and come, follow me." . . . And Jesus looked around and said to his disciples, "How hard it will be for those who have riches to enter the kingdom of God!" And the disciples were amazed at his words. But Jesus said to them again, "Children, how hard it is to enter the kingdom of God! It is easier for a camel to go through the eye of a needle than for a rich man to enter the kingdom of God." And they were exceeding astonished, and said to him, "Then who can be saved?" Jesus looked at them and said, "*With men it is impossible,* but not with God; for all things are possible with God."[3]

In a primary sense salvation is not merely "hard" but "impossible," even for the one who is prepared to work for it. Jesus is teaching his disciples that human law keeping and righteous activity is useless given the extreme nature of God's justice. However, in a secondary sense, salvation is easy in that it is to be located in God's mercy. Thus, Jesus' soteriological position is ultimately based on the volition and discretionary work of God—God justifies whomever he wants.

However, Jesus does place value on human attitudes and practices like mercy and forgiveness. Jesus taught in his Sermon on the Plain:

> Be merciful, even as your Father is merciful. Judge not, and you will not be judged; condemn not, and you will not be condemned; forgive, and you will be forgiven; give, and it will be given to you . . . . *For the measure you give will be the measure you get back.*[4]

But, while this line of thought is generally compatible with what was probably a contemporary tradition later recorded in the Mishnah—"with what measure a man metes it shall be measured to him again"[5]—clearly the two conceptual traditions, when understood in their totality, are separated by a very basic difference. The relationship that must and can be mended between God and man is not just a two-party covenantal affair in Jesus' recorded thought, but it involves a third person. In his words, "the Son of man has authority on earth to forgive sins."[6] With this claim Jesus has generated an idea that is clearly divergent from the soteriological reflections developed in contemporary Pharisaic or early Rabbinic circles.[7] G. Boccaccini has neatly summarized the distinction between the two as follows:

> For the Pharisees . . . salvation is a consequence of obedience to the law on the part of humankind and of an interaction between mercy and justice in judgment on the part of God. For Jesus and his early followers, however, salvation is based on one's acknowledgment of being a sinner, on merciful and forgiving practices, and on the faithful hope of the merciful and forgiving intervention of God through the eschatological judge, the Son of man.[8]

Now considering both James and Paul in the light of Jesus' teachings, they also maintain the neutrality of Hebrew law as the means of atonement. However, Paul interprets this neutrality in one way and James in another. Paul stresses the fact that he is "captive" to the law of sin and thus cannot keep the law of God (Romans 17:1-19, 22-23).[9] In contrast to Paul, James maintains that human passions and desires create an internal war, but a war that can be fought with some success (4:1-3). The human heart is not completely captive to sin given its ability to wield the weapon of good works.[10] Man can choose to do the good and forestall the condemnation of evil. For James there is a "law of Liberty," which is a "perfect" and "royal" law. But what is this law? He claims:

> But he who looks into the perfect law, the law of liberty, and perseveres, being no hearer that forgets but a doer that acts, he shall be blessed in his doing (1:25) . . . . If you really fulfill the royal law, according to the scripture, "You shall love your neighbor as yourself," you shall do well (2:8)[11] . . . . So speak and so act as those who are to be judged under the law of liberty. (2:12)

Here James adds support to his thesis that good works are necessary by claiming that the essence of God's law is not to be found in Pharisaic rites, precepts of purification, or codes of morality, but in the simple teaching of liberating love.[12]

B. Reicke claims, however, that James' theology ought not to be presented in opposition to that of Paul. In his words:

> James' rejection of an empty Christianity which is in name only and of a faith which does not lead to works or deeds of love can hardly imply any polemic against Paul. The latter is not referred to at all in

the context. Paul's opposition was to works and observances of the law as tickets for entering the house of righteousness, but he was just as thoroughly convinced as James that the faith of those inside must express itself in works of love.[13]

Paul's own words, in this regard, help settle any doubt as to James' probable continuity with him. In his epistle to the Galatians, he said:

> For in Christ Jesus neither circumcision nor uncircumcision is of any avail, but *faith working through love* . . . . For you were called to freedom, brethren; only do not use your freedom as an opportunity for the flesh, but through love be servants of one another. For the whole law is fulfilled in one word, "you shall love your neighbor as yourself" (Galatians 5:6, 13-14).[14]

However, for both Paul and James, heavenly salvific intervention is still necessary. In Paul's case it is necessary because the situation is so hopeless. He says "Christ redeemed us from the curse of the law" (Galatians 3:3). Redemption is paid for by the blood of Jesus, and the individual's acceptance of the redeeming work of this event is the means of salvation (Romans 3:21-26; 5:18-19). In James' case intervention is necessary to conclude the war or finish a work in progress. However, man should not feel hopeless in the face of the law given the reality of human freedom. Salvation is ultimately found in the message of "the implanted word" (1:21) which is "the faith of our Lord Jesus Christ, the Lord of glory" (2:1). But such "faith by itself, if it has no works, is dead" (2:17). For "man is justified by works and not by faith alone" (2:24).[15] Thus, James' readers are informed that they must abide by the injunction to "be doers of the word, and not hearers only" (1:22). Acknowledging their essential similarity on the subject of salvation and the importance of faith, how might we articulate their difference? While for Paul it is faith primarily in the *work* of Christ as the means of atonement that is central to his soteriology, for James' soteriological perspective it is perhaps not only the work but, more to the point of his argument, the *word* of Christ that must be believed and acted upon.

No matter how similar or different Paul and James may appear to be on the subjects of the work and word of Christ, and of the doing of good deeds, both of them begin with the same idea, the absolute need for a divine salvific intervention. Now when it comes to Theophilus' thought as developed in *Ad Autolycum*, he is certainly closer to James than he is to Paul. But while he follows James' emphasis on the message and word of Jesus in terms of select moral teachings from the Sermon on the Mount, Theophilus' notion of nomos does not exactly parallel that of James either. In fact, there are four very essential differences that must be taken into account.

First, as we have already seen, in *Ad Autolycum* nomos does not appear to include Mosaic ritualistic or ceremonial law, but Mosaic moral law is undeniably fundamental to its soteriological system. However, while centered particularly on Mosaic moral teachings, Theophilian nomos is not exhausted by them.

Theophilian nomos is extended to include also the basic moral teachings of Solomon, the Prophets, Jesus and Paul. In the Epistle of James nomos has great sanctifying value,[16] but it is not the source of salvation as it is in *Ad Autolycum.*

Second, while *Ad Autolycum* argues the importance of interaction between faith and works, it does not promote faith in a divine person and his soteriological intervention, but faith in God's integrity. The bishop shows no interest, at least in *Ad Autolycum,* in promoting faith in Jesus Christ in either his atoning work (Paul) or his atoning word (James). There is, to be sure, divinely creative and inspirational intervention in the bishop's documentation of world history. As was argued in the fourth chapter, the activities of God personified in terms of the sophia, the pneuma and especially the logos, as divine agents, are introduced to explain the creation of the world and the source of nomos. However, Theophilus does not believe he has compromised God's oneness.[17]

Third, *Ad Autolycum* does not suggest anywhere that the occasional failure to keep the nomos, as he understood it, or the violation of a single commandment somehow leads to irrevocable condemnation. And last of all, *Ad Autolycum* does not put God's attributes of mercy and justice in opposition to each other, but recognizes their complementary nature. For *Ad Autolycum* the God who demands righteousness, nevertheless, dispenses mercy freely and wisely via the criterion of his just nature. Therefore, in *Ad Autolycum,* moral law keeping is, at least from the human point of view, an effective means of salvation.

Again, given that Theophilus is a bishop in the Christian church, given that he follows in a line of bishops which includes the incarnational christology and person-based soteriology of Ignatius, and given there is no evidence that the later orthodox Christian community saw him as a heretic or purveyor of "unorthodox" ideas, it seems logical to conclude that he promoted a Christianity which resembled the Epistle of James in terms of its teaching on the importance of good works and respect for moral law. However, under close scrutiny the soteriology of *Ad Autolycum* itself does not fully resemble the soteriology of the Epistle of James. There is for *Ad Autolycum* no necessity for faith in the unique divine intervention of "Jesus Christ, the Lord of Glory" (James 2:1). While the evidence does not recommend an *exact* parallel between Theophilus' and James' soteriologies, there are good reason to think that the bishop's thought does fall within the trajectory of this New Testament epistle.

Before drawing to a conclusion it might be wise, having briefly compared Theophilus' soteriology in *Ad Autolycum* with the soteriological perspectives of Paul and James in their New Testament epistles, to look at an important late second-century theologian with whom the bishop could have shared similar theological ideas. Theophilus is said to have written heresiologies on Hermogenes and Marcion. This claim alone should be enough to recommend a comparison with Irenaeus, Hippolytus and Tertullian, all of whom did the same. Although at some distance from Theophilus and each other in time and space, both Hippolytus (b. 170 in Italy) and Tertullian (b. ca. 160 in North Africa) would probably have been young men when Theophilus flourished (ca. 180). They certainly could have known Theophilus' works and used them in the preparation of their own treatises on the heretics in question. They could have fallen within the trajectory of Theophilus' heresiological theology. But without his heresiological works and with no mention of Theophilus by either of them, it seems unjustified for us to speculate much further on these connections.

However, Irenaeus is another matter. Born in Smyrna, Asia Minor sometime between 115 and 130, studying and teaching in Rome, he eventually became bishop of Lyons shortly after the local persecutions of 177.[18] He remained in office until his death around 200. Between 180-185 he composed his famous five books *Against Heresies (AH)* and a few years later wrote a small apologetic called *Proof of Apostolic Preaching,* but better known as simply *Demonstration.* Irenaeus was a true contemporary of Theophilus and, furthermore, several Theophilian motifs show up in Irenaeus' work (like the hands of God, the infancy of Adam, Adam's nature and destiny, and an emphasis upon morality).[19] Given the high probability of a conceptual relationship and source connection,[20] let us consider briefly Irenaeus' soteriological perspective to see if there is the slightest parallel with the soteriology of Theophilus.

To begin with, Irenaeus, like Theophilus, offers his own credal statement regarding the nature of his faith and that of his church:

> The Church, though dispersed throughout the whole world, even to the ends of the earth, has received from the apostles and their disciples this faith: She believes in one God, the Father almighty, maker of heaven and earth, and the sea, and all things that are in them; and in one Christ Jesus, the son of God, who became incarnate for our salvation; and in the holy spirit, who proclaimed through the prophets the dispensations of God, and the advents, and the birth from a virgin, and the passion, and the resurrection from the dead, and the ascension into heaven in the flesh of the beloved Christ Jesus, our Lord, and his future manifestation from heaven in the glory of the Father "to gather all things in one," and to raise up anew all flesh of the whole human race, in order that to Christ Jesus, our Lord, and God and saviour, and king according to the will of the invisible Father, "every knee should bow, of things in heaven, and things in earth, and things under the earth, and that every tongue should confess" to him, and that he should execute just judgment towards all. (*AH* 1.10.1)

While Irenaeus' creed shares some initial similarities with that of Theophilus (3.9),[21] the differences with *Ad Autolycum* are extensive. In contrast to Theophilus' extant books, Irenaeus' *Against Heresies* is written to the ecclesiastical community and thus represents a theology to educated believers rather than a theology endeavoring to entice belief. Thus, with Irenaeus we are not dealing with a theology that would have consciously avoided identifying Jesus with the preexistent logos, as did Theophilus. Irenaeus places Jesus Christ, the logos, at the center of his teachings. Furthermore, it is the logos as Christ Jesus, who is "the Son of God" and "became incarnate for our salvation." To use J. Daniélou's language, for Irenaeus, the logos as Christ Jesus is the nomos.[22]

Why was this sort of divine action necessary according to Irenaeus? Originally Adam and Eve were created "by the hands of the Father, that is, by the Son and the Holy Spirit" possessing both the "image and likeness of God" (*AH* 5.6.1). Irenaeus distinguishes the *imago Dei* from the *similitudo Dei*. By nature of his immaterial soul man is an *imago Dei,* but the *similitudo Dei* was the gift of the divine pneuma which man forfeited because of his disobedience. Nevertheless, restoration of man's original state can be achieved through faith in the work and word of Christ. The recovery of the *similitudo Dei* is actually the story of the righteous man's salvation (*AH* 3.11.8). What was surrendered by the first parents was to be regained. In Irenaeus' words: "What we had lost in Adam—namely, to be according to the image and likeness of God—that we might recover in Christ Jesus" (*AH* 3.18.1).

The following brief analysis of Irenaeus' soteriological statement observes his two central theses. To begin with, the bishop of Lyons speaks of the importance of the incarnation, saying:

> For in no other way could we have learned the things of God, unless our master, existing as the word, had become man . . . . We could have learned in no other way than by seeing our teacher, and hearing his voice with our own ears . . . having become imitators of his works as well as doers of his words. (*AH* 5.1.1)

According to Irenaeus' first thesis, it is necessary that the incarnation be understood as underlying human atonement. While in a qualified sense Theophilus could agree with Irenaeus when he spoke of the logos as dwelling in an individual so that he became a pedagogical voice, clearly Theophilus did not teach in *Ad Autolycum* that there was a need for the sort of salvific incarnation implied by Irenaeus. Irenaeus believes that the blessing of salvation is "the gift of immortality" (*AH* 5.1.1), a gift which is made possible not only by an incarnation but by the full meaning of the one unique incarnation in Christ Jesus. He says of this blessing:

> [It is] according to the ministration of the word, who is perfect in all things, as the mighty word, and very man, who redeeming us by his own blood in a manner consonant to reason, gave himself as a redemption for those who had been led into captivity. (*AH* 5.1.1)

Such an incarnation leads to redemption and to restoration:

> The word being made man *recapitulated* all things in himself; so that . . . taking to himself the pre-eminence, as well as constituting himself head of the church, he might draw all things to himself at the proper time. (*AH* 3.16.6)

The most detailed account of Irenaeus' notion of "recapitulation" is found in a passage where he also expands upon a highly developed parallelism between Eve and Mary. Whereas Paul originated the comparison of Adam and Christ,[23]

Justin the Martyr was the first to formulate a comparison of Eve and Mary.[24] Irenaeus reports in his account:

> That the Lord then was manifestly coming to his own things, and was sustaining them by means of that creation which is supported by himself, and was making a *recapitulation* of that disobedience which had occurred in connection with a tree, through the obedience which was exhibited by himself when he hung upon a tree, the effects also of that deception being done away with, by which that virgin Eve, who was already espoused to a man, was unhappily misled—was happily announced, through means of the truth spoken by the angel to the virgin Mary, who was also espoused to a man. For just as the former was led astray by the word of an angel, so that she fled from God when she had transgressed his word; so did the latter, by an angelic communication, receive the glad tidings that she should sustain God, being obedient to his word. And if the former did disobey God, yet the latter was persuaded to be obedient to God, in order that the virgin Mary might become the patroness (*advocata*) of the virgin Eve. And thus, as the human race fell into bondage to death by means of a virgin, so is it rescued by a virgin; virginal disobedience having been balanced in the opposite scale by virginal obedience. (*AH* 5.19.1)

Mary, as the mother of Jesus, has become the *advocata Evae*. She is the new mother of humanity, and thus the birth of Christ can be described as "the pure one opening purely that pure womb which regenerates men unto God" (*AH* 4.33.11).[25]

With the preceding thesis regarding the importance of the incarnation clearly in mind, we can now consider his second thesis regarding the source of salvation. Following the Apostle Paul, and in contrast to Theophilus' *Ad Autolycum*,[26] Irenaeus says:

> For as by the disobedience of the one man who was originally moulded from virgin soil, the many were made sinners, and forfeited life; so was it necessary that, by *the obedience of one man,* who was originally born from a virgin, many should be justified and receive salvation. (*AH* 3.18.7)

According to Irenaeus' second thesis, following both Paul and James, salvation is the direct result of the work and word of the man Christ Jesus. While Theophilus' ecclesiastical theology, which was probably more fully developed within his own heresiological works, might have agreed on some level with this thesis, clearly the protreptic theology of *Ad Autolycum* does not express it. *Ad Autolycum* promotes salvation as the product of nomos keeping by "whoever will" (2.27).

This contrast between Irenaeus and Theophilus' soteriologies may be most noticeable in their institutional concerns. According to W. H. C. Frend, "the Eucharist [for Irenaeus] united God and creation by imparting Christ's divine life to believers and guaranteed the regeneration of the flesh."[27] In Irenaeus' own words:

> But vain in every respect are they who despise the entire dispensation of God, and disallow the salvation of the flesh, and treat with contempt its regeneration, maintaining that it is not capable of incorruption. But if this indeed do not attain salvation, then neither did the Lord redeem us with his blood, nor is the cup of the Eucharist the communion of his blood, nor the bread which we break the communion of his body. (*AH* 5.2.2-3)[28]

For Irenaeus it is the elements of the Eucharist that demonstrate the reality of the incarnation and the passion of Christ, and within this institution believers identify and participate with Christ and his resurrection, thus becoming known as Christians.[29] While the earlier Antiochene bishop, Ignatius, could have provided the grist for Irenaeus' theological mill in this instance—wanting to "imitate the passion of God" (*Romans* 6:3),[30] and thus celebrating the Eucharist as the "medicine of immortality" and the "antidote to death" (*Ephesians* 20:2)—there is no language like his in *Ad Autolycum* to suggest that Theophilus even performed this sacrament. To the contrary, Christianity appears in *Ad Autolycum* to be a matter of morality, the precepts of which were revealed by the logos, not a matter of faith in the atoning work of the divine passion.

But for Irenaeus, much as for James and Theophilus, faith in God and commitment to morality are inseparable. The bishop of Lyons claims:

> Action, then, is preserved by faith, because "unless you believe," says Isaias, "you shall not continue"; and faith is given by truth, since faith rests upon reality: for we shall believe what really is, as it is, and, believing what really is, as it is forever, keep a firm hold on our assent to it. (*Demonstration* 3)

Irenaeus is saying that "what really is" must correspond to behavior, to a normative pattern of "action."[31] And how does he describe this normative pattern?

> This beloved, is the preaching of the truth, and this is the manner of our salvation, and this is the way of life, announced by the prophets and ratified by Christ and handed over by the apostles and handed down by the church in the whole world to her children. This must be kept in all security, with good will, and by being well-pleasing to God through good works and sound moral character. (*Demonstration* 98)

Based on these last two passages, it can be said that Irenaeus' theory of atonement, like that of Theophilus, is a version of the so-called "educational view."[32] However, for *Ad Autolycum* atonement is reconciliation built on the work of the logos as the illuminator or the teacher or the reminder of salvific nomos, and not explicitly on the work of Christ or exclusively on the word that was ratified by him. For *Ad Autolycum* atonement is dependent upon a studious lifestyle, that is, keeping faith with this fundamental truth: "It is necessary to become a student of the legislation of God" (2.17). It is such legislation that Theophilus is trying to teach Autolycus, if he would only pay attention. Irenaeus' soteriology, conversely, is dependent upon a uniquely divine intervention which is the work and word of Christ, and thus it is not so very different from that of the New Testament authors, Paul and James.

The orientation toward law in the Epistle of James and the concern with morality based on biblical law in the *Demonstration* of Irenaeus suggest that Theophilus' thought falls within a similar trajectory. Nevertheless, without depreciating this plausible connection, I have argued here that the sanctifying value James places on "good works" is different from the soteriological value of "nomos" in Theophilus' *Ad Autolycum*. And furthermore, Irenaeus, who complements James' emphasis on the logos as the word of nomos, exceeds Theophilus' teaching in *Ad Autolycum,* by identifying the logos as also the salvific Christ figure. In other words, for Irenaeus, the logos is much more than the provider of salvific nomos. In fact, while James and Irenaeus, as well as Paul, Ignatius, Justin, Tatian and Athenagoras, all important figures in Catholic tradition, can be said to esteem nomos, it is the logos in the person of Jesus the Christ who is, in the final analysis, salvific for them. However, *Ad Autolycum* portrays the logos as primarily the provider of salvific nomos. This shift in *Ad Autolycum* from salvific logos to salvific nomos was not acknowledged by Eusebius or Jerome and, therefore, the modern reader should not be too hasty to dislodge the bishop himself from his traditional place in the stream of Catholic tradition. Moreover, while Theophilus appears to be an anomaly within that stream, I believe that this perceived difference is owing to his protreptic project in *Ad Autolycum*. With these comparisons in mind, consider the following schematic of Theophilus ideological location in the development of Catholic Christianity:

THEOPHILUS' PLACE IN CHURCH HISTORY

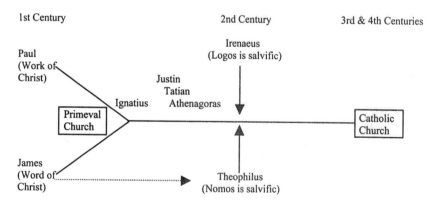

On the basis of the evidence of his three substantial books, I have concluded that Theophilus promoted a religion which was, in respect to the soteriological value of nomos, closer to the emphasis of Hellenistic Judaism than was any other form of New Testament Christianity. While Theophilus was a self-confessed Christian, presumably in good standing with the larger church, he emphasized and promoted to a greater extent than other second-century Christian theologians a moral decalogue that included the teachings of Jewish Wisdom literature. For Theophilus' *Ad Autolycum,* it is obedience to this moral law of God (nomos keeping) that leads to salvation. That is to say, human righteousness and salvation are inseparably bound in the teachings of *Ad Autolycum.*

It was the purpose of this book to lay out the focus of Theophilus' thought, particularly his soteriology, in terms of the protreptic nature and nomistic emphasis of *Ad Autolycum,* rather than attempt to identify his specific brand of Christianity. Nevertheless, I hope that the results of my research as epitomized in the final paragraph of this book will help us better understand the bishop's theological home.

In the light of the protreptic nature of *Ad Autolycum,* can we draw a complete picture of Theophilus' Christianity? It is admittedly difficult and perhaps even rash to try with so little evidence about the bishop's ecclesiastical thought. I think with some confidence we can say he was an erudite pastor who studied and practiced literary, historical and philosophical criticism, and promoted a nomos-based soteriology. I doubt that Theophilus' theological integrity was compromised by his intention to present his readers with an attractive invitation to his Christian religion. With intensity of conviction he commended the hearing and doing of nomos as the only effective means of salvation. Therefore, I take Theophilus to be a representative of a type of Christianity that, sharing with the Epistle of James and the work of Irenaeus, condemned empty Christianity and cheap Grace, a brand of Christianity that is best identified as nomistic Christianity.

Notes

1. See B. Reicke, *The Epistles of James, Peter and Jude,* The Anchor Bible (New York: Doubleday, 1964), 3-10; H. Koester, *Introduction to the New Testament Volume Two: History and Literature of Early Christianity* (Philadelphia: Fortress, 1982), 156-157; and particularly S. G. Wilson's *Related Strangers: Jews and Christians 70-170 C.E.* (Minneapolis: Fortress, 1995), 154-55.

2. While both Paul and James are not talking about moral law only, but also ritual or ceremonial law, it is possible that their polemic originates from an anti-moralistic stance toward what they perceive to be the Pharisaic interpretation of Hebrew sacred literature.

3. Mark 10:17, 21 and 23-27. Cf. Matthew 19:16-26 and Luke 18:18-27.

4. Luke 6:36-38. Cf. Matthew 7:1-2 and Mark 4:24. See J. A. Fitzmyer, *The Gospel According to Luke I-IX,* The Anchor Bible (New York: Doubleday, 1981), 641.

5. Mishnah Sotah 1:7-9, in H. Danby, *The Mishnah* (New York: Oxford University Press, 1987), 294.

6. Mark 2:10; Matthew 9:6 and Luke 5:24.

7. S. M. Wylen, *The Jews in the Time of Jesus* (New York: Paulist Press, 1996), 147, has said of the Pharisaic notion of salvation: "The Pharisees taught that the Torah was the means to salvation through observance of the divine commandments. They taught the Jews that they had an available means of salvation even without the temple sacrifices. . . . The Pharisees saw the source of human suffering in the failure of humankind to obey God's laws. Renewed piety and obedience to the Torah would cause a merciful God to send the messiah. . . . The Pharisees were flexible in interpreting the Torah. They made it relevant to the new age. The Pharisees used their interpretive powers to update Torah law first for Hellenistic society, then for post-temple Judaism."

8. G. Boccaccini, *Middle Judaism: Jewish Thought 300 B.C.E. to 200 C. E.* (Minneapolis: Fortress, 1991), 220. However, while useful in the context of this brief comparison with Theophilus' thought, these are generalizations on the parts of Wylen and Boccaccini. A. F. Segal, in his *Rebecca's Children: Judaism and Christianity in the Roman World* (Cambridge, MA: Harvard University Press, 1986), pp.165-71, points out that "the official doctrine of Jewish salvation is not outlined fully in any one place in Rabbinic literature." Segal, discussing the Jewish model of universalism in contrast to a Christian one, claims that "Rabbinic Judaism did not impose a single doctrine of the meaning of salvation on all its practitioners," and yet by consensus "the critical Rabbinic doctrine was the openness of salvation to all mankind: the doing of good deeds and repentance defined salvation. Anyone, Jew or Gentile, who was able to do good deeds gained the reward of them." Segal says of Rabbinic thought that "both conversion and repentance stress intention and motivation to change one's behavior as a fundamental component of moral development" and that the rabbis specifically "linked the salvation of the Gentiles explicitly to the covenant made with Noah." Thus, the "Noahide Commandments," which number from six to ten, depending on the midrashic version, "include what the rabbis considered to be universally recognizable moral imperatives."

9. Cf. Romans 2:6, 13; 3:20; 7:10.

10. See James 1:26-27.

11. James is quoting Leviticus 19:18.

12. See B. Reicke, *The Epistles of James, Peter and Jude*, 24 and 29.

13. B. Reicke, *The Epistles of James, Peter and Jude*, 5. H. Koester, in his *Introduction to the New Testament Volume Two*, 157, disagrees with Reicke, claiming that James possesses a developed "polemic against Paul's doctrine of justification by faith (Jas 2:14-26)." However, mediating Reicke and Koester, James could be read as a polemic against an exaggeration of certain Pauline ideas which he may have encountered in his later context. Nevertheless, this hardly constitutes a polemic against Paul's recorded teachings themselves.

14. Notice that Paul quotes Leviticus 19:18 as did James 2:8 above.

15. Cf. Philippians 2:12: "Therefore, my beloved, as you have always obeyed . . . *work out your own salvation* with fear and trembling; for God is at work in you, both to will and to work for his good pleasure." James would have supported this advice and claim.

16. See H. Koester, *Introduction to the New Testament Volume Two*, 157.

17. For instance, in James, Jesus Christ is Lord (1:1 and 2:1) and it is "the honorable name" of this Lord which is "invoked" over the Christian (2:7). In addition to this, it is the παρουσία τοῦ κυρίου (5:7), "the coming of the Lord" who is clearly Christ, which is eagerly anticipated in his soteriological scheme. This language of salvific intervention is not found in the bishop's system of thought as it is propounded in *Ad Autolycum*. In other words, while he may have practiced this invocation and believed in some sort of

παρουσία, nothing in *Ad Autolycum* or its protreptic system seems to demand such language or ideas.

18. See W. H. C. Frend, *The Rise of Christianity* (Philadelphia: Fortress, 1984), 244-50 and especially J. Quasten, *Patrology. Volume One: The Beginnings of Patristic Literature* (Utrecht and Brussels: Spectrum, 1950), 287-13 for two brief overviews of Irenaeus. Also consider both W. A. Meeks, *The Moral World of the First Christians* (Philadelphia: The Westminster Press, 1986), 154-60 and R. M. Grant, *Jesus After the Gospels: The Christ of the Second Century* (Louisville, KY: Knox, 1990), 96-110 as appropriate studies regarding Irenaeus' emphasis on morality and connection with Theophilus, respectively. Also see the works of G. Wingren, *Man and Incarnation: A Study in the Biblical Theology of Irenaeus* (Philadelphia: Muhlenberg, 1959); J. T. Nielsen, *Adam and Christ in the Theology of Irenaeus of Lyons* (Assen: Van Gorcum, 1968); and Y. de Andia, *Homo Vivens: Incorruptibilité et divinisation de l'homme selon Irénée de Lyon* (Paris: Etudes Augustiniennes, 1986).

19. Irenaeus, *AH* 3.21.10, 4 preface 4, 4.20.1, 5.1.3, 5.5.1, 5.6.1, 5.28.4 and *Demonstration* 11 are the key passages. According to R. M. Grant, *Jesus,* 99: "Like Theophilus (1.5, 2.18), Irenaeus speaks of God's hands at work in creation, especially the creation of Adam. But while Theophilus defined the 'hands' as God's logos and sophia (2.18), Irenaeus is careful to identify them as son and spirit (*AH* 4 preface 4, 5.6.1, 5.28.4) or logos and spirit (5.1.3) or to explain that logos and sophia are the same as son and spirit (4.74, 4.20.1). He knows that the combination son-spirit is biblical, while logos-sophia is not." See also J. Mambrino, "Les Deux Mains de Dieu' dans l'oeuvre de saint Irénée," *Nouvelle Revue Théologique* 79 (1957), 355-70. R. M. Grant, *Jesus,* 102, also says: "Like Theophilus (2.25-27) [Irenaeus] strongly emphasizes Adam's free will and refers to deification and immortality as the result of obedience to God (*AH* 4.37-39)."

20. A case has been made for Irenaeus' intentional use of Theophilus by F. Loofs, *Theophilus von Antiochien Adversus Marcionem und die anderen theologischen Quellen bei Irenaeus* (Texte und Untersuchungen zur Geschichte der altchristlichen Literatur 46.2, 1930). His theory of a literary and conceptual connection between Theophilus and Irenaeus has been criticized by F. R. M. Hitchcock, "Loofs' Theory of Theophilus of Antioch as a Source of Irenaeus," *Journal of Theological Studies* 38 (1937), 130-39. However, R. M. Grant, *Jesus,* 99-100, has gone even further, suggesting that Irenaeus consciously corrected the Antiochene bishop.

21. Irenaeus promotes one God who is the Father and Creator.

22. J. Daniélou, *The Theology of Jewish Christianity. A History of Early Christian Doctrine before the Council of Nicea II* (Philadelphia: The Westminster Press, 1977), 163-64, where he discusses the identity of logos as nomos, saying: "Judaism at the time of Christ regarded the Torah as a divine reality existing before the world . . . the law is so to speak the visible sacrament of the presence of the divine word. For the Jew the Torah is the true incarnation, as the Koran was to be for the [Muslim]." I think the teaching of *Ad Autolycum* is best understood in terms of the idea that the logos provides through various individual men the truth of nomos as an effective means of salvation.

23. Roman 5:12-21 and I Corinthians 15:22 and 45-49.

24. Justin, *Dialogue with Trypho* 100. Cf. Irenaeus, *AH* 3.22.4, where Mary, as the *causa salutis,* is contrasted to Eve.

25. In this regard, it is interesting to compare the "virgin birth" story of the Gospel of James with the canonical "virgin conception" stories.

26. See Romans 5:15-21 and *AA* 2.27.

27. W. H. C. Frend, *The Rise of Christianity,* 249.

28. This remarkable passage continues: "For blood can only come from veins and flesh, and whatsoever else makes up the substance of man, such as the word of God was actually made. By his own blood he redeemed us, as also his apostle declares, 'In whom we have redemption through his blood, even the remission of sins (cf. Colossians 1:14).' And as we are his members, we are also nourished by means of the creation (and he himself grants the creation to us, for he causes his sun to rise, and sends rain when he wills). He has acknowledged the cup (which is a part of the creation) as his own blood, from which he bedews our blood; and the bread (also a part of the creation) he has established as his own body, from which he gives increase to our bodies. When, therefore, the mingled cup and the manufactured bread receives the word of God, and the Eucharist of the blood and the body of Christ is made, from which things the substance of our flesh is increased and supported, how can they affirm that the flesh is incapable of receiving the gift of God, which is life eternal, which flesh is nourished from the body and blood of the Lord, and is a member of him?"

29. See *EEC*, 320-24 and 777-78 on the Eucharist. Irenaeus' primitive version of transubstantiation, "made the Eucharist an important argument against Gnostics" (777), who denied a real physical body to Christ. Such a problem is not reported by Theophilus in his extant works even though he must have been aware of it in his heresiologies. For Theophilus "the regeneration of the flesh," or the resurrection, is proven by his analogies with nature.

30. Cf. *Smyrnaeans* 6-8 and *Philadelphians* 4.

31. W. A. Meeks, *The Moral World of the First Christians*, 155-56.

32. See F. Young, "Atonement," in *EEC*, 115-21, where he addresses several theories of atonement. He says of the "educational view": "Christian teaching is presented as the true morality . . . . Christ was the embodiment of the logos, the underlying rationality of the cosmos, the divine reason; he therefore confirmed and fulfilled the teaching of the great prophets and philosophers of all time and provided the final revelation of truth and goodness. In a culture that believed that sin was ignorance and virtue knowledge, a kind of skill that could be taught, it is not surprising that this could be regarded as the fundamental necessity for human beings, to be attracted away from wickedness and restored to communion with the divine." Thus, "reconciliation with God required repentance, a turning to the living God and abandonment of idolatry and immorality, which was brought about by Christ's revelation of the truth."

Select Bibliography

I. Editions & Translations

Bardy, G. *Théophile d'Antioche: Trois livres à Autolycus*. Paris: Du Cerf, 1948.
Dods, M. "Theophilus of Antioch to Autolycus." Pp. 87-121 in *The Ante-Nicene Fathers* 2. Grand Rapids: Eerdmans, 1953.
Grant, R. M. *Theophilus of Antioch: Ad Autolycum*. Oxford: Oxford University Press, 1970.
Otto, J. C. T. *Corpus apologetarum christianorum saeculi secundi: Theophili episcopi Antiocheni Ad Autolycum libri tres* 8. Jenae: Prostat apud Libraria Dufft, 1861.

II. Studies on Theophilus

Bentivegna, J. "A Christianity without Christ by Theophilus of Antioch." *Studia patristica* 13 (1975): 107-30.
Bergamelli, F. "Il languaggio simbolico delle immagini nella catechesi missionari di Teofilo di Antiochia." *Salesianum* 41 (1979): 273-97.
Bolgiani, F. "L'ascesi di Noe: A proposito di Theophilo ad Autolyco, III, 19." Pp. 295-333 in *Forma futuri: Studi in onore del cardinale Michele Pellegrino*. Torino: Bottega d'Erasmo, 1975.
———. "Sullo scritto perduto di Teofilo D'Antiochia Contro Ermogene." Pp. 77-118 in *Paradoxos Politeia: Studi patristici in onore di Giuseppe Lazzati*, edited by R. Cantalamessa and L. F. Pizzolato. Milan: Vita e Pensiero, 1979.
Cury, C. "The Theogony of Theophilus." *Vigiliae Christianae* 42 (1988): 318-26.
Grant, R. M. "Notes on the Text of Theophilus, Ad Autolycum III." *Vigiliae Christianae* 12 (1958): 136-44.
———. "Scripture, Rhetoric and Theology in Theophilus." *Vigiliae Christianae* 13 (1959): 33-45.
———. "The Bible of Theophilus of Antioch." *Journal of Biblical Literature* 66 (1947): 173-96.
———. "Theophilus of Antioch to Autolycus." *Harvard Theological Review* 40 (1947): 227-56.
———. "The Problem of Theophilus." *Harvard Theological Review* 43 (1950): 179-96.
———. "The Textual Tradition of Theophilus of Antioch." *Vigiliae Christianae* 6 (1952): 146-59.
Hitchcock, F. R. M. "Loofs' Theory of Theophilus of Antioch as a Source of Irenaeus." *Journal of Theological Studies* 38 (1937): 130-39.
Loofs, F. *Theophilus von Antiochien Adversus Marcionem und die anderen theologischen Quellen bei Irenaeus. Texte und Untersuchungen zur Geschichte der altchristlichen Literatur* 46.2, 1930.

Marcovich, M. "Theophilus of Antioch: Fifty-five Emendations." *Illinois Classical Studies* 4 (1979): 76-93.

Martin, J. P. "Filon Hebreo y Teofilo Cristiano: la continuidad de una teologia natural." *Salmaticensis* 37 (1990): 302-17.

———. "La antropología de Filón y la de Teófilo de Antioquia: sus lecturas de Genesis 2-5." *Salmaticensis* 36 (1989): 23-71.

———. "La presencia de Filón en el Hexámeron do Teófilo de Antioquía." *Salmaticensis* 33 (1986): 147-77.

McVey, K. E. "The Use of Stoic Cosmogony in Theophilus of Antioch's Hexaemeron." Pp. 32-58 in *Biblical Hermeneutics in Historical Perspective: Studies in Honor of Karlfried Froehlich on his Sixtieth Birthday,* edited by M. S. Burrows and P. Rorem. Grand Rapids: Eerdman's, 1991.

Nautin, P. "Ciel, pneuma et lumiére chez Théophile d'Antioche (notes critiques sur Ad Auto. 2, 13)." *Vigiliae Christianae* 27 (1973): 165-71.

———. "Notes critiques sur Théophile d'Antioche, Ad Autolycum Lib. II." *Vigiliae Christianae* 11 (1957): 212-25.

Norris, F. W. "Theophilus." Pp. in *Encyclopedia of Early Christianity* edited by Everett Ferguson. New York: Garland, 1990.

Ogara, F. "Aristidis et epistolae ad Diognetum cum Theophilo Antiocheno cognatio." Rome: *Gregorianum* 25 (1944): 74-102.

Quispel, G., and R. M. Grant. "Note on the Petrine Apocrypha." *Vigiliae Christianae* 6 (1952): 31-32.

Schoedel, W. R. "Theophilus of Antioch: Jewish Christian?" *Illinois Classical Studies* 18 (1993): 279-297.

Simonetti, M. "La sacra scrittura in Teofilo d'Antiochia." Pp. 197-207 in *Epektasis: Mélanges Jean Daniélou.* Paris, 1972.

Vermander, J. M. "Théophile d'Antioche contre Celse: A Autolycos III." *Revue des Études Augustiniennes* 17 (1971): 203-25.

Zeegers-Vander Vorst, N. "La création de l'homme (Gn 1, 26) chez Théophile d'Antioche." *Vigiliae Christianae* 30 (1976): 258-67.

———. "Les Citations du Nouveau Testament dans les livres à Autolycus de Théophile d'Antioche." *Texte und Untersuchungen zur Geschichte der altchristlichen Literatur* 115 (1975): 371-82.

———. "Notes sur quelques aspects judaïsants du Logos chez Théophile d'Antioche." Pp. 69-87 in *Actes de la XIIe Conférence Internationale d'Études Classiques.* Amsterdam, 1975.

———. "Satan, Eve et le serpent chez Théophile d'Antioche." *Vigiliae Christianae* 35 (1981): 152-69.

III. Some Related Studies

Brown, R., and J. P. Meier. *Antioch and Rome: New Testament Cradles of Catholic Christianity.* New York: Paulist Press, 1983.

Charlesworth, J. H. "The Jewish Roots of Christology: The Discovery of the Hypostatic Voice." *Scottish Journal of Theology* 39 (1985): 19-41.

Corwin, V. *St. Ignatius and Christianity in Antioch.* New Haven: Yale University Press, 1960.

Daniélou, J. *The Theology of Jewish Christianity: A History of Early Christian Doctrine before the Council of Nicea I.* Philadelphia: The Westminster Press, 1977.

Downey, G. *A History of Antioch in Syria from Seleucus to the Arab Conquest.* Princeton: Princeton University Press, 1961.

Grant, R. M. "Conflict in Christology at Antioch." *Studia Patristica* 18 (1983): 141-50.

———. *Greek Apologists of the Second Century.* Philadelphia: The Westminster Press, 1988.

———. *Jesus After the Gospels: The Christ of the Second Century.* Louisville, KY: Knox, 1990.

———. "Jewish Christianity at Antioch in the Second Century." *Recherches de Science Religieuse* 60 (1972): 97-108.

———. *Les êtres Intermédiaires dans le judaisme tardif. Studi e Materiali di Storia delle Religioni* 38 (1967).

Hann, R. R. "Judaism and Jewish Christianity in Antioch: Chrisma and Conflict in the First Century." *The Journal of Religious History* 14 (1987): 341-60.

Klijn, A. F. J. "The Study of Jewish Christianity." *New Testament Studies* 20 (1973/74): 419-31.

Klijn, A. F. J., and G. J. Reinink. *Patristic Evidence for Jewish Christian Sects.* Leiden: Brill, 1973.

Kraeling, C. "The Jewish Community at Antioch." *The Journal of Biblical Literature* 51 (1932): 130-60.

Laeuchli, S. *The Language of Faith: An Introduction to the Semantic Dilemma of the Early Church.* New York: Abingdon, 1962.

Liebeschuetz, J. H. W. G. *Antioch: City and Imperial Administration in the Later Roman Empire.* Oxford: Clarendon, 1972.

Mambrino, J. "Les Deux Mains de Dieu' dans l'oeuvre de saint Irénée." *Nouvelle Revue Théologique* 79 (1957): 355-70.

Meeks, W. A. *Origins of Christian Morality in the First Two Centuries.* New Haven: Yale University Press, 1993.

———. *The Moral World of the First Christians.* Philadelphia: The Westminster Press, 1986.

Meeks, W. A., and R. L. Wilkens. *Jews and Christians in Antioch in the First Four Centuries of the Common Era.* Society of Biblical Literature Sources for Biblical Study 13. Missoula, MT: Scholars Press, 1978.

Mühl, M. "Der λογός ἐνδιάθετος und προφορικός von der älteren Stoa bis zur Synode von Sirmium 351." *Archiv für Begriffsgeschichte* 7 (1962): 7-56.

Norris, F. W. "Antioch of Syria." Pp. 265-69 in vol. 1 of *The Anchor Bible Dictionary,* edited by D. N. Freedman. New York: Doubleday, 1992.

———. "Antioch-on-the-Orontes as a Religious Center: Paganism" Pp. 2322-79 in vol. 2.18.4 of *Aufstieg und Niedergang der römischen Welt,* edited by H. Temporini and W. Haase. Berlin: de Gruyter, 1990.

Quispel, G. "The Discussion of Judaic Christianity." *Vigiliae Christianae* 22 (1968): 81-93.

Ruiz, G. "L'enfance d'Adam selon saint Irénée." *Bulletin de Littérature Ecclésiastique* 89 (1988): 97-111.

Wallace-Hadrill, D. S. *Christian Antioch: A Study of Early Christian Thought in the East.* Cambridge: Cambridge University Press, 1982.

Wilson, S. G. *Related Strangers: Jews and Christians 70-170 C.E.* Minneapolis: Fortress Press, 1995.

Zeegers-Vander Vorst, N. *Les citations des poètes grecs chez les apologistes chrétiens du IIe siècle.* Louvain: Publications Universitaires, 1972.

Index

About the Author

Rick Rogers (Ph.D., The University of Michigan) teaches courses in religion and history in the History and Philosophy Department at Eastern Michigan University. He also has taught at The University of Michigan, Albion College, and Concordia College. A former minister to students at the University Reformed Church in Ann Arbor, Rogers is a member of the Society of Biblical Literature, the American Academy of Religion, the North American Patristics Society, and the Detroit-based National Conference for Community and Justice. He is married to Susan Kesling Rogers and lives in Dearborn, Michigan.